Antonia Clare

JJ Wilson

speakout

Pre-intermediate
Students' Book

CONTENTS

CONTENTS

LISTENING/DVD	SPEAKING	WRITING
listen to people talk about what makes them happy	talk about what makes you happy; ask and answer personal questions	
	talk about relationships; talk about past events	write about an important year in your life; improve your use of linking words
	start/end a conversation; sound natural	
BBC Blackpool: watch an extract from a drama	talk about important people in your life	write a competition entry about your best friend
listen to people talk about how companies motivate staff	talk about work/studies	write an email about work experience
	talk about dangerous jobs; talk about work routines	
listen to interviews about jobs	discuss likes/dislikes; respond and ask more questions to keep the conversation going	
BBC The Money Programme: Dream Commuters: watch an extract from a documentary about commuting	describe your work/life balance	write a web comment about work/life balance
listen to a radio programme about young people having fun	talk about your future plans	write an email invitation
	ask and answer questions for a culture survey	
listen to four phone calls	make and receive phone calls; learn to manage phone problems	
BBC Holiday 10 Best: Cities: watch an extract from a travel programme about visiting Barcelona	plan a perfect day out	write an email invitation
listen to two people describing their secret talents	talk about your talents	write a competition entry about talents; check your work and correct mistakes
	talk about what you did at school; talk about obligations	
listen to a radio programme giving advice about language learning	give and to respond to advice	
BBC Horizon: Battle Of The Brains: watch an extract from a documentary about brain power	discuss five top tips for tests	write advice for a problem page
	describe journeys	
listen to a radio programme about travel items	talk about travel	write an email describing a trip or weekend away; learn how to use sequencers
listen to a man describing a special place in a city; understand and follow directions in a city	ask for and give directions; learn to show/check understanding	
BBC Full Circle: watch an extract from a travel programme about a trip across the Andes	present ideas of a journey of a lifetime for an award	write an application for an award
	talk about your health	
listen to a radio interview with a food expert	discuss food preferences; make predictions for the future	write about food; improve your sentence structure
listen to conversations between a doctor and her patients; predict information	explain health problems	
BBC The Two Ronnies: watch an extract from a short comedy about squash	ask and answer questions about sports for a survey	write about a sporting memory

COMMUNICATION BANK page 160   AUDIO SCRIPTS page 168

CONTENTS

CONTENTS

CLASSROOM LANGUAGE

1A Complete the questions with the words in the box.

> say to does you are do

1 What _____ this mean?
2 How _____ you spell it?
3 What page _____ we on?
4 What's the answer _____ number 6?
5 Can _____ repeat that, please?
6 How do you _____ this word?

B Match questions 1–6 above with answers a)–f).

a) OK. Which part? The whole sentence?
b) It's a type of food.
c) Page 63.
d) You don't say the 'k'. Listen: 'knee'.
e) The answer is b.
f) B-a-n-a-n-a.

SPELLING

2A ▶ L.1 Listen and write down the words you hear.

B Listen again to check.

C Write down ten words in English.

D Work in pairs and take turns. Student A: say your word and then spell it out. Student B: write it down.

PARTS OF SPEECH

3 Match the parts of speech in the box with the words in bold.

> ~~verb~~ adjective auxiliary adverb noun article preposition of place

1 I **studied** here last year.   *verb*
2 We have **a** new teacher.
3 This is a great **school**.
4 The class is **in** Room 14.
5 **Do** you like speaking English?
6 The teachers are **helpful**.
7 I work **quickly**.

TENSES AND STRUCTURES

4 Find one example of each of these things in the text below.

1 present simple
2 present continuous
3 present perfect
4 past simple
5 *going to* for future plans

> My name is Yoko. I was born in Japan, but at the moment I'm living in the United States. I've been here for six months. I'm going to visit my uncle in Canada next year.

QUESTION WORDS

5 Complete the questions with the words in the box.

> who   where   what   when
> why   how

1 _____ is your name?
2 _____ do you know in this class (which students)?
3 _____ do you come from?
4 _____ is your birthday?
5 _____ do you come to school: by car or by public transport?
6 _____ are you studying English? Do you need it for your job?

AUXILIARY VERBS

6 Underline the correct alternative.

1 What *do/does/are* you do?
2 Where *do/does/is* she live?
3 What *do/does/did* they do yesterday evening?
4 I *am not/don't/doesn't* know the answers to these questions.
5 The library *don't/not/doesn't* open on Sundays.
6 We *don't/didn't/weren't* go on holiday last year.
7 *Is/Are/Do* you studying at the moment?
8 John *doesn't/isn't/aren't* using the computer, so you can use it.

VOCABULARY

7 Complete the word webs with the words in the box.

> car   shop assistant   bookshop
> lawyer   bakery   uncle
> tomato   grandmother   bike
> doctor   supermarket   sugar
> train   cousin   pasta

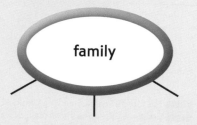

family

food

jobs

shops

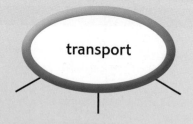

transport

UNIT 1

UNIT **1**

SPEAKING
> Talk about what makes you happy
> Ask and answer personal questions
> Start/end a conversation
> Talk about important people in your life

LISTENING
> Listen to people talk about what makes them happy
> Understand routine exchanges
> Watch an extract from a BBC drama

READING
> Understand two newspaper articles about relationships

WRITING
> Write about an important year in your life
> Write about your best friend
> Improve your use of linking words

BBC CONTENT
> Video podcast: What do you look for in a friend?
> DVD: Blackpool

life

VOCABULARY free time

1A Complete phrases 1–5 below with the verbs in the box.

~~go~~ eat have play spend

1   _go_   shopping/on holiday
2   _____ time with family/money
3   _____ out/with friends
4   _____ time off/a barbecue
5   _____ (a) sport/a musical instrument

B Work in pairs. Which activities from Exercise 1A can you see in the photos? Add some more activities to the list.

LISTENING

2 ▶1.1 Listen to people talking about what makes them happy. Match speakers 1–6 with photos A–F above.

1 _____
2 _____
3 _____
4 _____
5 _____
6 _____

3 Complete the sentences. Then listen again to check.

1 Alana

The thing that makes me happy is [1] _____. I like it when I can go out and spend money on the things I really, really want. Yeah, going [2] _____ makes me happy.

2 Marie

I love being in the [3] _____. Being on holiday and going to the [4] _____. Swimming in a pool. That makes me really happy. You just forget all your problems and enjoy the sun.

3 Josh

Being with [5] _____ and family. Eating a nice meal with your friends, or having a barbecue. Watching the children, you know, play around and have a good time.

4 Paul

Having time off work, like I am now. Listening to [6] _____ or reading a good [7] _____. Just spending time on my own makes me really happy.

5 Dan

I love playing [8] _____. When my team wins a basketball game, for example. It doesn't always happen, but when it does, I'm so happy.

6 Jenny

Being somewhere beautiful makes me happy. Being near nature, by the [9] _____, or in the mountains. Just walking somewhere beautiful.

4 Work in pairs. Which people in Exercise 3 enjoy the same things as you?

SPEAKING

5A Read the questions. Think about your answers.

1 What small things in life make you happy?
2 What made you smile today?
3 Where do you feel happiest?
4 What things in your house make you happy?
5 Are you happy right now? Why/Why not?
6 When did you last laugh a lot? Where were you?

B Work in groups. Ask and answer the questions.

GRAMMAR question forms

6A Complete the questions in the tables.

Questions with auxiliaries			
question word	auxiliary	subject	infinitive
Where	1 _____	you	feel happiest?
2 _____	did	you	(last) laugh a lot?

Questions with *be*			
question word	*be*	subject	adjective/noun/ verb + -*ing*, etc.
	3 _____	you	happy (right now)?
4 _____	were	you?	

B Circle the correct word in bold to complete the rules.

> **Rules:**
>
> 1 In questions with auxiliaries put *do/does/did* **before/after** the subject.
>
> 2 In questions with *be* put *am/are/is/was/were* **before/after** the subject.

➤ page 128 **LANGUAGEBANK**

PRACTICE

7A Put the words in the correct order to make questions.

1 many / are / your / how / in / people / family?
2 see / often / you / parents / how / your / do?
3 family / with / you / spending / do / your / time / enjoy?
4 last / your / when / celebration / was / family?
5 you / do / with / live / who?
6 you / often / eat / do / friends / how / out / with?
7 friend / your / live / where / best / does?

B ▶1.2 Listen and check.

C Look at audio script 1.2 on page 168. Underline the stressed words. Listen again and repeat.

D Work in pairs. Ask and answer the questions.

SPEAKING

8A Work in pairs. Look at the photos and prompts below and make questions about each topic.

B Work in groups. Ask and answer the questions.

Hobbies/Interests

1. What / do / free time?
2. Have / hobbies?
3. When / start?
4. Why / enjoy?

Holidays

5. Where / usually / go / holiday?
6. Do / holiday / friends or family?
7. How long?
8. What / do?

Weekend

9. What / like / do / weekend?
10. Do / ever / work or study / weekend?
11. Where / go out?
12. What time / get up?

| ▶ **GRAMMAR** \| past simple | ▶ **VOCABULARY** \| relationships | ▶ **HOW TO** \| talk about past events |

SPEAKING

1 Work in pairs. Discuss the questions.

1 Do you believe in love at first sight? Why/Why not?

2 Where are good places to meet new people?

3 What things can cause problems in a relationship?

READING

2A Look at the photos and the headlines. Answer the questions.

1 What do you think the stories are about?

2 Do you think it was difficult for the tallest man in the world to find a girlfriend? Why/Why not?

3 What do you think 'third time lucky' means?

B Read the stories to check your ideas.

TALLEST MAN FINDS LOVE

The world's tallest man married a woman who is twenty-five years younger than he is – and much shorter. Bao Xishun, who is 2.36m tall, married Xia Shujian, 1.70m.

Bao, who comes from Inner Mongolia, became famous when he appeared in the *Guinness Book of Records* as the world's tallest man in 2006.

Before that Bao was very shy. He didn't go out much and he didn't have a girlfriend. He worked in a restaurant, but he didn't make much money.

But when he became famous Bao started to earn good money doing advertisements. He decided to look for a wife. He advertised all over the world, but fell in love with a saleswoman from his home town, Xia.

After just one month Xia and Bao got married.

Third time lucky

Jean and Bert Jolley from Blackburn, UK, recently married for the third time. The couple first married in 1972. 'I liked her straight away,' said Bert.

He asked her to marry him and she accepted. But eight years later they started to have problems. They argued a lot, so they got divorced in 1980. But a few months later they remarried.

Unfortunately, the couple started arguing again. So in 1986 they divorced for the second time. Then they got back together again – but did they get married? No, they didn't. 'He asked me, but I said no,' explained Jean. When Bert fell ill, Jean changed her mind. 'That's why we decided to marry again.' On Friday the couple married for the third and final time. 'I still don't like wedding cake,' said Bert, 'and I've tried a few!'

3 Read the stories again. Are the statements true (T) or false (F)?

1 Bao Xishun looked all over the world for a wife.

2 He had lots of girlfriends before he became famous.

3 Bao asked Xia to marry him four weeks after they met.

4 When Jean and Bert first met they didn't get on well.

5 They got divorced because they argued, but then they got back together again.

6 Jean decided to remarry Bert when she discovered he was ill.

4 Discuss. Which do you think is the best love story? Why?

VOCABULARY   relationships

5A Read sentences 1–10 below. Whose love story do they describe?

1 They **met**.

2 They **got on well**.

3 He didn't **have a girlfriend**.

4 They **fell in love**.

5 They **got married**.

6 They **argued**.

7 They **got divorced**.

8 They **got back together again**.

9 He **asked her to marry him**.

10 She **accepted**.

B Match definitions a)–g) with the phrases in bold above.

a) had a good relationship

b) disagreed

c) began to love each other

d) have a romantic relationship with a girl

e) said yes

f) ended their marriage

g) started their relationship again

◖ speakout TIP

Words like *get* and *have* are used in lots of different phrases in English. Keep lists of these phrases and add new phrases when you learn them. Write down all the phrases you know with *get*. Compare your list with your partner's.

GRAMMAR past simple

6A Underline examples of verbs in the past simple in the texts in Exercise 2.

B Complete the tables below with the correct form of the verbs in the past simple.

Past simple			
regular		irregular	
work	_worked_	become	_____
start	_____	fall	_____
decide	_____	get	_____
marry	_____	say	_____

negative	He _____ have a girlfriend.
question	_____ they get married again?
short answer	No, they _____./Yes, they did.

7A ▶1.3 Listen to three different ways to pronounce regular past simple verbs.

1 /d/ **lived** They lived in Africa.

2 /t/ **asked** He asked her to marry him.

3 /ɪd/ **started** They started a family.

B ▶1.4 Listen and put the words in the box in the correct column in the table below.

worked   wanted   stopped   smiled   walked   needed   talked studied   helped   decided

/d /	/t/	/ɪd/
lived	asked	started

➧ page 128 **LANGUAGEBANK**

PRACTICE

8A Complete the sentences with the correct form of the past simple.

go (x2)   stay   see   cook   spend

1 I _____ my best friend three months ago.

2 I _____ to a wedding last summer.

3 I _____ up all night.

4 I _____ on holiday last month.

5 I _____ a meal for some friends last night.

6 I _____ the day with my sister on Monday.

B Make *When did you last ... ?* questions for each sentence in Exercise 8A.

When did you last see your best friend?

C Work in pairs and take turns. Ask and answer the questions.

A: *When did you last go on holiday?*

B: *It was a few months ago. I went to Malta with some friends.*

SPEAKING

9A Write down five important dates in your life. Prepare to talk about them.

B Work in pairs and take turns. Ask and answer questions about the dates. Try to guess what happened.

A: *19th July 2006.*

B: *Did you get married?*

A: *No, I didn't.*

B: *Did you start work?*

A: *Yes, I did.*

WRITING linking words

10A Match 1–4 with a)–d) to make sentences. Link the phrases with a word from the box below.

and   so   but   because

1 In 1998 I finished my degree ...

2 I moved house in 2002 ...

3 I wanted to learn Italian ...

4 They wanted to buy a house, ...

a) they didn't have enough money.

b) I could travel around the country.

c) started my first job.

d) I didn't like my flat-mate.

B Complete the web comment with linking words *(and, but, so, because).*

2006 was an important year [1]_____ I met my wife, Ania. We met in an internet chatroom [2]_____ we got on immediately. We started to chat and send emails, [3]_____ we lived in different countries [4]_____ it was difficult for us to be together. Now we live in the UK with our two children.

C Write about an important year in your life. Use linking words *(and, but, so, because).*

VOCABULARY conversation topics

1A Work in pairs. Discuss the questions.

1 When did you last meet someone new?

2 Where did you meet them?

3 What did you talk about?

B Look at the topics in the box below. Tick the topics which are OK for a conversation with someone that you don't know very well.

> films cars your age sport something you want to sell politics
> your new computer your last holiday your health problems
> your family the weather your work/studies your weekend

C Compare your ideas with other students.

D Work in pairs. Ask and answer questions about the topics in Exercise 1B.

READING

2A Read the article. Which tips do you think are good advice? Is there any bad advice?

The art of conversation

Do you ever find that you have nothing to say at a party? Read our top tips to improve your conversation skills.

DO...

... ask questions. Try 'FORE' – ask about Family, Occupation, Recreation, Education.

... listen. Listen to what people tell you and show you are interested.

... talk about technology. In pubs almost half the conversations nowadays are about computers.

... read film reviews. Read reviews so you know what people are talking about and have something to say.

DON'T...

... talk about 'dangerous' topics. Make sure you know who you are talking to before talking about religion or politics.

... interrupt. Don't interrupt an interesting conversation to ask about the weather.

... sell. Don't use social time to sell your latest product.

B Work in pairs. Cover the article. How many tips can you remember?

1 This is my friend, Rachel.

6 Did you have a good weekend?

7 Did you watch the match last night?

FUNCTION making conversation

3A Look at the pictures and questions/comments 1–12. Choose a response a)–l).

a) I'd love a coffee, thank you.

b) Oh, we work together.

c) I'm an architect.

d) Yes, it's lovely.

e) Yes, I'll probably see you on Wednesday.

f) Yes, it was terrible. We lost 3–0.

g) Hi. Nice to meet you.

h) Yes, let's keep in touch.

i) Yes, it was OK. I didn't do much.

j) No, I'm just visiting.

k) It was nice to meet you, too.

l) Woodbridge. It's a small town near Ipswich.

B ▶1.5 Listen and check.

4 Work in pairs and take turns. Student A: look at page 160. Student B: look at page 162.

▸ page 128 **LANGUAGEBANK**

LEARN TO sound natural

5A ▶1.6 Listen to these phrases again. Notice how words are linked.

1 Would you like a drink?

2 Did you have a good weekend?

3 This is my friend Rachel.

4 I'd love a coffee, thank you.

5 Yes it was OK.

6 It was nice to meet you.

B Listen again and repeat.

speakout TIP

Use *so* to help a conversation when you ask another question. *Poland? So, where exactly in Poland do you come from?* You can also use it when you want to change the topic. *So, did you watch the match last night?* Can you add *so* to any questions in Exercise 3A? Practise saying the questions.

SPEAKING

6A Work in pairs. You are going to a party to meet students from another class. Prepare five questions to ask the new students.

So, why are you learning English?

Where exactly do you live?

So, what do you do in your free time?

B Imagine you are now at the party. Talk to as many different students as possible. Start and finish conversations with them using the flowchart and your questions from Exercise 6A.

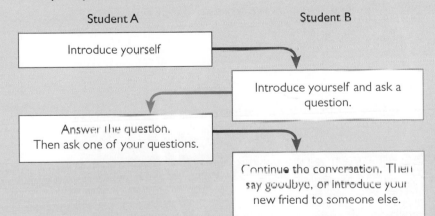

Student A — Student B

Introduce yourself

Introduce yourself and ask a question.

Answer the question. Then ask one of your questions.

Continue the conversation. Then say goodbye, or introduce your new friend to someone else.

▶ DVD PREVIEW

1A Work in pairs and discuss the questions.

1 Where is a good place to meet a new friend/partner?

2 Where is a good place to go on a first date?

3 What kinds of things can you talk about on a first date?

B Read the programme information and answer the questions.

1 What is Peter Carlisle's job?

2 Where did Natalie and Peter first meet?

3 Where do they meet again?

BBC Blackpool

This BBC drama is set in Blackpool, UK. Peter Carlisle is a detective who is investigating a murder. He goes to the Samaritans* to talk about some personal problems and he meets a woman called Natalie. In this episode, he follows Natalie into a supermarket, so that he can talk to her again. Will he ask her out? Will she accept?

> *** The Samaritans** – an organisation which tries to help people who are experiencing problems in life.

▶ DVD VIEW

2A Watch the DVD. Then number the scenes in the correct order.

a) Peter is waiting for the woman to leave the building. _1_

b) He follows Natalie into a supermarket. __

c) They arrange to meet in a bar. __

d) He pretends to do some shopping, because he wants to talk to her. __

e) He asks her if she wants to go out. __

B Work in pairs and answer the questions.

1 Does Peter want the things he puts in his basket?

2 What is tofu? Does he like it?

3 What do you think will happen next?

3 Watch the DVD again. Who says sentences 1–5: Peter (P) or Natalie (N)?

1 'So, what are you doing?'

2 'I wondered if you were doing anything tonight?'

3 'It really, really wouldn't be a good idea.'

4 'It's not going to happen.'

5 'A bar called Funny Girls, 8.30.'

speakout a special person

4A Think about people you know. Who is the best person to:

- go on holiday with?
- talk to about your problems?
- borrow money from?
- go out for an evening?
- invite to your house for dinner?
- work/live with?
- go to a concert/art gallery with?

B Work in pairs and discuss your answers.

5 You are going to talk about an important person in your life. Think about questions 1–6.

1 Who is this person?
2 What is their relationship to you?
3 How did you meet?
4 How often do you see them?
5 What kind of things do you do together?
6 Why is this person important to you?

6A ▶ 1.7 Listen to someone describing a friend and answer the questions.

1 How do they know each other?
2 Why are they good friends?

B Listen again and tick the key phrases you hear.

---

keyphrases

I've known (name) for …

We met …

He/She is one of my best friends because …

One thing I like about (name) is …

The only problem with (name) is …

We get on well because …

We both enjoy …

We keep in touch by …

We will always …

C Work in pairs and take turns. Student A: tell your partner about your special person. Use the key phrases to help. Student B: ask questions to find out more information about him/her.

writeback a competition entry

7A Read the competition entry below. Underline three reasons why Julie is the writer's best friend.

Is your friend the 'best friend in the world'? Tell us why.

Julie is the best friend in the world because she is always there for me. Julie is the person I call when I have a problem, or if I need to borrow money. She has helped me through some difficult times. We have known each other for nearly twenty years, so we know everything there is to know about each other. We argue sometimes but we have the same sense of humour, so our arguments don't last very long. I can talk to Julie about anything and I know she will be a friend forever.

B Write an entry for the competition about your best friend or someone special. Use the questions in Exercise 5 to help you.

FREE TIME

1A Complete the questions with the missing word.

1 How often do you _____ a barbecue?

2 What do you usually do when you have time _____ work/ from your studies?

3 How do you usually _____ time with your family?

4 What kinds of things do you hate spending money _____?

5 Where do you usually _____ out with friends?

6 Where do you like to _____ shopping?

B Work in pairs. Ask and answer the questions.

QUESTION FORMS

2 Work in pairs. Complete the application form for your partner. Ask and answer questions using the words in brackets.

APPLICATION FORM
Name: (what) *What is your name?*
Age: (how)
Place of birth: (where)
Marital status: (married)
Address: (where)
Telephone number: (what)
Mobile: (have got)
Email: (what)
Occupation: (do)
Hobbies: (have)

3A Choose some of the topics in the boxes below. Write five questions to ask other students.

love   home   family
work   food   holidays

B Work in groups. Ask and answer the questions.

RELATIONSHIPS

4A Answer the questions.

1 When was the last time you argued with someone?

2 Who do you get on well with at the moment?

3 How did your parents meet?

4 Where did your parents get married?

5 Do you think it's possible to fall in love the first time you see someone?

6 Have any of your friends or family had children recently?

B Work in pairs and compare your answers.

PAST SIMPLE

5A Put the words in the correct order to make questions.

On your last holiday:

1 did / go / where / you?

2 why / there / did / go / you?

3 in / you / a / stay / did / hotel?

4 do / day / during / did / you / the / what?

5 evenings / out / the / you / go / in / did?

6 the / weather / hot / was?

7 you / language / speak / what / did?

8 you / friends / make / new / any / did?

B Work in pairs. Ask and answer the questions.

6A Write a list of ten verbs you learnt in Unit 1. What are the past simple forms?

B Work in pairs and take turns. Student A: say a verb. Student B: say the past simple form.

A: *meet*

B: *met*

C Now use the verbs from Exercise 6A to make questions.

D Ask and answer the questions.

A: *When did you meet your partner?*

B: *We met in 2006.*

MAKING CONVERSATION

7A Complete the conversations.

Conversation 1
A: Hi, (name) ____. How ____ you?
B: Fine, ____.

Conversation 2
A: This is my ____, (name) ____.
B: Hi. ____ to meet you.

Conversation 3
A: So, ____ you work here?
B: No, I'm just ____.

Conversation 4
A: Where exactly do you ____ from?
B: I come from (place) ____.

Conversation 5
A: How do you know (name) ____?
B: Oh, we ____ together.

Conversation 6
A: It was nice to ____ you.
B: Nice to ____ you, too.

Conversation 7
A: I ____ we meet again soon.
B: Yes, let's ____ in touch.

Conversation 8
A: ____ you again.
B: ____ probably see you later.

B Work in pairs and practise the conversations.

SPEAKING

> ❯ Talk about what motivates you at work
> ❯ Talk about dangerous jobs
> ❯ Discuss likes/dislikes
> ❯ Describe your work/life balance

LISTENING

> ❯ Listen to interviews about jobs
> ❯ Watch an extract from a BBC documentary about commuting

READING

> ❯ Read a newspaper article about dangerous jobs
> ❯ Understand a survey about work/life balance

WRITING

> ❯ Write an email about work experience
> ❯ Write a web comment about work/life balance

BBC CONTENT

> ☐ Video podcast: What do you do?
> ◉ DVD: Money Programme: Dream Commuters

UNIT **2**

work

▶ **GRAMMAR** | present simple and continuous   ▶ **VOCABULARY** | work   ▶ **HOW TO** | talk about work/studies

VOCABULARY work

1 Discuss the questions.

1 What are the people doing in the photo?

2 What sort of company is it?

3 Would you like to work for a company like this? Why/Why not?

2 A Work in pairs. Match the words in the box with definitions 1–8.

> ~~company~~ employee salary office
> customer staff task boss

1 a business that makes or sells things or provides services
company

2 a person who buys products or uses services

3 money for doing a job

4 a place where many people work at desks

5 a worker

6 a job you need to do

7 a person who manages the workers in the company

8 everyone who works in the company

B ▶ 2.1 Listen to the words and repeat.

LISTENING

3 A Work in pairs. Discuss. How do you think companies use the things in the pictures below to motivate staff?

> **mo·ti·vate** /ˈməʊtəveɪt
> $ ˈməʊtə,veɪt/ *verb* to make someone want to do something:
> *Teachers should motivate students to stay in school.*

From Longman Wordwise Dictionary.

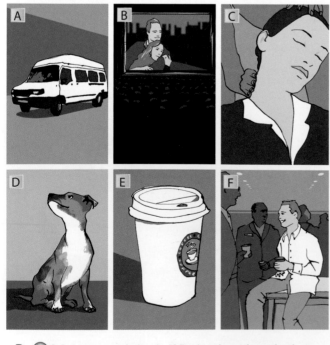

B ▶ 2.2 Listen and check. Which other ideas do they talk about? Which ideas do you think are the best?

4 A ▶ 2.3 Listen to three employees describing what they are doing. Tick the activities they mention.

> watching a film   choosing a CD   fishing   studying
> waiting for a customer   having a massage
> checking emails   making coffee

B Listen again. Answer the questions.

1 What is the 'agreement' between the two shops?

2 What does the company pay for?

3 Why can the woman start work at 1p.m.?

GRAMMAR present simple and continuous

5 A Read sentences a) and b). Answer the questions.

a) This is the clothes shop.

b) I'm having a break.

1 Which sentence describes something that is always true?

2 Which sentence describes a temporary situation?

3 Which sentence uses the present simple?

4 Which sentence uses the present continuous?

B Read sentences a)–d). Answer the questions.

a) I'm choosing my free CD for the week.

b) I'm checking my emails.

c) I'm studying history.

d) Six of us are doing online courses.

1 Which two sentences refer to this exact moment?

2 Which two sentences refer to the general present but not at this moment?

▷ page 130 **LANGUAGE**BANK

PRACTICE

6 Make two sentences or questions with the prompts. Use the present simple and present continuous.

1 you / work   on a special task at the moment?
                              on Saturdays?

Are you working on a special task at the moment?
Do you work on Saturdays?

2 I / look   for a job at the moment
                           at my emails when I get to work

3 I / not / use   English for my job
                           the photocopier at the moment

4 you / watch   the news on TV every day?
                           TV right now?

5 I / not / read   any good books at the moment
                           a newspaper every morning

6 you / have   a good time at this party?
                           a company car?

7 I / sell   my house
                           IT products to companies in Asia

7A Make *you* questions with the prompts. Use the present simple or present continuous.

1 think / your salary / good?
   Do you think your salary is good?
2 speak / any other languages?
3 why / learn English?
4 study for / an exam / now?
5 work on / a special project / at the moment?
6 have / your own / office?
7 like / your / boss?

B Work in pairs and take turns. Ask and answer the questions above.

SPEAKING

8A Work in pairs. Discuss. What are the most important things for people who work? Number the items below in order of importance. 1 = very important. 7 = not important at all.

interesting tasks

flexible hours/long holidays

a chance to develop your skills

a big salary

good relationships with other employees/customers

a friendly boss

working for a big company

B Compare your ideas with other students.

WRITING   starting/ending an email

9A Look at the phrases below. Which are formal (F) and which are informal (I)?

Starting an email

Dear colleagues   *F*   Dear Sir   Hi   Dear Dr Bryce
Hello   Dear All   Hi everyone

Introducing the main topic

I am writing about …   It's about …   Regarding …

Ending an email

See you soon   Best wishes   Bye for now
I look forward to hearing from you   Best regards
Speak soon   Take care   Cheers   Love   Yours sincerely

B Read the advertisement. Answer the questions.
1 What does Fox Ltd produce?
2 What sort of people is Fox Ltd looking for?

Do you need work experience?

Fox Ltd is a leader in fashion and design. With offices in London, Paris, Rome and Madrid, we make high quality clothes and shoes for successful professionals. We are looking for people who want work experience in all areas.

Write to Richard Moore at rmoore@foxltd.com.

C You are interested in the advertisement above. Write an email to Fox Ltd using the prompts below and phrases from Exercise 9A.
1 Introduce yourself (name, home town, etc.).
2 Say why you're writing.
3 Say what you're doing now (studying English, etc.).
4 Ask for information about Fox Ltd's work experience programme.
5 End the email.

VOCABULARY jobs

1A Match the jobs with photos A–G.

> sales rep   fashion designer   IT consultant
> foreign correspondent   personal trainer
> rescue worker   motorcycle courier

B ▶ 2.4 Listen and repeat. Underline the stressed syllables.

sales rep

speakout TIP

The stressed part of a word or phrase sounds l o n g e r, LOUDER and ^higher^ than the other parts. Practise saying new vocabulary, focusing on the stressed parts.

C Work in pairs. Discuss. Which are the best/worst jobs? Think about:

- meeting people
- opportunities to travel
- problems to deal with
- tasks
- hours of work
- salary

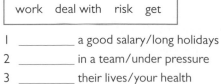

▶ page 152 **PHOTOBANK**

2A Complete the phrases with the words in the box.

> work   deal with   risk   get

1 _____ a good salary/long holidays
2 _____ in a team/under pressure
3 _____ their lives/your health
4 _____ problems/customers

B Use the phrases to talk about the jobs in Exercise 1.

IT consultants get a good salary.

3A Complete sentences 1–6 with the words in the box.

> get   team   under   deal with   holidays   risk

1 People work better when they _____ a good salary.
2 People work better _____ a lot of pressure.
3 It's important that employees get long _____.
4 People who _____ their lives at work should get more money.
5 It's more enjoyable to work in a _____ than alone.
6 These days people usually _____ their own IT problems.

B Work in pairs. Discuss. Which of the sentences above do you agree/disagree with? Why?

READING

4A Work in pairs. Discuss. Which of the jobs in Exercise 1A do you think is the best paid, most interesting or most dangerous? Why?

B Work in groups. Student A: read the text below. Student B: read the text on page 160. Student C: read the text on page 162. Make notes on:
- job
- country
- people interviewed
- why the job is dangerous
- special memories/stories

C Tell your group about your text using the notes.

Danger rating 8/10

In Brazil, they are called motoboys and on average one of them dies in traffic every day. Foreign correspondent Tom Gibb met the motoboys of São Paulo. He learnt that accidents are not the only problem – there are also robberies. It happened twice to Luis Carlos de Gatto.

'The first time was terrible, a really bad memory. I lost everything. I had no insurance and the company didn't give me anything.' The motoboys usually earn just $300 a month.

Gibb asks, 'Why do you drive so crazily when you know it's dangerous?' De Gatto says it's because they often work under time pressure. 'It's dangerous, but what can we do?'

Motorbike courier, Brazil

Gibb also spoke to some car drivers. One said, 'The motorcycle couriers are crazy – they never respect the people walking in the streets.' Another said, 'They drive so fast and many are too young to work in this job.'

Once in a while, they try to change the traffic laws – they want the motoboys to drive like everyone else. But the changes all failed, so the motoboys continue to risk their lives in one of the most dangerous jobs in the world.

GRAMMAR adverbs of frequency

5A Look at sentences 1–9 below. Put the words in bold in the correct place on the line.
1 He **never** worries.
2 **Often** the people they rescue are frightened.
3 The mountain rescuers **sometimes** get angry.
4 It **usually** involves a few broken bones.
5 Life as a jockey is **rarely** safe.
6 These people **always** risk their lives.
7 The people they rescue **hardly ever** say thank you.
8 **Once in a while** jockeys even die during a race.
9 **Occasionally** they get a surprise.

occasionally/once in a while		always
0%		100%
(none of the time)		(all the time)

B Read your text again. Underline all the adverbs or expressions of frequency. Look at the other texts to find more examples.

➡ page 130 **LANGUAGEBANK**

PRACTICE

6A Find and correct the mistakes in sentences 1–6 below. There is one mistake in each sentence.
1 I work always at night.
2 Once on a while I study at weekends.
3 I ever hardly study alone.
4 I work at home occasional.
5 It is sometime difficult to study and work at the same time.
6 I don't usual miss classes because of work.

B Write three true sentences and three false sentences about your job or studies.
I deal with customers once in a while.

C Work in pairs and take turns. Student A: read out your sentences. Student B: guess which are true.

SPEAKING

7A Work in groups. You are making a TV programme about dangerous jobs. Discuss the questions and choose three jobs for your programme.
1 Which jobs are dangerous? Why? How often are the people in dangerous situations?
2 Which jobs are the most interesting for your TV audience?
3 Who will you interview for the programme? What questions will you ask them?

B Work with another group and compare your ideas.

▶ **FUNCTION** | expressing likes/dislikes ▶ **VOCABULARY** | work ▶ **LEARN TO** | respond and ask more questions

FUNCTION expressing likes/dislikes

1A ▶ 2.5 Listen to a man talking about his job. What does he like about it?

B Listen again and complete the sentences.
1 I like _____ outside.
2 I **can't stand** _____ at a desk all day.
3 I **absolutely love** _____ .
4 I **don't like** _____ in a team. I prefer working alone.
5 I **don't mind** _____ my hands dirty.
6 I'm **keen on** _____ new things.
7 I **hate** _____ under pressure.
8 I'm **not very keen on** _____ for a company. I want to be my own boss.

C Read the sentences. Which phrases in bold are positive (**+**)? Which are negative (**−**)? Which are not positive or negative (**?**)?

2A Which of the statements in Exercise 1B is true for you?

B Work in pairs. Find out three things that your partner loves/likes/hates and write sentences about them. Use the phrases in Exercise 1B to help.
Maria can't stand smoking.

▸ page 130 **LANGUAGEBANK**

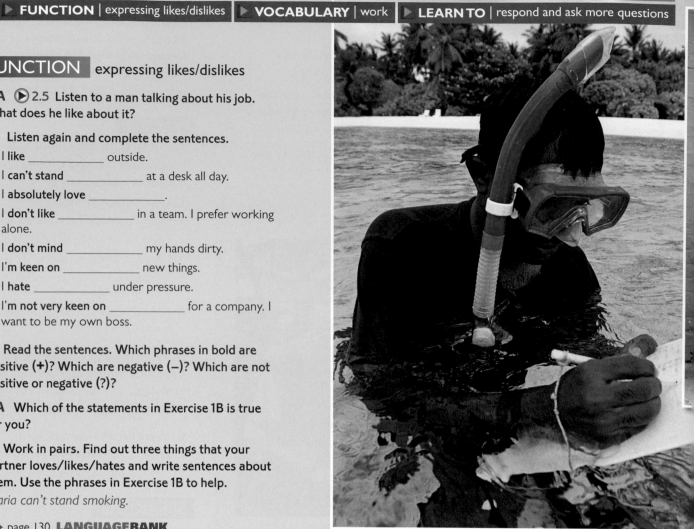

VOCABULARY types of work

3A Work in pairs. Look at the types of work below. Answer the questions.

education
sales and marketing
accounts
retail
the entertainment industry
the fashion industry
the tourist industry
the food industry

1 Which industry does a chef, cook and waiter work in?
2 Which industry does a model and fashion designer work in?
3 What types of jobs are there in the entertainment industry?
4 What types of jobs are there in retail?

B Work in pairs. Discuss. Which types of work in Exercise 3A are good for you/your partner? Why?
I should work in sales and marketing because I don't mind working under pressure.

LISTENING

4A Read the notes about a company and answer the questions below.
1 What is special about the company?
2 Who do you think uses its services?

NAME OF COMPANY: VocationVacations

HEADQUARTERS: Portland, Oregon, USA

FOUNDED: 2004

SERVICE: holidays where you can try doing different jobs

B ▶ 2.6 Listen and check.

5A Listen again and answer the questions.
1 How does the company help you find your 'dream job'?
2 What type of jobs can you try?

B Work in pairs. Discuss the questions.
1 Do you like the idea of VocationVacations?
2 What job would you like to try with VocationVacations?

LEARN TO respond and ask more questions

6A ▶ 2.7 **Read and listen to the extracts from the audio script. Notice how the listener responds.**

A: But during the holiday you try out a different job – your dream job.

B: Oh, I see. That sounds interesting.

A: So if you can't stand your job any more, you can try something new!

B: Great. So how does it work?

A: The holiday is usually just one weekend. You work one to one with an expert who shows you how to do the job …

B: Right.

A: Say, for example, you want to be a cheese maker. You spend the weekend with a real cheese maker who teaches you all about cheese.

B: That's great. So how many jobs can you try?

A: I looked on their website. There's a lot, actually. You can try over seventy-five jobs.

B ▶ 2.8 **Listen and repeat the phrases in bold. Copy the intonation to sound interested.**

C ▶ 2.9 **Listen and respond using the phrases in Exercise 6A.**

D **Look at audio script 2.6 on page 168. Underline other examples of comments and questions. Write them in the table.**

comments	*Oh I see. That sounds interesting!*
questions	*So how does it work?*

7A **Work in pairs. Student A: complete sentences 1–4. Student B: complete sentences 5–8.**

1 I got a new job as a _____.

2 Yesterday I bought a new _____.

3 I'm going on holiday to _____.

4 Last night I saw _____.

5 I've always wanted to _____.

6 Yesterday I learnt how to _____.

7 I watched a great film about _____.

8 This morning I met _____.

B **Work in pairs and take turns. Student A: read a sentence. Student B: respond and ask a follow-up question.**

A: *I just got a new job as a ski instructor!*

B: *Really?! When do you start?*

SPEAKING

8A **Work in pairs. Plan a new vacation for VocationVacations. Make notes on:**

* the career

* necessary likes/dislikes

* where the vacation is

B **Work with other students and take turns. 'Sell' your vacation. Ask questions to find 'buyers'.**

Do you like taking risks? Are you keen on working flexible hours? I have a perfect vacation for you!

DVD PREVIEW

1 Work in pairs. Discuss the questions.

1 How do you get to college/work?

2 How long does it usually take? Is it usually a good or bad journey? Why?

2A Read the programme information and answer the questions.

1 Why did Justin get fed up with his life?

2 What did he decide to do?

BBC The Money Programme: Dream Commuters

The *Money Programme* is a BBC documentary series. *Dream commuters* tells the story of a man who was **fed up with** his journey to work and his lifestyle. Every day there was a lot of **traffic** on the roads and the **commute** to work took a long time. He wasn't happy with his work/life balance. So he bought a **property** in France and took his family to live there. He now takes cheap **flights** to work. He is one of a growing number of **commuters** who live in another country. He says it has **transformed** his life.

B Match the words in bold with definitions 1–7 below.

1 completely changed

2 journeys in a plane

3 people who travel to work

4 cars, motorbikes, etc., on the road

5 journey to work

6 a building or land that you own

7 unhappy with something, so you want to change it

▶ DVD VIEW

3 Watch the DVD and choose the correct alternative to complete sentences 1–4 below.

1 More and more people are choosing to live abroad *and commute to their jobs in the UK/but buy property in Britain.*

2 The way we live is changing because of *cheaper houses in Europe and budget flights/commuter trains and traffic.*

3 Justin's commute costs about *£138/£38.*

4 Justin's journey home is about *700 miles/70 miles.*

4 Watch the DVD again. Who says sentences 1–5: the presenter (P), Justin Saunders (J) or Rebecca Saunders (R)?

1 'I get fed up with the traffic.'

2 'He's one of a group of commuters who take the same flight to Toulouse every week.'

3 'We looked on the internet and we saw properties available much cheaper than in Britain.'

4 'That's the house down there. With the terrace.'

5 'We've just transformed our lifestyle.'

5 Work in pairs. Discuss the questions.

1 Would you like to be a 'dream commuter'?

2 What are the benefits and the problems?

speakout work/life balance

6 Read the text and discuss the questions.

In the UK people work 43.5 hours per week on average. Men work 46.9 hours. In France the average working week is 35 hours. Research also shows that 16 percent of UK workers work over 60 hours per week. At home in the UK, working parents play with their children for only 25 minutes per day. 1 out of 8 (12.5 percent) fathers see their children only at the weekend.

1 Is the work/life balance the same in your country?
2 Do you think people work too much? What problems can this cause?
3 Are you happy with your work/life or study/life balance? Why/Why not?

7 ▶ 2.10 Listen to an interview with a student. Does she have a good work/life balance? Tick the key phrases you hear.

keyphrases

How much time do you spend … (sleeping/ relaxing/commuting)?

I spend a lot of time … (working/doing exercise)

Do you ever … (have a holiday)?

What about your … (social life/weekends)?

How do you spend your weekends?

8A Write some questions about work/life balance. Use the things in the box below to help you.

exercise/sport   social life   family   weekends
enjoyable hobbies   holidays   work/study habits

How much time do you spend with your family?

B Work in groups and take turns. Ask and answer your questions. Find someone who has a similar work/life balance to you.

writeback a web comment

9A Read the entry to www.worklife247.com. Answer the questions.
1 Is this a stressful job? Why/Why not?
2 Would you like a job like this?

I'm a personal trainer. I eat well and I do a lot of exercise. I spend about five hours a day working with clients. In general, I think my work/life balance is good. I take time off every few months just to relax, and I rarely get stressed. Once in a while I go out partying. For me, a balanced lifestyle is really important. When I was younger I worried if I missed a day of exercise. These days I don't worry about it.

My only problem is the one-hour commute. I hate taking the train every day and it's expensive. I'm planning to move house so I can live near the gym where I work and walk to work every morning.

B Think about your work/life balance and write a comment for www.worklife247.com.

PRESENT SIMPLE AND CONTINUOUS

1 Work in pairs. Which verb can you use for a) and b)? Put each verb into the present simple or present continuous.

1 a) Don't switch off the TV! I'*m watching* it.

  b) I love that programme! I *watch* it every week.

2 a) Can you call me back later? I _____ my homework.

  b) I try to keep fit. I _____ yoga and aerobics every day.

3 a) I love tennis but I _____ badly.

  b) Sorry, I can't hear you because Matthew _____ the piano.

4 a) I _____ about twenty text messages a day, usually to friends.

  b) She _____ a book. It will be published next year.

5 a) Daddy can't come home now. He _____ late at the office.

  b) Usually he _____ from 9a.m. to 5p.m. from Monday to Friday.

6 a) I like to spend time with friends. That's what _____ me happy.

  b) I _____ some coffee. Do you want some?

7 a) She loves the school. She _____ a lot of friends there.

  b) Jill _____ some problems with her phone. Can you check it?

8 a) He only met his real father last month. They _____ to know each other now.

  b) In the UK about 50 percent of married couples _____ divorced.

9 a) She always _____ a book to her son before he goes to sleep.

  b) I _____ his new book at the moment. It's really good.

10 a) Hi Tim! I'm in town for a week. I _____ an old friend.

  b) When we go to London we usually _____ the National Gallery.

2A Make six true sentences about your life/job. Use a word from each box.

at home   my friends   in bed
at the weekend   in the bath
on Friday evening   my family
during my holidays   at my desk

work   drink   play   do   sing   eat
write   talk   call   visit

often   sometimes   rarely   never
always   usually   once in a while
occasionally   hardly ever

B Work in pairs and compare your sentences.

A: *I rarely work at my desk.*

B: *Do you often work at home?*

ADVERBS OF FREQUENCY

3A Match questions 1–7 with answers a)–g).

1 How often do you play sport?

2 Do you usually get up before 7a.m.?

3 How often do you phone your mother?

4 Do you eat a lot of meat?

5 How many texts do you send in a week?

6 Do you ever go camping?

7 How often do you read a newspaper?

a) Yes, my children wake me up at 5.30a.m.

b) I don't know. Maybe twenty.

c) Very rarely. I watch the news on television.

d) I play football once in a while.

e) No, hardly ever. I prefer fish.

f) Once a week. We always speak on Sundays.

g) Yes, occasionally. But it usually rains.

B Work in pairs and take turns. Ask and answer questions 1–7.

EXPRESSING LIKES/DISLIKES

4A Work in pairs. How well do you know your partner? Think of questions for answers 1–6:

1 I absolutely love it.

2 I can't stand it.

3 I don't like it very much.

4 I don't mind it.

5 I'm not very keen on it.

6 I like it.

B Ask your partner the questions. Ask follow-up questions to find out more.

A: *Do you like Italian food?*

B: *I absolutely love it.*

A: *What's your favourite dish?*

B: *Spaghetti Bolognese.*

A: *Really? How often do you eat it?*

WORK AND JOBS

5 Work in pairs and take turns. Student A: choose a word/phrase from the box. Student B: choose another word/phrase and explain the connection between them.

IT consultant   office   sales rep
foreign correspondent   staff
work in a team   risk their lives
fashion designer   boss
deal with customers   task
motorcycle courier   company
get a good salary   opportunity
rescue worker   personal trainer
deal with problems

A: *IT consultant*

B: *An IT consultant deals with problems related to technology.*

BBC VIDEO PODCAST

Download the podcast and view people talking about their jobs.

Authentic BBC interviews

www.pearsonlongman.com/speakout

SPEAKING
› Talk about your future plans
› Discuss your favourite types of culture
› Make and receive phone calls
› Plan a perfect day out

LISTENING
› Listen to a radio programme for gist and detail
› Understand a radio programme about young people having fun
› Watch an extract from a BBC travel programme about visiting Barcelona

READING
› Read an arts quiz

WRITING
› Write an email invitation

BBC CONTENT
▯ Video podcast: What do you like doing in your freetime?
⦿ DVD: Holiday 10 Best: Cities

UNIT
3

time out

▶ **London for free**   p28

▶ **Weird or wonderful?**   p30

▶ **Can I take a message?**   p32

▶ **Barcelona**   p34

▶ **GRAMMAR** | present continuous/*be going to* for future   ▶ **VOCABULARY** | time out   ▶ **HOW TO** | talk about plans

VOCABULARY time out

1A Complete the word webs with the verbs in the box.

> have   go   get   see   go to

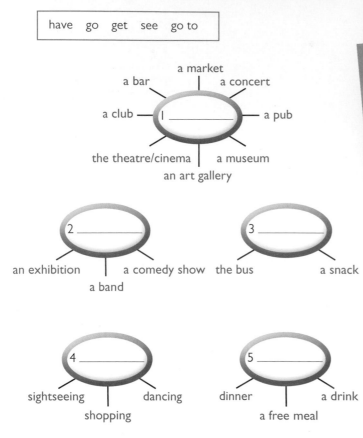

1 _____
- a market
- a bar
- a concert
- a club
- a pub
- the theatre/cinema
- a museum
- an art gallery

2 _____
- an exhibition
- a comedy show
- a band

3 _____
- the bus
- a snack

4 _____
- sightseeing
- dancing
- shopping

5 _____
- dinner
- a drink
- a free meal

B Work in pairs and take turns. Ask and answer questions using the phrases above.

A: How often do you go to a museum?

B: Not very often.

▊▶ page 153 **PHOTOBANK**

LISTENING

2A Work in pairs. Look at the photos and discuss. What can you do in London? Which of these places can you visit for free?

B ▶ 3.1 Listen to the first part of a radio programme. Complete the notes.

1 Visit famous _____ and _____.

2 Go _____: see Big Ben or Trafalgar Square.

3 For a great view of London, walk through one of London's many _____.

4 Go shopping: try one of London's famous _____, like Camden or Covent Garden. Or try the flower market in Columbia Road.

5 Entertainment: see a _____ show, or go to the theatre. There are free classical music _____, too.

C Work in pairs and compare your answers. Then listen again to check.

London Eye

Big Ben

British Museum

3A Work in pairs. Discuss the questions.

1 How much money do you usually spend when you go out for an evening?

2 Can you have a good night out for £15 in your town?

3 Where can you go? What can you do?

B ▶ 3.2 Listen to the second part of the radio programme and complete the notes.

> DOMINIQUE
>
> 6.30–7.15p.m. Art exhibition: Tate Modern
> Price: ¹_____.
> 7.45–9.30p.m. ²_____ at The King's Head.
> Price: FREE. Drinks – £6.
> 10.00–10.45p.m. ³_____ in Brick Lane.
> Price: FREE.
> Bus home. Price: £1.50
> TOTAL: £7.50
>
> ROB
>
> 6.00–6.45p.m. National ⁴_____. Price: FREE
> 7.15–8.15p.m. Street Entertainers in Covent
> Garden. Price: ⁵_____
> 9.30–10.45p.m. Comedy Club. Price: ⁶_____
> TOTAL: £8

C Work in pairs. Discuss. What do you think of the two plans? Which things would you like/not like to do?

Theatreland

Camden Market

Green Park

GRAMMAR present continuous/be going to

4 Read sentences a)–d) and answer the questions.

a) I'm going to see a free art exhibition.

b) I'm meeting some friends.

c) I'm going to watch some comedy.

d) I'm not having dinner. There isn't enough time.

1 Do the sentences refer to the present or the future?

2 Is there a definite time and place for the plans?

3 What tenses do the sentences use?

▶ page 132 **LANGUAGE**BANK

PRACTICE

5A Make sentences or questions with the prompts. Use the present continuous or *be going to.*

1 we / go / cinema / Friday

2 you / go / stay / at / home / this evening?

3 she / not / work / this weekend

4 what time / we / meet / tomorrow?

5 I / go / watch / football match / later

6 they / go out / for a pizza / Saturday

B Change two sentences so they are true for you.

C Work in pairs and compare your ideas.

SPEAKING

6A Think about your future plans. Make notes about:
- places/people you plan to visit
- a film you want to see
- something delicious you want to eat

	you	your partner
tonight	*visit friend*	
this weekend		
next week/month		
later this year/next year		

B Work in pairs and take turns. Ask and answer questions about your plans. Add notes to the table.

A: *What are you going to do tonight?*

B: *I'm going to visit an old friend.*

WRITING invitations

7A Put the emails in the correct order.

> Hi Sonia – I'm going to be in London next week. Sue and I are meeting for a drink on Tuesday evening at 6.30p.m. Would you like to come?
>
> Anabel _1_

> I'd love to. Sounds great! See you there. ___
>
> S

> Great to hear from you. I'm sorry, but I'm busy. I'm doing an exercise class from 6p.m. to 7.30p.m. What are you doing afterwards? ___
>
> Sonia

> We're going out for a meal. Do you want to meet us for dinner? We're having a pizza at La Fontana at 8p.m. ___
>
> A

B Look at the emails. Underline two phrases for inviting and two responses.

C Write emails with the prompts.

> Hi Matt,
> What / you / do / tonight? A few people / come / watch / football / my house. want / come?
> All

> Great / hear. love / to. time / everyone / come?
> Matt

> Tilly,
> What / do / weekend? Would / like / dancing / Saturday night?
> Frank

> sorry / busy / Saturday evening. want / go cinema / Sunday?
> T

> That / great / idea. love / to. What / want / see?
> Frank

D Work in pairs. Choose an activity from Exercise 6 and write an email inviting another pair to the event.

VOCABULARY the arts

1A Complete the sentences in any way you choose.

> One of my favourite singers/bands/artists is _____.
> I like him/her/them because _____. The best thing
> he/she/they did was called _____. I first saw/heard
> it in _____. I like it because _____.

B Work in groups and compare your sentences. Did anyone in the group choose something or someone similar?

2A Work in pairs. Put the words in the box into the correct word web. Which words can go in more than one word web?

> ~~painting~~ (n) ~~play~~ (n) jazz rock art gallery audience
> band actor sculptor singer concert hall painter
> songwriter sculpture artist pop exhibition classical
> performance composer concert

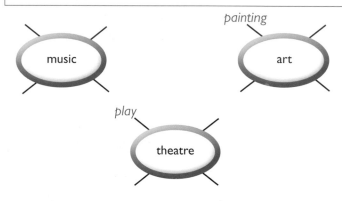

painting

music

art

play

theatre

B Work in groups. Answer the questions.

1 Which of the words in Exercise 2A are people?

2 Which are places?

3 Which can you see in the photos?

C Work in pairs and take turns. Make true sentences using pairs of the words in the box.

An <u>audience</u> goes to a <u>concert</u>.

3A ▶ 3.3 Listen to the words in the box in Exercise 2A. Underline the stressed syllables.

<u>pain</u>ting

B Listen again and repeat.

READING

4A Work in pairs. Discuss the questions. Which art form(/s) (e.g. *art, music, theatre, dance*) do you like the best/least? Why?

B Work in pairs. Do the *Culture Quiz*.

C ▶ 3.4 Listen and check your answers.

D Listen again and answer the questions.

1 Which artist does the man guess for question 3?

2 Which question did the woman get wrong?

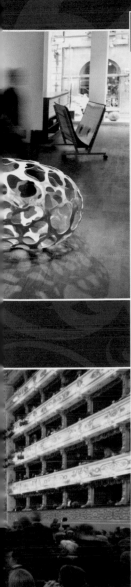

CULTURE QUIZ

1 Which artist spent four years on his back painting the Sistine Chapel?
  (a) Salvador Dali
  (b) Michelangelo
  (c) Leonardo da Vinci

2 Who became famous as a five-year-old singer in a band of five brothers and later married Elvis Presley's daughter?
  (a) Kanye West
  (b) Justin Timberlake
  (c) Michael Jackson

3 Who became famous for dropping and throwing paint to produce paintings?
  (a) Pablo Picasso
  (b) Édouard Manet
  (c) Jackson Pollock

4 Which song about Marilyn Monroe has sold over 35 million copies, and was played by Elton John at Princess Diana's funeral?
  (a) *Candle in the Wind*
  (b) *Thriller*
  (c) *Your Song*

5 Which painting was upside down for two months in New York's Museum of Modern Art before anyone noticed?
  (a) *Water Lilies* by Claude Monet
  (b) *Sunset on Rouen* by J W Turner
  (c) *The Boat* by Henri Matisse

6 Which concert in 2005 took place in ten cities at the same time (including Rome, Berlin, Paris, London and Moscow) and had over 1,000,000 people in the audience?
  (a) Band Aid
  (b) Live 8
  (c) Led Zeppelin

7 Which Beatles song title changed to become *Yesterday*?
  (a) *Tomorrow*
  (b) *Heavenly*
  (c) *Scrambled Eggs*

8 Whose play, called *Breath*, lasts just thirty-five seconds and consists of no words?
  (a) George Bernard Shaw's
  (b) William Shakespeare's
  (c) Samuel Beckett's

GRAMMAR questions without auxiliaries

5 Read questions a)–d) and answer questions 1–3 below.

a) Which artist spent four years on his back painting the Sistine Chapel?
b) Who became famous as a five-year-old singer?
c) What did Michelangelo do?
d) When did Michael Jackson become famous?

1 Which questions ask us to name the subject (the person who does the action)?
2 Which questions ask for other information about the subject?
3 Compare questions a) and b) with questions c) and d). Which extra words are in c) and d)?

▶ page 132 **LANGUAGEBANK**

PRACTICE

6A Write questions for the underlined answers. Two questions use auxiliary verbs (does/did).

1 The first of The Beatles to die was <u>John Lennon</u>.
   Which of The Beatles died first?
2 The singer Bjork comes from <u>Iceland</u>.
3 <u>Samba music</u> became popular in Brazil in the twentieth century.
4 Shakespeare's longest play is <u>Hamlet</u>.
5 <u>Beethoven</u> continued composing music after he became deaf.
6 Afrobeat was invented by musician <u>Fela Kuti</u>.
7 Frida Kahlo painted <u>fifty-five</u> self-portraits.
8 <u>Fernando Botero's</u> art is famous for its fat people.
9 Alberto Giacometti's sculptures are famous <u>because of their long, thin people</u>.

B Work in pairs and compare your answers. Which questions use auxiliary verbs?

SPEAKING

7A Ask questions to find out:

1 who listens to music most frequently?
   How often do you listen to music?
2 who has the biggest CD collection?
3 who has an iPod or MP3 player with them now?
4 who can name more than five classical composers?
5 who has been to the theatre or cinema in the last six months?
6 who has been to an art exhibition in the last year?
7 who regularly goes to art galleries and/or concerts?
8 who has bought a painting?

B Discuss. Who is the most/least interested in culture?

▶ **FUNCTION** | making a phone call   ▶ **VOCABULARY** | collocations   ▶ **LEARN TO** | manage phone problems

SPEAKING

1 Work in pairs. Discuss the questions.

1 Look at the pictures? Who do you think each person is talking to? What do they want?

2 Do you prefer speaking on the phone or in person?

3 Have you ever made a call or taken a message in English? What happened?

VOCABULARY collocations

2A Look at phrases 1–7 below. Which of the things have you done in the last 24 hours?

1 have a chat

2 arrange to meet friends

3 book a table

4 cancel a booking/reservation

5 check information

6 change a ticket

7 talk business

B Work in pairs and compare your answers.

A: *Have you had a chat in the last 24 hours?*

B: *Yes, I had a chat with my sister last night.*

3A ▶ **3.5 Listen to four people making phone calls. Why are they phoning? Choose from the reasons in Exercise 2A.**

B Listen again and complete the notes.
Conversation 1

✦ KING'S RESTAURANT ✦
Notes to manager
Friday: Rodney Collins, table for _____ people.
Day: Saturday. Time: _____.

Conversation 2

🏛 HIGH TOWER PRODUCTIONS
2 tickets for Judy _____.
Original date: _____.
New date: _____.

Conversation 3

Dinner with Wendy and the gang,
Zanzibar's at _____
on _____ night.

Conversation 4

Date: 28th May.   Thomson & Co
To: Sarah Hobbs. Caller: Andy Jones.
Time: 3.30.
Message: Cancel _____. Please call back.

FUNCTION making a phone call

4 Complete the phrases in the table with the words in the box.

it's   back   for   leave   here   take   can

	caller	receiver
start the call	Hello, this is Andy. Hello, [1]_____ Andy. (NOT ~~I am Andy~~)	Hello, Paul speaking.
ask to speak to someone/ find out who is speaking	[2]_____ I speak to … ?	Who's calling?
when the person the caller wants isn't there	Can I [3]_____ a message?	I'm afraid she's not [4]_____ at the moment. Can I [5]_____ a message? I'll ask her to call you [6]_____.
finish the call	See you soon. Good bye.	Thanks [7]_____ calling. See you soon. Good bye.

5A Complete the phone conversations.

Conversation 1

Receiver — Caller

Hello. Jane ¹_____

Hi, ²_____ Mike.

Hi, Mike. How are you?

I'm fine. How about you?

Very well, thanks.

Are you busy at the moment? Do you want to have lunch in the Japanese restaurant?

That sounds good. What time?

One o'clock?

Great.

OK. ³_____ you soon.

Conversation 2

Receiver — Caller

Lupini Products.

Hello, can I ¹_____ to the managing director?

One moment. Who's ²_____?

It's Jane Walker here.

I'm afraid he ³_____ here at the moment. I think he's at lunch. Can I take a ⁴_____?

Please tell him I'm waiting for him in the Japanese restaurant and I'm ordering right now!

B Work in pairs and practise the conversations. Take turns to change roles.

⟫ page 132 **LANGUAGEBANK**

LEARN TO manage phone problems

6A Look at the phrases in bold in the audio script below and match them to problems a)–d).

a) we need to hear something again   2   5
b) the speaker is speaking too fast
c) the speaker is speaking too quietly
d) when we are not sure the information is correct

Extract 1

C: OK, one moment. ¹**Can I just check?** What's the name please?
D: The tickets are booked in the name of Judy Starr.
C: ²**Sorry, I didn't catch that.** Did you say Starr?
D: Judy Starr. S-t-a-double r.
C: There's nothing on the sixth or seventh. There are two seats for the eighth but they're separate. We have …
D: ³**Sorry, can you slow down, please?**

Extract 2

F: Are you doing anything on Saturday? Because a few of us are going out for dinner.
E: Sorry, Wendy, ⁴**can you speak up, please?** I'm on Oxford Street and I can't hear a thing.

Extract 3

H: It's 0988 45673.
G: ⁵**Can you repeat that, please?**

B ▶ 3.6 Listen and repeat the phrases.

7A ▶ 3.7 Listen and write an appropriate response to each phrase.

1 _____
2 _____
3 _____
4 _____

B ▶ 3.8 Listen to check.

SPEAKING

8 Work in pairs. Student A: turn to page 160. Student B: turn to page 162.

speakout TIP

Before you make a phone call, think carefully about the words you will use. How will you start the conversation? What information do you want? Write down some key words that you will use and expect to hear.

DVD PREVIEW

1 Work in pairs and discuss. Which are the most exciting cities in the world to visit?

2A Work in pairs and discuss.
1 What do you know about Barcelona in Spain?
2 Would you like to go there? Why/Why not?

B Read the programme information. What things do you think the presenter will talk about?

BBC Holiday 10 Best: Cities

Holiday 10 Best takes a journey to different cities around the world to find out what they have to offer. They go to the coolest, hippest*, biggest and most exciting places on the planet and discover what makes a city truly great. In this programme Ginny Buckley gives us her ideas for how to spend the perfect day in Barcelona.

* **Hippest** – the most fashionable

▶ DVD VIEW

3 Watch the DVD. Tick the activities that Ginny suggests for her perfect day in Barcelona.

10:00	a) breakfast with coffee and toast
	b) breakfast with hot chocolate and 'churros' ✓
11:00	a) sightseeing – La Sagrada Familia
	b) shopping in a market
13:00	a) have lunch – try some tapas
	b) have a picnic on the beach
16:00	a) have a snack
	b) go shopping
18:00	a) visit the beach
	b) get a drink
22:00	a) go to bed
	b) go out for the evening (eating, drinking, dancing)

4A What does Ginny say about each suggestion? Match what she says to the time she is talking about.

10:00 a) Now one thing that will probably surprise you about Barcelona is that it's got beaches. Five of them.

11:00 b) What can I say? I'm a northern girl and I love my markets, and this is the best one I've found anywhere in the world.

13:00 c) Now you don't want to start your day too early because it's going to be a long one …

16:00 d) The way to approach a night out in Barcelona is to take a drink here, a nibble of tapas there, and then repeat until you get tired, or the sun comes up.

18:00 e) First stop on my sightseeing tour: La Sagrada Familia.

22:00 f) People always think that a siesta is about sleeping. Not true. In Barcelona, it means a nice, long lunch, and that means it's time for tapas.

B Watch the DVD again to check.

5 Work in pairs. Discuss the questions.
1 Would you enjoy any of the things the presenter talks about? Which ones?
2 When did you last do any of these things? Where were you?

speakout a perfect day

6A ▶ 3.9 **Listen to Dana talking about her plans for a perfect day out and answer the questions.**

1   Which city is she planning to visit?

2   Number the activities in the order she talks about them.

a) see a concert ____

b) go to a market ____

c) go sightseeing ____

d) walk through the old city ____

e) have dinner in a restaurant ____

f) relax in a park ____

B   Listen again and use the key phrases to complete sentences 1–5.

1   … walk through the old city.

2   … fantastic!

3   … in the main square.

4   … go to a classical music concert.

5   … going to relax in the park.

C   Work in groups. You are going to plan 24 hours in a city of your choice. Plan your day in detail. Use questions 1–6 to help you.

1   Which city are you planning to visit?

2   What are you going to do there?

3   How are you going to get around?

4   What are you going to eat/drink? Where?

5   What are you planning for the evening?

6   What is going to make the day so special?

D   Work with other students and tell them about your plans for a 'perfect day out'.

E   Listen to other students' plans. Which do you think are the best?

writeback an invitation

7   Write an invitation. Describe your perfect day out and give it to someone in another group. Use the emails on page 29 to help you.

TIME OUT

1 Cross out one phrase which is not possible in each sentence.

1 I went to *a bar/~~sightseeing~~/the market*.

2 Do you want to get *the bus/a snack/ an art gallery*?

3 They went to *the art gallery/ the museum/a snack*.

4 She has gone *a pub/sightseeing/dancing*.

5 Can we have *a club/dinner/a drink*?

PRESENT CONTINUOUS/ *BE GOING TO* FOR FUTURE

2A Put the words in the correct order to make questions.

1 are / what / doing / tonight / you?

2 you / weekend / are / this / doing / special / anything?

3 dinner / evening / is / this / your / who / cooking?

4 you / holiday / are / on / going / when?

5 are / going / city / you / to / visit / which / next?

6 after / to / are / lesson / going / the / / what / do / you?

B Work in pairs and take turns. Ask and answer the questions.

THE ARTS

3 Work in pairs and take turns. Student A: choose a word from the box and use the prompts to describe it. Student B: guess the word.

painting (n)   play (n)   jazz   rock
art gallery   audience   band
actor   sculptor   singer   concert
hall   painter   songwriter
sculpture   artist   pop
exhibition   classical   performance
composer   concert

It's a person who …
It's a place where …
It's something that …
It's a type of …

A: *It's a person who works with stone or wood and makes art.*

B: *It's a sculptor.*

QUESTIONS WITHOUT AUXILIARIES

4A Make questions with the prompts. Add a question word and put the verb into the correct form.

1 famous works / include / *Romeo and Juliet* and *Hamlet*?

Whose famous works include Romeo and Juliet *and* Hamlet?

2 be / an actor / before / he became US President?

3 1975 Queen album / include / the song *Bohemian Rhapsody*?

4 be / a fourth great Renaissance painter, besides Leonardo, Michelangelo and Titian?

5 'John' / win / an Oscar for his song *Can you Feel the Love Tonight* from *The Lion King*?

6 Bob Marley song / include / the words 'Let's get together and feel alright'?

7 watery Italian city / have / an international art exhibition every two years?

8 member of the Dion family sell / 200 million records before 2007?

9 hit songs include / *I'm like a bird*, *Promiscuous* and *Maneater*?

B Do the quiz. Each answer begins with the last two letters of the previous answer.

1 Shakespe<u>are</u>

2 Re _ _ _ _

3 _ _ight at the Ope_ _

4 _ _pha_ _

5 _ _t_ _

6 _ _e Lo_ _

7 _ _ni_ _

8 _ _ li _ _

9 _ _ lly Furtado

C Check your answers on page 160.

MAKING A PHONE CALL

5A Complete the phone call with the words in the box.

here   it's   back   like   can

A: Hello there, ¹_____ Billy Blue.

B: Hello, Billy. How are you?

A: I'm absolutely fine, thank you.

B: So, Bill, what ²_____ I do for you?

A: I'd ³_____ to speak to Mrs Chow.

B: Sorry, she's not ⁴_____ right now.

A: Any idea when she'll be ⁵_____?

B: Never. Today she got the sack.*

*If you *get the sack*, it means you lose your job.

B Complete the message with the words in the box.

call   leave   this   message   busy

Hello, ¹_____ is Pete and Paul.

Sorry, there's no one here at all.

We're probably ²_____, in a meeting,

Or maybe in a restaurant, eating,

Or maybe in a bar watching a game,

But ³_____ a ⁴_____ and your name.

We'll ⁵_____ you back some time soon,

And pigs might fly* around the moon.

Pigs might fly is an idiom that means 'it will never happen'.

C Work in pairs and take turns. Read the conversation in Exercise 5A and the message in Exercise 5B. Concentrate on the rhythm.

UNIT 4

great minds

► **GRAMMAR** | present perfect + *ever/never*   ► **VOCABULARY** | *make* and *do*   ► **HOW TO** | talk about your talents

Have you ever ...

... **made a speech** in front of other people?
... **made friends** with someone from another country?
... **made a meal** for five people or more?
... **made a phone call** in another language?
... **made a terrible mistake**?
... **made a difficult decision**?
... **done a project** that took more than one week?
... **done something interesting** with a group of friends?
... **done a dangerous sport**?
... **done business** in another language?
... **done well/badly** in an exam?
... **done your homework** on the bus?

VOCABULARY *make* and *do*

1A Work in pairs. Read the questionnaire above. What do the phrases in bold mean? Which can you see in the picture above?

B Work in groups and take turns. Ask and answer the questions. Then make sentences with the prompts.

None of us ⎫
One of us ⎬ has/have made ...
A few of us ⎬   done ...
All of us ⎭

None of us has done a dangerous sport.

C Which group has made/done the most things?

GRAMMAR present perfect + *ever/never*

2A ▶ 4.1 Listen and read the conversation below. Which tenses do the speakers use?

A: Have you ever made a speech in public?

B: No, never. Have you?

A: Yes, I have. I made a speech at work.

B: Really? When did you do that?

A: At a conference last year. I was really nervous.

B: I'm not surprised. OK, have you ever made friends with someone from another country?

A: No, I haven't, but my brother has. He met a woman from Chile in 2006. In fact, they got married a week ago!

B Answer the questions about the conversation.

1 Underline two questions about general experiences (where the exact time is not important). How are they formed?

_____ you (*ever*) + past participle ... ?

2 Find two sentences which say <u>when</u> the actions happened in the past. Which verb tense is used?

3 Circle the three short answers to *Have you ... ?* questions.

C Listen again. Notice how *have* is pronounced in the questions. How is it different in the short answers?

▰▰▶ page 134 **LANGUAGEBANK**

PRACTICE

3A Underline the correct alternative.

1 She *has been/was* on TV yesterday.

2 *Have you ever written/Did you ever write* a speech?

3 I've *never eaten/never ate* snails.

4 Last night I *have finished/finished* the book.

5 *Have you ever been/Did you ever go* to the USA?

6 He *has finished/finished* the project this morning.

B Complete the sentences.

1 I've ...

2 Yesterday I ...

3 I've never ...

4 I've always ...

5 When I was a child I ...

C Work in pairs and compare your answers.

4A Write the past participles in the table below. Check your answers on page 127.

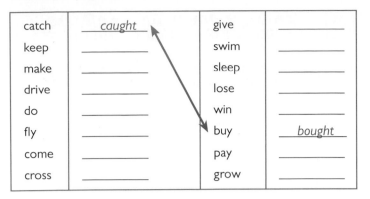

catch	_caught_	give	
keep	_____	swim	
make	_____	sleep	
drive	_____	lose	
do	_____	win	
fly	_____	buy	_bought_
come	_____	pay	
cross	_____	grow	

B ▶ 4.2 Match the verbs which have rhyming past participles. Then listen and check.

caught /kɔːt/ – bought /bɔːt/

C Work in pairs. Use the verbs above to make six _Have you ever … ?_ questions. Use the ideas in the box to help you.

> fish   anything expensive   a bus   a prize   all day
> a plane   plants   in a river

D Work in pairs and take turns. Ask and answer the questions.

A: _Have you ever caught a fish?_
B: _Yes, I have. I caught three last weekend!_

LISTENING

5 Read the advertisement and answer the questions.

1 What is a talent show?
2 How many people will be on the show?

> ### DO YOU HAVE A SECRET TALENT?
> Maybe you tell jokes, sing, dance,
> or touch your nose with your tongue?
> ### Here's your chance to become famous!
> Write seventy-five words about your talent.
> Six lucky winners will appear on _The Talent Show_ next July.

6A ▶ 4.3 Listen to two people who entered the competition and complete the table.

1 What is his/her talent?
2 Has he/she ever done it in public?
3 Is there a special way to do it?
4 Does he/she practise?

	Ralph	Carly
1		
2		
3		
4		

B Work in pairs and compare your ideas. Then listen again to check.

SPEAKING

7A Read the advertisement in Exercise 5. Think about a talent you have or someone else has. Answer the questions.

1 What is the talent?
2 Have you ever done it in public?
3 Is there a special way to do it?
4 Do you practise?

B Work in groups and take turns. Describe your talent. Decide who should enter the competition.

I can remember long numbers. I started doing this when I went to school.

WRITING   correcting mistakes

8A Read the competition entry below. Find eight mistakes and correct them. Use these symbols:

gr = grammar   p = punctuation   sp = spelling

> ### My secret talent
> My talent is that I can do impressions of famous people. I can to speak like Lenny Henry, George Bush, Hugh Grant and many others. I first discovered this abillity when I was child. I often watched cartoons and then 'did' the voices myself I have donc it many times at parties and in front of friends. They always think it's funy. There is no magic secret, I just listen carefully and am practising.

B Write your own competition entry.

C Work in groups. Read the entries and correct any mistakes.

speakout TIP

Don't make the same mistake twice! Look through your corrected written work. Do you repeat your mistakes? Write down the correct form in a different colour.

▶ **GRAMMAR** | *can, have to, must*   ▶ **VOCABULARY** | education   ▶ **HOW TO** | talk about obligations

VOCABULARY education

1 Work in pairs. Discuss the subjects in the box. Which were you good at/not good at when you were at school? Which are you interested in now?

> maths science history literature art
> languages   IT (information technology)

▷ page 154 **PHOTOBANK**

2A Complete the phrases with the verbs in the box.

> make   wear   do/take   give   play   study

1 _____ art/music
   a foreign language
   online

2 _____ sport
   games
   a musical instrument

3 _____ mistakes
   friends

4 _____ a test
   exams

5 _____ a performance

6 _____ a school uniform

B Which of the things above did you do at school? Did you enjoy them? Write (+), (−) or (?)(no experience), next to each one.

C Work in pairs and compare your answers. Did you have similiar experiences?

READING

3A Work in pairs. Discuss. Are traditional ways of learning the best?

B Read the text. Match paragraphs 1–3 with topics a)–c) below.

a) very young children learn to play the violin
b) a school where children can study at night
c) a school where children don't do exams

C Read the text again. Discuss. Which of the ideas in the text do you think is the best? Which is the worst idea?

ARE TRADITIONAL WAYS OF LEARNING THE BEST?

Read about some alternative schools of thought . . .

1. 24-HOUR TEACHING

One school in Hampshire, UK, offers 24-hour teaching. The children can decide when and if they come to school. The school is open from 7a.m. to 10p.m., for 364 days a year and provides online teaching through the night. The idea is that pupils don't have to come to school and they can decide when they want to study. Cheryl Heron, the head teacher, said 'Some students learn better at night. Some students learn better in the morning.' Cheryl believes that if children are bored, they will not come to school. 'Why must teaching only be conducted in a classroom? You can teach a child without him ever coming to school.'

2. LEARN BY LISTENING

Steiner schools encourage creativity and free thinking, so children can study art, music and gardening as well as science and history. They don't have to learn to read and write at an early age. At some Steiner schools the teachers can't use textbooks. They talk to the children, who learn by listening. Every morning the children have to go to special music and movement classes called 'eurhythmy', which help them learn to concentrate. Very young children learn foreign languages through music and song. Another difference from traditional schools is that at Steiner schools you don't have to do any tests or exams.

3. STARTING YOUNG

A child learning music with the Suzuki method has to start as young as possible. Even two-year-old children can learn to play difficult pieces of classical music, often on the violin. They do this by watching and listening. They learn by copying, just like they learn their mother tongue. The child has to join in, but doesn't have to get it right. 'They soon learn that they mustn't stop every time they make a mistake. They just carry on,' said one Suzuki trainer. The children have to practise for hours every day and they give performances once a week, so they learn quickly. 'The parents must be involved too,' said the trainer, 'or it just doesn't work.'

GRAMMAR *can, have to, must*

4 Read sentences 1–6 and put the verbs in bold in the correct place in the table.

1 Children **can** decide when they come to school.
2 At some Steiner schools, the teachers **can't** use textbooks.
3 The children **have to** practise for hours every day.
4 At Steiner schools you **don't have to** do any tests.
5 They **mustn't** stop every time they make a mistake.
6 The parents **must** be involved, too.

possible/allowed	not possible/not allowed
can	
necessary	not necessary

➠ page 134 **LANGUAGEBANK**

PRACTICE

5A Complete the text with *have to/don't have to, must/mustn't, can/can't*. There may be more than one possible answer.

'Do I have to go to school today?'

They ¹_____ (not necessary) wear a uniform, and they ²_____ (not necessary) wait for the school bus. These are two of the advantages of being home-schooled. But there are more. 'You ³_____ (possible) choose which subjects you want to study,' says Jasmin, aged fourteen. 'You ⁴_____ (necessary) work hard, but you ⁵_____ (possible) choose to work when you feel like it.' Jasmin is one of 55,000 children in the UK who doesn't go to school. She stays at home for her education, and she's much happier. 'School is all about rules: you ⁶_____ (necessary) be at school at 8.30a.m., you ⁷_____ (not allowed) wear trainers, you ⁸_____ (not allowed) use your mobile phone in class, etc. I prefer being at home.' Jasmin's mother, Terry, educates her four children at home. 'Some people think that children who study at home ⁹_____ (not allowed) go to the exams and get the same qualifications, but they ¹⁰_____ (allowed), and they do!'

B ▶ 4.4 Listen and check. Notice the pronunciation of *have to*.

They don't have to ... /ˈhæftə/

C Listen again and repeat.

6A Work in pairs. Write a list of things that home-schooled children *can/have to/must* do and things they *don't have to/can't/mustn't* do.

B Discuss. Do you think home-schooling is a good idea? Why/Why not?

SPEAKING

7A Do you think these statements are true (T) or false (F)?

1 In the UK children don't have to learn a foreign language at school.
2 In the UK you can take exams in art, cooking and sport at school.
3 Children in Thailand have to sing the national anthem in the morning.
4 In Singapore children must learn most subjects (maths and science) in English.
5 In France children don't have to wear uniforms to school.
6 In Japan children mustn't be late for school, or they can't get in.
7 In Spain children don't have to eat at school. They can go home for lunch.
8 In the UK children have to eat a vegetarian meal at lunch.
9 Children in Poland must repeat the year if they fail their exams.

B Work in pairs. Discuss the questions.

1 Are these rules and customs the same or different in your country?
2 Do you think they are good or bad ideas?

▶ FUNCTION | giving advice   **▶ VOCABULARY** | language learning   **▶ LEARN TO** | respond to advice

SPEAKING

1A Read the quotes about learning. Do you agree with any of them? Why/Why not?

> We learn by doing.

> A little knowledge is a dangerous thing.

> The best way to learn is to teach.

> Anyone who stops learning is old, whether at twenty or eighty.

B Compare your ideas with others students.

VOCABULARY language learning

2A Read sentences 1–7. Then match the words in bold with definitions a)–g).

1 I **reread** articles we use in class.
2 I **look up** new words in a dictionary.
3 I watch films with **subtitles**.
4 I **visit** English websites to read the news.
5 I **chat** to other learners.
6 I **practise** grammar on the internet.
7 I listen to English songs and I try to **memorise** them.

a) find information in a book/on a computer
b) read again
c) talk on the internet
d) study until you remember
e) words on a film which translate what a character says
f) do something regularly to improve your skill
g) spend time in a place (or website)

B Work in pairs. Discuss the questions.

1 Which of the activities above do you do? How often?
2 Which do you think are the most important/useful?
3 Do you have any other ideas on how to improve your English?

FUNCTION giving advice

3A Read the website message below and think of three things Tomasz can do to improve his English.

Hi – Can you help me? I'm studying English at a language school, but I'm going to start work for an international company next month. I need to improve my English quickly! Has anyone got any good ideas? Looking forward to hearing from you.

Tomasz

B Work in pairs and compare your answers.

4 Read the replies and discuss. Which ideas have you tried? Which do you think are the most useful ideas?

Hi Tomasz – I think you should study online. Use message boards to chat with people all over the world and practise your English. You will make new friends, too!
Pepped

Tomasz – Read news websites every day. And look up new words in a dictionary.
Beatriz20

You should get a good grammar book and do the exercises.
DimaD

I think it's a good idea to focus on listening. Why don't you watch films in English (without the subtitles!)?
jenpen61

p.s. You shouldn't worry about grammar. It doesn't matter if you make mistakes.

Tomasz – I don't think you should study on your own. You should talk to people. Find someone who speaks English, and talk to them.
Smith1894

5A Look at the replies in Exercise 4 again. Complete phrases 1–6 below.

1 I _____ you should …

2 You should …

3 You shouldn't …

4 Why _____ you … ?

5 I (don't) think it's a good _____ to …

6 Find/Write/Do …

B Discuss. Which phrases have the same meaning?

6A ▶ 4.5 Listen to a radio programme. Complete the notes in the table.

	problem	advice
Andy	Too frightened to speak. 1 _____ not good.	2 _____ to yourself 3 _____ _____ about making mistakes
Olivia	4 _____ _____ native speakers. They 5 _____ too fast.	6 _____ listening skills (podcasts, etc.) 7 _____ and 8 _____ at the same time

B Work in pairs. Discuss the questions.

1 Do you have these problems?

2 What do you think of the advice?

LEARN TO respond to advice

7A Look at the radio presenter's responses. Mark them (✓) I agree, (✗) I disagree or (?) I agree but not completely.

1 That's a good idea.

2 I suppose so.

3 You're right.

4 I'm not sure that's a good idea.

B Listen again. Write the response for each piece of advice.

1 I think Andy should practise speaking to himself.

2 Andy should try it.

3 Andy shouldn't worry about making mistakes.

4 Olivia should listen to English as much as possible.

▶ page 134 **LANGUAGEBANK**

8A Look at pictures A–D below. What do you think the problems are?

A: I think _____ more salad. It's good for you. (you / eat)

B: That's _____ idea. (good)

A: You _____ so much time on the computer. (not / spend)

B: _____ right.

A: _____ we go for a five kilometre run every morning? (why)

B: I _____ a good idea. (not sure)

A: I think _____ idea if we go shopping together. (good)

B: I _____ . (suppose)

B Complete the conversations in pictures A–D using the words in brackets.

9 Work in groups and take turns to ask for and respond to advice. Student A: turn to page 160. Student B: turn to page 162. Student C: turn to page 164. Student D: turn to page 167. Read your situation and explain it to the group. *I've got this problem …*

DVD PREVIEW

1 Work in pairs and discuss the questions.

1 Have you ever done a driving test/school exam/intelligence test (IQ test)?

2 How did you prepare? Did you do well? Why/Why not?

2 Work in pairs. Match 1–6 with a)–f) to make sentences. Use a dictionary to check the meaning of the phrases in bold.

1 You need to be very **bright**

2 The intelligence test is a good test of **mental**

3 **On average**, about 50 percent

4 All school children have to **sit an**

5 When the examiner gives you the **instructions**, he also

6 1,000 students **did the test** and

a) **exam** at the end of the school year.

b) most of them were **successful**.

c) of people **fail** this exam the first time they do it.

d) **ability** and the results show your **IQ score**.

e) to **pass the exam**.

f) tells you the **time limit**.

3A Read the programme information. What is the programme about?

BBC Horizon: Battle Of The Brains

Horizon is a BBC documentary series. This programme follows a group of people who agree to repeat a test that they did when they were children. In 1932 every eleven-year-old in Scotland did an intelligence test. Nearly seventy years later, at the age of seventy-nine or eighty, hundreds of the same people did the test again. The results were very interesting, and maybe they can tell us about the type of people who live the longest.

B Are statements 1–3 below true (T) or false (F)?

1 In 1932 all adults in Scotland did an intelligence test.

2 Many of the same people are doing the test again.

3 The programme can tell us how to live longer.

▶ DVD VIEW

4A Watch the DVD and answer the questions.

1 Did people get a better score the second time or when they were children?

2 What type of people did well in the test?

B Underline the correct alternative. Watch again to check.

1 *A special exam for children was/ The results of the 1932 test were* 'rediscovered' in an Edinburgh basement.

2 Professor Ian Deary says the instructions, the test and the time limit are *the same as they were in 1932/ easier than in 1932.*

3 The two old men and the old woman are talking about *schools eighty years ago/ the exam they have done.*

4 People who did *well/ badly* in the IQ test as a child are the people who are still alive today.

5 Work in pairs. Discuss. Can you remember any tests you did as a child? What would be easier/more difficult now?

speakout tips for tests

6 Work in pairs. Look at the tips for taking tests. Do you think these are good or bad ideas? Why/Why not?

1 Study with friends at the same time every day.
2 Don't eat too much before the exam.
3 Don't study too hard the night before the exam. Have a break.
4 Go to bed early the night before.
5 Answer all the questions even if you don't know the answers.

7A ▶ 4.6 Listen to two people discussing some of the ideas. Answer the questions.

1 Which idea do they think is very good?
2 Which idea do they disagree about?
3 What is the third idea they talk about?

B Listen again and tick the key phrases you hear.

keyphrases

How about this one?
In my opinion, this is a really good idea.
I think this is great advice.
I agree with this one.
It depends.
I'm not sure about this advice.
This is obvious.
This idea is similar to that one.

8A Work in pairs. Make a list of your five 'top tips' for taking tests.

B Tell the rest of the class about your tips. Do you all agree?

writeback a problem page

9A Read the problem below and answer the questions.

1 What does Barry do?
2 What's his problem?

help.org

It's the season of blue skies, sunshine, strawberries, Wimbledon and EXAMS! Read Barry's problem and write your reply. The three best replies will win a free copy of my best-selling book, *Work It Out*.

Hi!

I'm a language student. I have an exam in one month but I'm having problems studying for it. I share a bedroom with my thirteen-year-old brother, who is very noisy. I've tried studying in the library (the hours aren't very good – it closes at 7.00), in the park (too windy) and at school (also noisy). I really want to do well in my exam but I just can't find the right place to study. Also, I have problems concentrating. I can read for an hour but after that I get bored and I can't concentrate. Any advice?

Barry Kidd

B Think of some advice and write a reply for www.help.org.

MAKE AND DO

1A Complete the questions with *makes* or *does*.

Who in your family …

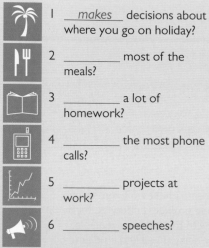

1 ___makes___ decisions about where you go on holiday?

2 _____ most of the meals?

3 _____ a lot of homework?

4 _____ the most phone calls?

5 _____ projects at work?

6 _____ speeches?

B Work in pairs and take turns. Ask and answer the questions.

PAST SIMPLE OR PRESENT PERFECT + *EVER/NEVER*

2A Complete the sentences with the correct form of the verb in brackets.

Questions

1 _____ in the sea? (you / ever swim)

2 _____ on holiday last year? (you / go)

Negatives

3 _____ Africa. (I / never visit)

4 _____ last night. (I / not go out)

Affirmatives

5 _____ in more than one country. (I / live)

6 _____ in a restaurant last weekend. (I / eat)

B Work in pairs and take turns. Guess your partner's answers to questions 1–2.

C Are sentences 3–6 true for your partner? Ask and answer questions to find out.

EDUCATION

3A Match 1–7 with a)–g) to make questions.

1 Do you play
2 When you take
3 How do you feel when you make
4 At school, did you
5 Have you ever given a
6 Do you ever study
7 Did you study

a) online?
b) performance of anything?
c) exams, do you get nervous?
d) study art?
e) any sport particularly well?
f) a foreign language at school?
g) mistakes?

B Work in pairs and take turns. Ask and answer the questions.

CAN, HAVE TO, MUST

4A Underline the correct alternative to complete the sentences.

1 In Australia, you *must/can/don't have to* drive on the left.

2 In the UK, you *have to/can/can't* smoke in pubs and restaurants.

3 You *can't/have to/must* talk on your mobile phone during an examination.

4 Children are lucky. They *don't have to/must/can* worry about paying bills!

5 In the UK, you *have to/can't/mustn't* be 17 years old before you can ride a motorcycle.

B Write down one thing:

- you can/can't do in your country
- you have to do next week
- mustn't do during an exam
- you don't have to do at the weekend
- you must do when learning a language
- you mustn't do while driving
- you have to do every day
- you don't have to do when you are a child

C Work in pairs and compare your ideas.

LANGUAGE LEARNING

5A Complete the questions.

1 Do you r__r_____ articles to help you understand them?

2 How often do you pr_____ your English?

3 Do you like watching films with sub_____? Why/Why not?

4 Have you ever used a ch_____ room in English?

5 Which words from this unit are you going to mem_____?

B Work in pairs and take turns. Ask and answer the questions.

GIVING ADVICE

6A Complete the tables below with phrases for giving/responding to advice.

giving advice

responding to advice

B Work in pairs. Complete the conversation in different ways.

A: Why don't we _____?
B: That's a _____.
A: I think/don't think _____.
B: OK. Let's _____.

C Practise and act out your conversation.

UNIT 5

travel

The Rabbit Proof Fence

The Motorcycle Diaries

VOCABULARY transport

1 Work in pairs and answer the questions.

1 How many types of transport can you think of? Make a list.

2 What do you think is the best way to travel? Why?

➡ page 155 **PHOTOBANK**

READING

2 Work in pairs. Look at the photos and discuss the questions.

1 What type of transport do you think the people are using?

2 Where do you think the people are going?

3 How do you think these words are connected to their journeys?

cow rabbit fence oxygen crash experiments

3 Work in groups. Student A: read the text on this page. Student B: read the text on page 161. Student C: read the text on page 163. As you read, make notes about your text.

1 Who made the journey?

2 Where did they go?

3 What problem(s) did they have on the journey?

4 What happened at the end of the journey?

The motorcycle diaries

Before he became a famous revolutionary, Che Guevara was simply Ernesto Guevara de la Serna from Argentina, a student looking for fun. He was studying medicine when he decided to travel across Latin America by motorbike with his friend Alberto.

They slept on floors, met girls and drank beer. They walked through deserts and up mountains and spent some time working in a leper colony* in Peru. Their only problem was with transport, once crashing a motorbike into a cow! But it was an amazing journey. They travelled 5,000 miles in four months.

While he was travelling, Ernesto met many poor people from Chile, Peru and Bolivia, and this opened his eyes to the lives of poor people. At the end of the journey, he stopped studying to be a doctor, and began his life's work – fighting for the poor. Later, Guevara and his friend Alberto wrote books about this journey, and in 2004 the story was made into a film, *The Motorcycle Diaries*.

*leper colony – a place where people with leprosy (a very serious illness) go to live.

4 Take turns to tell your group about your text. Make notes about the other texts as you listen. Were your answers to Exercise 2 correct?

speakout TIP

Make short notes. Don't write full sentences. Choose only important information. Try to use your own words. *The sun was shining when they began their journey that Friday morning → Sunny when they left.* Find a sentence in one of the texts. Make a note of the main idea in three or four words.

5 Discuss the questions.

1 Which (parts of the) journeys sound interesting/enjoyable/terrible/frightening?

2 Why do you think the stories were made into films?

3 Can you think of any other journeys that have been made into films?

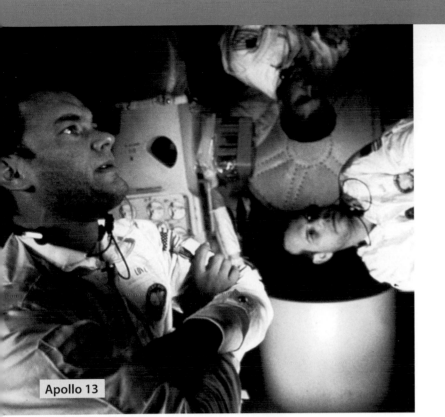

Apollo 13

GRAMMAR past simple and past continuous

6A Look at sentences a)–c) and answer the questions.

a) He **was studying** medicine when he **decided** to travel.

b) But while they **were travelling**, something **went** wrong.

c) One night when it **was raining**, the girls **decided** to escape.

1 What tenses are the verbs in bold?

2 Which action started first in each sentence (*study* or *decide*, etc.)?

B Underline the correct alternative to complete the rules.

Rules:

1 Use the *past simple/past continuous* for actions that continue.

2 Use the *past simple/past continuous* for completed actions.

C Find one more example of the past simple and the past continuous in the same sentence in your text.

➡ page 136 **LANGUAGEBANK**

PRACTICE

7A Make sentences with the prompts.

1 I / run / start to snow. So …

I was running when it started to snow. So I went home!

2 I / wait for a bus / meet my boss. So …

3 I / watch TV / recognise my best friend! So …

4 I / walk home / find $5,000 in a bag. So …

5 We / travel by plane / a man with a gun stand up. So …

6 We / ride our bicycles / a cow walk across the road. So …

7 We / eat in a restaurant / see a mouse. So …

8 I / study in my room / hear loud music next door. So …

B Work in pairs and compare your ideas.

8A ▶ 5.1 Listen to some ideas for Exercise 7A. Are they similar to yours?

B Listen again. Notice how *was* and *were* are pronounced. Then listen and repeat the first part of the sentences.

9 Work in pairs and take turns. Student A: make sentences with the past simple and the past continuous. Use a prompt from A and a prompt from B. Student B: respond with another sentence beginning with *So …* .

A: *I was sleeping in my bed when I heard a strange noise.*

B: *So I called the police.*

A

sleep

ride my motorbike

go for a drink

feel sick

deal with a problem

make a call

sit in a train

go to a concert

have some time off

watch a film

B

get hungry

buy a speedboat

crash

decide to change job

start to feel tired

fall asleep

see the love of my life

check my voicemail

read your email

hear a strange noise

SPEAKING

10A Describe something that happened to you on a trip or journey. Think about questions 1–8 and make notes.

1 Where and when did you go?

2 Who were you with?

3 What was the form of transport?

4 How long did the trip take?

5 What places did you see during the journey?

6 Did anything go wrong during the journey?

7 What happened while you were travelling?

8 How did you feel?

Last summer I went on holiday to Greece with a friend. We stayed in Athens for two days and then we visited some of the islands. One day, while we were travelling by boat, I dropped my bag into the water. I lost my camera, my money and my passport. It was a disaster!

B Work in groups. Tell your stories. Which were the most interesting and/or funniest stories you heard?

| ▶ **GRAMMAR** \| verb patterns | ▶ **VOCABULARY** \| travel items | ▶ **HOW TO** \| talk about travel |

VOCABULARY travel items

1 Work in pairs. Discuss the questions.

1 Do you travel light?

2 What do you usually pack when you go away for a short trip/long holiday?

2A Work in pairs. Look at the words in the box and choose two things for travellers 1–3 below.

| suitcase notebook digital camera souvenirs waterproof clothes dictionary walking boots sunhat rucksack money belt binoculars map umbrella |

1 a grandmother visiting her grandchildren in Australia

2 a student travelling around the world

3 a tourist visiting the sights in New York

B ▶ 5.2 Listen and repeat the words. Underline the stressed syllables.

C Work in pairs. Discuss. Which of the things in Exercise 2A do you own? Which do you take on holiday with you?

▸ page 155 **PHOTOBANK**

LISTENING

3A Read the introduction to a radio programme. Which of the items in Exercise 2A do you think the travellers will mention?

> **What do experienced travellers take on holiday?**
>
> *The Holiday Show* asks the experts to name one thing they always take on holiday.

B ▶ 5.3 Listen and check.

4A Work in pairs and complete the notes.

1 I try to learn _____.

2 I love _____.

3 I take a lot of _____.

4 I usually spend my holidays in

_____.

5 I sometimes travel in _____ places.

6 I don't carry too much _____.

7 I write things down because I like to

_____ them.

B Listen again to check.

GRAMMAR verb patterns

5A Look at sentences 1–9 below and underline the verb + verb combinations.

1 We always <u>expect to hear</u> English.

2 I always <u>want to talk</u> to local people.

3 I <u>love walking</u> when I go on holiday.

4 I always seem to take hundreds and hundreds of photos.

5 I usually choose to go to a warm place.

6 I enjoy travelling in wild places.

7 If you decide to go walking, a rucksack is easier to carry.

8 It's best to avoid carrying too much money.

9 I need to write things down.

B Complete the table below with the verbs in the box.

| ~~expect~~ want seem choose enjoy decide avoid need |

verb + *-ing*	verb + infinitive with *to*
	expect

C Work in pairs. Add the verbs in the box below to the table above. Which two verbs can go in <u>both</u> columns?

| hope finish imagine hate would like love |

▸ page 136 **LANGUAGEBANK**

PRACTICE

6 Cross out the verb combination that is <u>not</u> possible in each sentence.

1 I *hope/~~enjoy~~/expect* to get a free plane ticket.
2 I *want/would like/imagine* to visit Australia.
3 She *loves/avoids/needs* travelling.
4 Where did you *like/decide/choose* to go on your next holiday?
5 They *hate/want/love* working with tourists.
6 He doesn't *seem/need/enjoy* to know this area well.
7 Do you *like/expect/love* going to different countries?
8 Why did you *avoid/decide/hope* to become a travel writer?

7A Complete the sentences and make them true for you. The next word must be either the infinitive with *to* or the *-ing* form of a verb.

1 When I travel:
  I always avoid …
  I hate …
  I love …

2 On my last holiday:
  I chose …
  I decided …
  I enjoyed …

3 For my next holiday:
  I want …
  I hope …
  I would like …

B Work in pairs and compare your ideas.

SPEAKING

8 Work in pairs. Discuss the questions.

1 What type of holidays can you see in the photos? Which do you prefer? Why?
2 Is there anything that you really love doing when you are on holiday?
3 When you travel, do you try to learn about the place, its customs and its language? Why/Why not?
4 Do you enjoy visiting tourist areas, old cities, new cities, or none of these?

A: *I really like sightseeing holidays. I love spending time looking at beautiful old buildings.*
B: *I love taking photos. I put these on my Facebook page when I get back.*
A: *Me, too!*

WRITING using sequencers

9A Work in pairs. Read an email describing a trip and discuss. What were the good/bad things about the trip?

To:	mmazuri@yahoo.com
From:	CelineB@soutain.fr

Hi Mohamed,

I've just got back from my trip to Southern Africa. It was great. <u>First</u> we flew to Lesotho from Johannesburg. Then we took a boat down the river for two weeks. We saw lots of interesting animals and plants. After a while, it started raining heavily so I'm glad I had my waterproof clothes! After that, we went to Cape Town for a week to recover. Finally, we caught the plane back home. I loved the trip but I got tired of living out of a rucksack!

Speak soon.

Love,

Celine

B Underline five words/phrases that help us to understand the order of events. The first one has been done for you.

C Write an email to a friend about a trip or a weekend away. Use the words you underlined.

D Read other students' emails. Who had the most interesting trip?

▶ **FUNCTION** | asking for/giving directions ▶ **VOCABULARY** | tourism ▶ **LEARN TO** | show/check understanding

VOCABULARY tourism

1 Work in pairs. Look at the words in the box. Which things can you see in the photos?

| tour guide | boat trip | coach tour | tourists |
| sightseeing | natural wonder | tax-free shopping |

READING

2A Look at the title of the text. Discuss. What do you think the man does? Why do you think he works in three countries everyday?

B Read the text to find out.

C Discuss. Would you like Juan's job? Why/Why not?

FUNCTION asking for/giving directions

3A ▶ 5.4 Listen to Juan talking about one place in the city. What is special about it?

B ▶ 5.5 Listen and follow the routes on the map. For each route write the destination on the map.

C Listen again and read audio script 5.5 on page 171. Underline useful phrases for giving directions.

The man who works in three countries every day

JUAN OLIVEIRA was born in Argentina, grew up in Paraguay and now lives in Brazil. He says he loves the three countries equally, and he works in all three of them every day.

Juan is a tour guide in Foz do Iguaçu, a Brazilian town which is close to the borders of both Argentina and Paraguay. He takes tourists around the Iguaçu Falls, one of the great natural wonders of the world.

First, he shows tourists the waterfall from the Brazilian side. Then they cross the border to see the water from the Argentinian side. After that, they go on a boat trip which takes them under the waterfall. Finally, he takes them on the short journey to Ciudad del Este in Paraguay to do some tax-free shopping.

He says the Falls are amazing, especially in the rainy season. He sees them every day and he never gets tired of them.

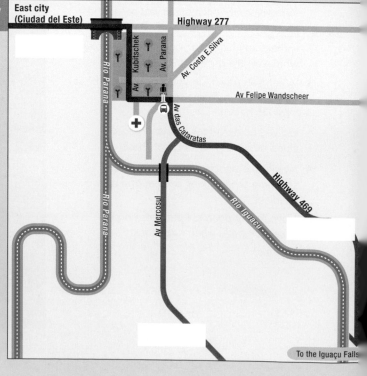

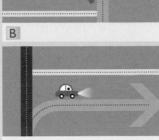

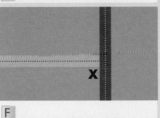

C go along the main road

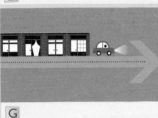

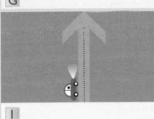

4 Label pictures A–J with the phrases in the box.

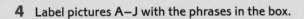

go along the main road   go straight on   in front of you
go past the turning   take the first right   go left
keep going until you reach (the border)   at the corner
go through the (centre of the town)   cross a bridge

5A ▶5.6 **Listen to three conversations. Are the statements true (T) or false (F)?**

1 Speaker 1 takes the bus.

2 Speaker 2 has a map.

3 Speaker 3 will see a restaurant before arriving at The Grand Motel.

B Complete the notes. Listen again to check.

Conversation 1 Carnival

It takes _____ minutes. Go straight on. You'll hear the _____ !

Conversation 2 Plaza Hotel

Go past the cinema. Take the first _____. Keep going for _____ minutes. You'll see the _____.

Conversation 3 The Grand Motel

Go to the end of the street. Go _____ and go past the _____ It's on the _____.

▌▶ page 136 **LANGUAGE**BANK

LEARN TO show/check understanding

6A ▶5.7 **Read and listen to the extracts from the audio script. Are the phrases in bold asking for information (A), explaining directions (E) or showing understanding (U)?**

Extract 1

A: Can we walk? *A*

B: Yes, it takes about ten minutes from here. *E*

Extract 2

C: Excuse me, can you help me? I'm looking for the Plaza Hotel. **Is this the right way?**

D: Um … Plaza Hotel, Plaza Hotel. Yes, **keep going, past the cinema and take the first left.**

C: OK.

D: **Then keep going for about fifteen minutes until you reach the end of the road.** And **you'll see the sign for the hotel. You can't miss it.**

C: OK. **Can you show me on the map?**

D: Sure.

Extract 3

E: Excuse me, we want to get to The Grand Motel. **Is it far?**

F: Umm … sorry, I've no idea. Jim, do you know?

G: What?

F: The Grand Motel?

G: The Grand Motel? Yeah, it's just over there. **Just go to the end of this street. Go left and go past the … um … there's a restaurant. Go past the restaurant and it's on the left.**

E: On the left. **So I need to** go to the end of the street, turn left, go past the restaurant and it's on the left.

B Which phrases mean:

1 Am I going in the right direction?

2 Continue.

3 It's easy to see it.

C ▶5.8 **Listen and repeat the phrases.**

7 Work in pairs. Look at audio script 5.6 on page 171 and practise the first two conversations.

SPEAKING

8 Work in pairs. Student A: look at the map on page 161. Student B: look at the map on page 163. Ask for and give directions.

A: *How do I get to the station?*

B: *Go straight on until you reach the Greek restaurant then turn right.*

DVD PREVIEW

1 Read the programme information and answer the questions.

1 What does Michael Palin do?

2 Where does he travel to in *Full Circle*?

3 How does he travel in this episode?

BBC Full Circle

Michael Palin is an actor and travel writer. In *Full Circle* he went on a journey through the seventeen countries along the Pacific coast. While travelling 50,000 miles in ten months, he saw and discovered things beyond his dreams. He learnt how to cook eggs in a volcano and how to make music with horses' bones in Chile! In this episode Michael travels across the Andes from Arica in Chile to La Paz in Bolivia in a small train.

▶ DVD VIEW

2A Look at the photos. Do you think it was an enjoyable journey? Think about food/comfort/weather/other passengers.

B Watch the DVD and tick the problems the people mention.

• the food is terrible
• the train gets very hot
• the air is thin and it's difficult to breathe
• the train is very noisy
• the train stops a lot because of animals/cars on the track
• the train is very slow

3A Work in pairs. Use a dictionary to check the meaning of the words/phrases in bold.

a) **Twice a week**, a railway service leaves Arica. _1_

b) We've **reached** the Bolivian border. ___

c) It's going to **take two hours**. ___

d) Some passengers are **local**. ___

e) Is it the **journey of a lifetime**? ___

f) It's the **journey of (everyone's) dreams**. ___

g) We've **crossed** the Andes at 16.4 miles an hour. ___

B Watch the DVD again. Number the sentences in Exercise 3A in the order you hear them.

4 Work in groups. Discuss the questions.

1 What do you think of this journey?

2 Would you like to do it? Why/Why not?

speakout an award

5A Read the text and answer the questions.
1 What is the award?
2 What will the winner do?

Journey of my Dreams is an award of €5,000 for the best idea for an original and inspiring journey anywhere in the world. The winner will receive training in film-making and will record their experiences for a future programme.

B ▶ 5.9 Listen to someone describing her journey of a lifetime and answer the questions.
1 Where does she want to go?
2 What does she want to do there?

C Listen again and tick the key phrases you hear.

keyphrases

We would like to go to …
The trip is going to take …
Some of the problems we're going to face include …
We want to experience the local culture …
Our plan is to speak to the local people …
We hope to find out about their traditions …
It should be an inspiring trip.
This is the journey of my/our dreams.

6A You are going to apply for the award. Work in pairs. Decide:
• where/how you are going to travel
• what you would like to experience/see/do
• which people you are going to stay/work with
• why you deserve the award

B Present your ideas to the class. Use the key phrases to help you. Who should win the award?

writeback an application

7A Read the application. Match paragraphs 1–3 with headings a)–c).
a) Goals and objectives
b) Details of the plan
c) Introduction

APPLICATION FORM

1 _____
We would like to go to Easter Island to live with the local people for three months. Easter Island is one of the great mysteries of the world. It has many famous stone statues of heads, but no one knows who made them or why.

2 _____
Our plan is to talk to the islanders about their history and about their present and future. We will ask them about their lives and what they think of the statues. We want to learn how the world's most isolated people live: what they eat, what they do for entertainment and what they think of the modern world of computers and other technology.

3 _____
We will record all of the interviews on film. We will also keep a diary of our own experiences on the island. Eventually, we hope to make a TV documentary and write a book about our time on the island.

B Write your application for the award. Use the model in Exercise 7A to help you.

55

TRANSPORT

1A Choose four types of transport from the box below. Write a sentence about each type. Don't mention the name.

> train tram minibus motorbike
> taxi ferry speedboat coach
> lorry helicopter

It travels through water and is very fast.

B Work in pairs and take turns. Student A: read your sentences. Student B: guess which type of transport it is.

A: It's a fast type of transport. It goes on the road. It has two wheels.

B: A motorbike.

PAST SIMPLE AND PAST CONTINUOUS

2A Put the verbs in brackets into the past simple or past continuous.

1 They (play) when the police (come).

They were playing when the police came.

2 They (run) away one night when it (rain).

3 While they (travel) by motorbike, they (meet) many people.

4 It (lose) oxygen for several hours before they (fix) the problem.

5 He (work) with the poor when he (decide) to change career.

6 While they (fly), some equipment (stop) working.

B Work in pairs. Discuss. Which films from Lesson 5.1 do the sentences go with?

3 Work in pairs and take turns. Ask and answer the question.
Where were you and what were you doing at these times yesterday?

TRAVEL ITEMS

4A Add the vowels.

1 stcs *suitcase*
2 rcksck
3 wtrprf clths
4 wlkng bts
5 sn ht
6 svnrs
7 bnclrs
8 ntbk
9 dgtl cmr
10 mny blt

B Work in pairs. Decide which of the items above are important for the holidays below.

beach   walking

sightseeing   adventure

A sun hat is important for a beach holiday.

VERB PATTERNS

5A Complete the sentences with the correct form of the verbs in brackets.

1 I sometimes choose _____ (go) somewhere on holiday because a friend recommends it.

2 I hope _____ (visit) more cities in my own country this year.

3 I seem _____ (have) good luck with the weather when I go on holiday. It never rains!

4 I want _____ (travel) to places where tourists never go.

5 I always avoid _____ (travel) by boat because I get sick.

6 I don't enjoy _____ (fly) very much.

7 I can't imagine _____ (go) on a camping holiday – I prefer hotels!

8 I wouldn't like _____ (have) a holiday with a big group of people.

B Work in pairs. Discuss. Are sentences 1–8 true for you? Why/Why not?

ASKING FOR/GIVING DIRECTIONS

6A Find and correct the mistakes. There are two mistakes in each conversation.

Conversation 1

A: Excuse me. I'm looking for the Natural History Museum. Is this right way?

B: Keep going until you reach the crossroads. It's in the right.

Conversation 2

A: Hello. We want to go to the Italian Embassy. Is far?

B: No. Just turn left and you'll see the sign for it. You can't miss.

Conversation 3

A: Excuse me, do you know where the university is?

B: Keep going long the main road. Then you'll see a sign and it's in front to you.

B Work in pairs and practise the conversations.

C Work in pairs and take turns.
Student A: ask for directions:

• from a well-known place in the town to Student B's house

• from Student B's house to the school

Student B: ask for directions:

• from the school to a nearby restaurant

• from a nearby restaurant to a well-known place in the town

A: OK. How do I get from the station to your house?

B: Well, you take the first right …

UNIT 6

SPEAKING
❯ Talk about your lifestyle
❯ Discuss food preferences
❯ Explain health problems
❯ Ask about sport for a sports survey

LISTENING
❯ Listen to a radio interview with a food expert
❯ Listen to conversations between a doctor and her patients
❯ Watch an extract from a BBC short comedy about squash

READING
❯ Identify specific information in an article about living longer

WRITING
❯ Write about food
❯ Write about a sporting memory

BBC CONTENT
▯ Video podcast: What do you do to keep fit?
◉ DVD: The Two Ronnies

UNIT

6

fitness

▶ **GRAMMAR** | present perfect + *for/since*   ▶ **VOCABULARY** | health   ▶ **HOW TO** | talk about your health

VOCABULARY health

1A Look at the words/phrases in the box. Are these things good (**+**) or bad (**−**) for your health?

> walking   junk food   fizzy drinks
> working with computers
> lots of sleep   fresh fruit/vegetables
> stress/worrying   city life   alcohol
> missing breakfast   smoking
> vitamins   exercise   caffeine
> oily fish   frozen food   fatty foods

B Work in pairs and compare your ideas. Can you add any more words/phrases to the box?

C Work in pairs and take turns. Ask and answer the questions.

1 What do you do to keep fit and healthy?

2 Do you do anything which is not healthy?

A: *What do you do to keep fit and healthy?*

B: *I get lots of sleep. How about you?*

A: *I cycle to work every day.*

B: *Do you do anything which is unhealthy?*

A: *Well, I probably eat too much junk food.*

READING

2A Look at the photos. Discuss. How do you think these things can help people to live longer?

B Read the texts to find out. Do they mention any of the things you talked about?

C What is the significance of these numbers in the texts?

> ~~94~~ 37   20%   80%   102   6   5–10
> 7   1997   900   3   3–4

94 – Dr Ellsworth Wareham is 94 years old.

D Work in pairs. Discuss the questions.

1 Do you want to live until you are 102? Why/Why not?

2 Do you agree with what the people in the texts do and what they think?

Laugh and live longer

Dr Ellsworth Wareham is a surgeon. He is a specialist in heart surgery and he has been a heart surgeon for 37 years. Now, he is 94 years old and he still performs surgery 3 or 4 times a week. But he doesn't tell his patients how old he is. He thinks that working hard and being active help you to live longer. So he also cuts the grass or helps his wife with the housework. He is a vegetarian, and has a large family. He thinks that these things help you to have 'peace of mind'.

Scientists have studied the people of Okinawa, an island in Japan, since 1970. They are trying to understand why Okinawans live longer than everybody else. It might be because of their diet. Okinawans eat lots of fruit, vegetables and soya. Or maybe it's because they eat 20% less food than people in Western countries. They have a saying 'hara hachibu' – it means 'eat until you are 80% full'. Scientists say that perhaps eating less gives you more energy and keeps you healthier.

Marge Jetton is 102 years old and lives in Loma Linda, California. She believes exercise and keeping fit helps you live longer. She rides 6 miles on a bicycle before breakfast! 'The whole world should be exercising,' she says. 'The television is full of it, everything is full of why you should exercise.' But there is something else. She is religious. Research shows that people who are religious may live longer, sometimes 5–10 years longer than everyone else.

People say that laughing every day makes you live 7 years longer, because it reduces stress. Dr Kataria, a doctor from Bombay, believes laughter is good for you. In 1997 he started Laughter Yoga. Since then he has travelled around the world and established hundreds of laughter clubs. In Bangalore more than 900 people attended a 'laughter conference' where they laughed for 3 days. One thing is certain: even if laughing doesn't make you live longer, it certainly makes you feel better.

GRAMMAR present perfect + *for/since*

3A Read sentences a) and b) and answer questions 1–3 below.

a) Scientists have studied Okinawans *since* 1970.

b) Dr Wareham has been a heart surgeon *for* 37 years.

1 When did scientists start to study Okinawans?

2 Do they still study Okinawans today?

3 How long has Dr Wareham been a surgeon?

B Underline the correct alternative to complete the rules.

Rules:
1 Use the present perfect to talk about things that happened *in the past and continue until now/in the past*.

2 Use *for/since* to talk about a period of time (how long) and use *for/since* to talk about a point in time (when something started).

C Complete the table with the phrases in the box.

2005   ~~ages~~   July   a long time   Saturday   I left university
two weeks/months/years   2p.m.   last night   an hour or two
I was a child/teenager

for	since
ages	2005

➡ page 138 **LANGUAGEBANK**

PRACTICE

4A Complete the sentences and make them true for you using the verbs in brackets.

1 I _____ (study) English for _____ /since _____.

2 I _____ (have) this phone for _____ /since _____.

3 I _____ (know) this teacher for _____ /since _____.

4 I _____ (live) this town/city for _____ /since _____.

5 I _____ (want) to buy a new _____ for _____ /since _____.

B Work in pairs and compare your sentences.

5A ▶ 6.1 Listen to the questions and write short answers with *for* and *since*. Don't write the questions.

1 *by the sea*

2 *for five years/since 2005*

B Work in pairs and compare your answers. Try to remember the questions.

6 ▶ 6.2 Listen and write the questions. Listen again and underline the stressed words.

SPEAKING

7A Write questions for each topic beginning *Do you … ?* and *How long have you … ?*

home

Do you …
live in the city centre?

How long have you …
lived there?

things you have (possessions)

Do you …
_____

How long have you …
_____

hobbies/sport

Do you …
_____

How long have you …
_____

work/study/school

Do you …
_____

How long have you …
_____

B Work in groups. Ask and answer the questions. Try to find out more information.

A: *Do you* have a car?

B: *Yes, I do.*

A: *How long have you* had it?

B: *It's very old. I've had it for about ten years.*

A: *What kind of car is it?*

B: *It's a VW Golf.*

C Tell the class about the students in your group.

► GRAMMAR | *may, might, will* **► VOCABULARY** | food **► HOW TO** | make predictions

VOCABULARY food

1A Work in pairs. How many types of food can you think of for each of the categories below? Make a list.

vegetables   meat

fruit   desserts

B Compare your lists with other students.
➡ page 156 **PHOTOBANK**

C Work in pairs. Discuss the questions.

1 What is your favourite food?
2 Do you ever eat food from other countries/cultures? If so, what?
3 Which of the dishes in the photos do you often/sometimes/never eat? Would you like to try any of them?

paella

sushi

burrito

falafel

LISTENING

2A Work in pairs. Look at the pictures and read the sentences about food. Do you think they are true (T) or false (F)?

1 In the future superfoods (very healthy foods, e.g. broccoli) may be the answer to our health problems.

2 In the future we will eat only food pills because they are healthier than normal meals.

3 In the future we might have food that can change its flavour for different people.

B ▶ 6.3 Listen to an interview with a food expert and check your answers.

C Complete sentences 1–6. Then listen again to check.

1 Superfoods are good for you because they have lots of v_____.
2 The most important thing is to eat healthy food every d_____.
3 In the past, astronauts ate a type of food pill when they were in s_____.
4 Food pills might become more p_____.
5 If you like chocolate ice cream, but your friend likes strawberry, you can eat the same ice cream and it will taste d_____ for each of you.
6 The technology might not replace normal drinks and food, but it may become c_____ in the future.

speakout TIP

When we aren't sure of a word we hear, we can often guess: What letter does the word begin with? How many syllables does it have? Do we recognise the ending of the word (e.g. *-tion, -y, -ed*)? Does the context tell us the type of word (e.g. noun, verb, adjective)? After guessing, check with a friend, your teacher or the audio script.

GRAMMAR *may, might, will*

3 Read sentences a)–d) and answer the questions about the phrases in bold.

a) Food pills **might become** more popular.

b) In the future we **may have** special food that can change its flavour.

c) Eating together is an important part of family life, and it **always will be**.

d) We **won't eat** only food pills in the future.

1 Which one is negative?

2 Which ones mean 'probably, but we don't know'?

3 Which one is a strong prediction about the future?

▮▮▶ page 138 **LANGUAGEBANK**

PRACTICE

4A Write responses to sentences 1–7. Use the prompts in brackets with *might/might not, may/may not* or *will/won't*.

1 We're having a picnic. (rain)   *It might rain.*

2 I'm becoming a vegetarian. (lose / weight)

3 Let's go to the best restaurant in town. (be / expensive)

4 I want to stop eating junk food. (feel / healthier)

5 Let's go to the café for breakfast. (not / be / open)

6 I want to try eating octopus. (not / like / it)

7 I'm going to do a cooking course. (enjoy / it)

B Work in pairs and take turns. Student A: say a sentence. Student B: respond. Try to continue the conversation.

A: *We're having a picnic.*

B: *It might rain.*

A: *Don't be so negative! The sun's shining.*

B: *That's true, but you should take an umbrella.*

SPEAKING

5A Work in pairs. Do you agree with sentences 1–8 below? Tick the four most interesting sentences.

1 In the future, nobody will be hungry for long.

2 People will eat more junk food.

3 People won't eat animals in the future.

4 More people might grow food to save money.

5 Families won't have time to eat together.

6 The next generation may not know how to cook; they will order food on the internet.

7 I might change my diet.

8 I might learn how to cook in the future.

B Compare your ideas with other students.

A: *Number 1 might happen, but it won't happen soon.*

B: *I agree. There is enough food in the world for everyone but it is not reaching the people who need it.*

WRITING sentence structure

6A Work in pairs. Read the extract from a blog below and discuss the questions.

1 Why is food important to Anusha?

2 What is her job?

3 How did she start?

How important is food in your life?

Anusha Jayasuriya, from Sri Lanka, talks about food.

I was eighteen years old when I came to England with my husband and I didn't know how to cook! I needed to learn quickly, so I read books and asked friends for help. I also went on a cooking course. I learnt to cook traditional Sri Lankan and Indian dishes. I also cooked English food. I really enjoyed it and became a chef.

My husband finished his degree in business and so we decided to use our skills together. We opened a Sri Lankan restaurant in 1990 and it became so successful that we opened a second restaurant seven years later.

Food is so important to me: it is my hobby and my passion and it never feels like a job.

B Compare the two examples. What do you notice about the length of the sentences?

I was eighteen years old. I came to England with my husband. I didn't know how to cook.

I was eighteen years old when I came to England with my husband and I didn't know how to cook!

speakout TIP

Short sentences may sound unconnected. Long sentences can be difficult to understand. Try to use *and* only once in a sentence. In the next sentence, use *also*. Look at your last piece of writing. Can you use this tip to improve sentence structure?

C Find two examples of the *and/also* pattern in the blog.

D Choose one of the topics in the box below and write a paragraph. Use different sentence lengths.

| cooking   restaurants   favourite food   family meals |

I love cooking.

One of my favourite restaurants is …

Every Sunday my family …

▶ **FUNCTION** | seeing the doctor   ▶ **VOCABULARY** | illness   ▶ **LEARN TO** | predict information

READING

1A Work in pairs. Look at the photo and discuss. What do you think the BBC Street Doctors do? Read the text to find out.

The BBC Street Doctors are back

Did you know that men are five times less likely to visit a doctor than women? The reason: they don't like waiting. Now the BBC Street Doctors have solved the problem. In this BBC programme, the Street Doctors travel to different cities around the UK and meet people on the street, at a market, in their offices, or wherever people want to meet them. With the Street Doctors, you don't have to wait; they will come to you. So, if you have a health problem, but you have no time to go to the doctor, let the BBC Street Doctors come to you.

B Discuss the questions.

1 Do you think it's a good idea for doctors to visit people on the street or in their workplace? Why/Why not?

2 Would you talk to a doctor on the street/ at work? Why/Why not?

VOCABULARY illness

2A Match problems 1–4 below with advice a)–d).

1 You **have got a headache/backache**.

2 You **have caught a cold/the flu**.

3 You **have broken your arm/leg**.

4 You **have a sore throat** and **a bad cough**. You also have **a high temperature**.

a) Take some **medicine/antibiotics**.

b) Go to the hospital for **an X-ray**.

c) Get some **rest**, and drink lots of hot drinks.

d) Take some **painkillers**.

B Work in pairs. Discuss. What do you do when you have a cold/headache/the flu to make yourself feel better?

A: *I usually go to bed with a hot drink. How about you?*

B: *I don't do anything. I just carry on working.*

FUNCTION seeing the doctor

3 ▶ 6.4 Listen to two conversations between a doctor and her patients. Answer the questions.

1 What problem(s) does the patient have?

2 What does the doctor suggest?

4A Complete sentences 1–6 below with the words in the box.

| ~~matter~~ problem hurt look worry pills |

1 What's the ___*matter*___ ?

2 How long have you had this _____?

3 I'll give you some _____.

4 Can I have a _____?

5 Where does it _____?

6 It's nothing to _____ about.

B Complete sentences 1–5 below with the words in the box.

| painful sleep sick hurts worried |

1 I feel _____ /terrible.

2 I can't _____.

3 I'm _____ about …

4 It _____ when I walk.

5 It's very _____.

C ▶ 6.5 Listen and repeat the phrases.

⟹ page 138 **LANGUAGEBANK**

5 Underline the correct alternative.

1 My head *hurts/pain/sore*.

2 I've got a really bad *flu/cold/sick*.

3 She feels *cough/sick/a temperature*.

4 I think I've *broken/sore/hurting* my arm.

5 Where does it *hurt/pain/sore*?

6 It's nothing to *problem/matter/worry* about.

7 I'll *give/take/look* you some pills.

8 How long have you had this *ill/matter/problem*?

LEARN TO predict information

6A Work in pairs. Look at the extracts from the conversations. What do you think the missing words are?

Extract 1

Doctor: Hello. I'm Dr Andrews. Now, ¹_____?

Woman: Well, doctor, ²_____. I get these ³_____ and I feel ⁴_____.

Doctor: Oh. How long ⁵_____?

Woman: A few ⁶_____ now. And I ⁷_____ at night because my ⁸_____ hurts.

Doctor: And are you very worried or under pressure at the moment?

Woman: No, I don't think so.

Doctor: ⁹_____ healthy diet?

Woman: Hmm. Quite healthy.

Doctor: ¹⁰_____ tea or coffee?

Woman: Yes, I do.

Extract 2

Doctor: Good morning. How can I help?

Man: Well, ¹_____ my foot.

Doctor: Your foot?

Man: Yes. It ²_____ walk.

Doctor: I see. ³_____ anything to it? ⁴_____ an accident?

Man: Um. Well, sort of.

Doctor: Can ⁵_____ a look?

Man: Yes, of course.

Doctor: Where ⁶_____? Here?

Man: Argh. Yes, there.

Doctor: Can you move it?

Man: Yes, a little, but it's ⁷_____.

Doctor: Hmm. I think ⁸_____ broken. It's nothing ⁹_____ about, but I think you should go ¹⁰_____ for an X-ray. I'll write you a note and if …

B Read audio script 6.4 on page 172 to check your answers.

speakout TIP

When you are going into a situation that you can plan for (a visit to the doctor, a trip to a restaurant, etc.), first try to predict the conversation. This will help you to understand words/phrases when you hear them.

7 Put the words in the correct order to complete the conversation.

Doctor: ¹ the / what's / matter?

Patient: ² cough / got / a / I've ³ terrible / I / feel

Doctor: ⁴ you / long / had / the / have / problem / how ?

Patient: ⁵ a / about / week.

Doctor: ⁶ I / a / can / look / have ?

Patient: ⁷ very / it's / painful

Doctor: ⁸ give / painkillers / I'll / some / you

8 Work in pairs. Student A: turn to page 161. Student B: turn to page 163. Role-play the conversations. Before you start, try to predict what the other person will say.

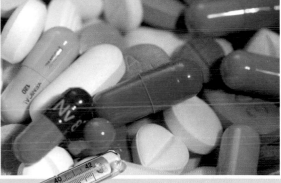

DVD PREVIEW

1A Work in pairs. Discuss. Which sports do you enjoy playing/watching?

B Look at the words in the box. Which words collocate with *play* (P) and which collocate with *go* (G)?

surfing basketball running badminton
horse racing jogging rugby cricket cycling
volleyball swimming squash rollerblading
football skiing windsurfing tennis

C Answer the questions with words from the box.

1 For which sport do you need:
   a) a ball b) a racket c) a bat?

2 For which sport do you score:
   a) a try b) points c) goals?

3 For which sport do you wear:
   a) boots b) trainers c) a swimsuit?

4 Which sport is played in these places in the UK:
   a) Wimbledon b) Lords c) Wembley d) Ascot?

➡ page 157 **PHOTOBANK**

2 Read the programme information about *The Two Ronnies*. Why do you think Ronnie Corbett is finding it difficult to keep calm?

BBC The Two Ronnies

The Two Ronnies was a very popular British comedy show which ran from 1971 to 1987. It featured Ronnie Barker and Ronnie Corbett who played many different characters. In this extract, Corbett and Barker have just played a game of squash. Barker has never played before. Corbett is the local squash champion and he is finding it difficult to keep calm.

Ronnie Barker   Ronnie Corbett

▶ DVD VIEW

3A Watch the DVD. Circle the correct answer.

1 Who won the match?
   a) The man in the suit.
   b) The man in sports clothes.

2 What does the man in the sports clothes (Ronnie Corbett) do during the conversation?
   a) He gets angry and hits the other man (Ronnie Barker).
   b) He gets angry and breaks his racket.

3 Are the two men going to play again?
   a) Yes, they are going to play another match the next day.
   b) No, they can't play again the next day. The man in the suit (Ronnie Barker) is going to play cricket.

B Work in pairs and compare your answers.

4 Watch the DVD again. Who makes comments 1–8: Barker (B) or Corbett (C)?

1 'It's a super game, isn't it? I can't understand why I've never tried it before.'   *B*

2 'How many goals did I get?'

3 'You won four games to love.'

4 'This is a racket, this is a ball, the game is called squash!'

5 'Will it work now you've done that?'

6 'I'm not going to be playing squash any more, ever.'

7 'I thought I might get a bit better.'

8 'I'm the secretary of this squash club. You know, I mean, I captain the A-team.'

speakout a sports survey

5A ▶ 6.6 **Listen to people answering questions for a sports survey. Number the questions in the order they answer them.**

a) Does exercise make you feel relaxed? ___1___

b) How much do you walk a day? ____

c) Do you have a sporting hero? ____

d) How much exercise do you do in a week? ____

B ▶ 6.7 **Listen and check. Tick the key phrases you hear.**

keyphrases

How often do you do sport/go swimming?

Do you like to watch sport on TV?

Have you ever run more than two kilometres?

It's difficult to find time to exercise, but …

I play football a lot/I don't play football very much.

I go to the gym once/twice/three times a week.

I prefer to walk.

I think he is one of the greatest (football) players ever.

Most people in the class like to do sport every day.

Nobody in the class plays tennis/golf.

C **Write a short answer for each question in the sports survey.**

6A **Work in pairs. Write your own sports survey (4–6 questions). Use the ideas below and the key phrases to help you. Think about:**

• your favourite sport

• sporting heroes

• a sport you enjoyed in the past

• a sport you would like to try

B **Interview as many people in the class as possible to complete your survey.**

C **What did you learn about people's attitudes to sport? Discuss.**

writeback a sporting memory

7 **Read the website entry and answer the questions.**

1 Is Louise a football fan?

2 What is her best sporting memory?

3 Where was she? What happened?

Italy wins the World Cup:

Louise Granger remembers

I remember when Italy won the World Cup in 2006. I was staying with some friends in Florence. We were having a meal on a hot summer's evening on a rooftop which had a fantastic view over Florence. Everything was quiet and beautiful. I didn't realise at the time that everybody was inside watching the match on television. Suddenly there was a huge noise. I didn't know what it was at first, but then I realised Italy had just scored and won the World Cup. Within minutes everyone was on the streets shouting, dancing, kissing and sounding their car horns. The party lasted all night long. I'll never forget that night.

8 **Write about a sporting memory for the website. Answer the questions.**

1 What was the event?

2 Where were you?

3 What happened?

4 Why was it so special?

HEALTH

1A Make questions with the prompts below for a class survey.

1 get lots of sleep
2 do exercise
3 eat junk food
4 work with computers
5 miss breakfast
6 take vitamins
7 drink caffeine
8 like oily fish

B Work in groups and take turns. Ask and answer the questions.

C Tell the class what you found out.

PRESENT PERFECT + FOR/SINCE

2A Write the name of:

1 a place you haven't been to since you were a child
2 something you have only had for a few months
3 someone you have known since you were a teenager
4 something you haven't done since you left school
5 something you have wanted to do for a long time
6 a sport/hobby you have done for more than five years

B Work in pairs and compare your ideas. Ask and answer questions about each thing.

A: *I haven't played tennis since I left school. Have you?*

B: *Yes, I love tennis.*

FOOD

3 Find twelve types of food in the word snake.

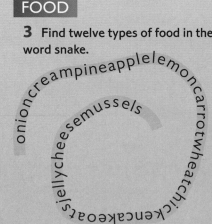

4A Work in pairs. Divide the food in Exercise 3 into these categories. There are two words for each category.

desserts	dairy
fruit	vegetables
grains	meat/seafood

B Add words to each category.

MAY, MIGHT, WILL

5A Match statements 1–6 to responses a)–f).

1 I've drunk eight cups of coffee.
2 I've started buying fresh vegetables.
3 I've stopped smoking.
4 I've stopped taking vitamins.
5 I've started doing yoga classes.
6 I've decided to run a marathon.

a) You won't cough all the time.
b) You might feel less stressed.
c) You may get more colds.
d) You may not be fit enough.
e) You will taste the difference.
f) You might not sleep well tonight.

B Work in pairs and take turns. Student A: use the prompts in the box below to make statements with *I've decided to … .* Student B: respond using *may/may not, might/might not, will* or *won't.*

buy a house in Monaco
give up eating meat   write a book
join a boxing club   get a pet tiger
become a dancer   live in Jamaica
do a degree in physics
marry an astronaut
go into politics

A: *I've decided to buy a house in Monaco.*

B: *It might be expensive!*

6 Work in groups and take turns. Ask and answer the questions.

1 What do you think may happen to your country in a few years' time?
2 Who do you think will win the next World Cup?
3 Where might you be in five years' time?
4 What job will you do in the future?
5 What will you do on your next birthday?
6 Where will you go on your next holiday?

SEEING THE DOCTOR

7A Complete the questions with the correct form of the verbs in the box.

catch   feel   give   break   can   have

1 Have you (or anyone in your family) ever _____ your arm/leg? Where? How?
2 Do you often _____ colds or the flu? What do you do to get better?
3 What do you do when you _____ got a headache?
4 Do you ever find you _____ not sleep? What do you do?
5 When was the last time the doctor _____ you some pills?
6 Is there any food that makes you _____ sick?

B Work in pairs and take turns. Ask and answer the questions.

UNIT 7

SPEAKING
> Talk about a life change
> Tell the story of a man's life
> Learn to find out information

LISTENING
> Listen to a radio programme about two women who changed their lives
> Understand short, predictable conversations
> Watch an extract from the beginning of a BBC film *My Family and Other Animals*

READING
> Read and predict information in a story

WRITING
> Use paragraphs to write about a change
> Write a blog/diary

BBC CONTENT
> Video podcast: How has your life changed in the last ten years?
> DVD: My Family And Other Animals

UNIT

7

changes

VOCABULARY verbs + prepositions

1A Work in pairs. Discuss. Would you like to change anything in your life? What would you change. Why?

B Read the text and circle the correct answer to complete sentences 1–3 below.

Radio Highlights: Life Change   **Saturday 7p.m.**

Are you bored with your life or your job? Do you do the same thing every day? Perhaps you're stuck in a rut, and it's time to **look for** something new.

Every year thousands of people **dream about** changing their lives. Many want to **give up** their jobs and start a new career, or move house or learn a new skill. Lots of people say they'd like to do something different, like **travel around** the world, or **move to** a new country. But only a few people actually follow their dreams. Around holiday times a quarter of the people in the UK **think about** changing jobs, but when the holiday finishes, they just **go back** to work as normal. Others **wait for** an opportunity their whole lives but it never comes. We talked to two women who were not afraid of changing their lives. Listen to their stories on *Life Change*.

---

1 To be *stuck in a rut* means:
   a) to work/live in a boring situation which never changes.
   b) to work/live in the same place for many years.

2 Most people who think about changing their lives:
   a) change one thing.
   b) don't change anything.

3 When twenty-five percent of people in the UK go on holiday:
   a) they have ideas about changing their jobs.
   b) they want to move to another country.

2A Complete the sentences with the phrases in bold from the text in Exercise 1.

1 I sometimes *think about* doing a different job.

2 I really enjoy travelling, but I wouldn't _____ another country to live.

3 I want to _____ my job, and _____ to studying.

4 I need to speak English because I want to _____ a better job. I _____ working as a famous journalist.

5 I should _____ a pay rise before I buy a new car.

6 I would love to _____ different countries.

B Tick the sentences you agree with. Work in pairs and compare your ideas.

Jasmin

LISTENING

3A Look at the photos. What life changes do you think these women have made?

B ▶ 7.1 Listen and check.

4A Read sentences 1–10 below. Are the sentences true (T) or false (F)?

Anita

1 Anita worked long hours in an advertising job.

2 She was nearly thirty years old when she decided to change her life.

3 She wanted to travel around the world.

4 She gave up her job to follow her dream.

5 She worked on a farm in South America.

Jasmin

6 Jasmin worked more than a hundred hours a week.

7 She looked after children in a hospital.

8 She played the piano well when she was a child.

9 She started piano lessons and learnt to write songs.

10 Now she plays her own music.

B Listen again to check.

5 Work in pairs. Discuss the questions.

1 Do you think it was a good idea for the women to make these life changes? Why/Why not?

2 Would you make any changes like this yourself?

Anita

GRAMMAR *used to*

6A Read sentences a)–c) and answer the questions.

a) Anita used to work in advertising.

b) Jasmin didn't use to have time for anything else.

c) Did you use to play the piano?

1 Did Anita work in advertising in the past?

2 Does she work in advertising now?

3 Did Jasmin have time for leisure activities in the past?

4 Does she have more time for these activities now?

5 Does question c) ask about the past or present?

B Look at your answers to questions 1–5 above and underline the correct alternatives to complete the rules.

> Rules:
>
> 1 *Used to* describes a habit or situation which was true in the past but it is not the same now. You can also use the *present/past simple* with the same meaning.
>
> 2 If something used to happen, it happened *once/ more than once.*

▐▐➡ page 140 **LANGUAGEBANK**

PRACTICE

7A Find and correct the mistakes. There are mistakes in four of the sentences.

1 When I was a child I used to cycle to school yesterday.

2 My brother always used listen to heavy metal music.

3 My family used to live in a different city.

4 I used to stay up all night dancing. Now I get tired at 10p.m.

5 We didn't used to have any pets.

6 We used to go skiing in the holidays last year.

B ▶ 7.2 Listen to check. Repeat the sentences.

C Change the sentences so they are true for you. Compare your sentences with other students.

SPEAKING

8A Make a note of three things that have changed in your life in the last ten years. Think about your appearance/home/work/ studies/free time.

B Work in pairs. Discuss. How have your lives changed?

WRITING paragraphs

9A Read about Ryan's life-changing decision. Put the sentences in the correct order to complete the paragraphs.

Paragraph 1

One of the best decisions I ever made was to go back to school. _1_

I've always thought that being a teacher would be interesting __

So I went back to college and did a teacher training course. __

Before that, I was working for a company, but I didn't enjoy my job. __

Paragraph 2

Doing the course wasn't easy. _1_

Now, I have a teaching qualification, and I'm doing the job I've always wanted to do. __

So I used to study in the evenings.

For example, I had to work to earn money, and find time to do coursework. __

B In each paragraph find sentences which:

1 contain the main idea

2 support the idea

3 finish or conclude the paragraph

C Write about a decision which changed your life. Write your story in paragraphs. Use sentences to introduce and support the idea and conclude the paragraph.

> One of the best decisions I ever made was _____.
>
> I wanted to _____. So I _____.
>
> _____ wasn't easy because _____.
>
> But _____. Now, I _____.

▶ **GRAMMAR** | purpose, cause and result ▶ **VOCABULARY** | collocations ▶ **HOW TO** | use phrases to connect ideas

READING

1 Read the definition of *impostor*. Do you know any stories about people who 'pretend to be someone else'?

> **im·pos·tor**, **imposter** /ɪmˈpɒstə
> $ ɪmˈpɒstɚ/ *noun* someone who pretends to be someone else in order to trick people

From *Longman Wordwise Dictionary*.

2A Look at the film poster. Who do you think this man pretended to be?

B Read the story. As you read, stop at each question and, with a partner, guess the answer. Then read to find out.

3 Work in pairs and discuss the questions.

1 Why do you think Demara did these things?
2 Do you think he was a good man?
3 Do you think people like Demara should be punished?

1 Ferdinand Waldo Demara was probably the greatest impostor in history. He was born in the USA in 1921. As a young man he pretended to be a doctor, an engineer, a lawyer, a university professor, a soldier, and a sailor. Demara's greatest adventure was during the Korean War.

What did he do?

a) He pretended to be a doctor on a ship.
b) He worked for the Korean government.
c) He pretended to be a politician.

Read 6 to find out →

2 Demara pretended to be a teacher and the police caught him. He spent six months in prison. After this, he played one more role. He appeared in a 1960 film (called *The Hypnotic Eye*) to make some money, acting as a doctor. But real fame arrived in 1961 when Hollywood made a film of Demara's life.

3 The bullet was very close to the soldier's heart. Demara studied from a book so that he could save the man's life. He removed the bullet and the soldier lived. In fact, while Demara's worked as a doctor, none of his patients died. But in the end he became too successful.

What happened?

a) He appeared on TV and his friends recognised him.
b) His photo and false name appeared in a newspaper.
c) He became a film star.

Read 5 to find out →

4 Demara didn't go to prison because people thought he was a hero. Instead the police released him and gave him extra money to say 'thank you' for his great work! But later the police arrested him for a different crime.

What did he do?

a) He robbed a bank.
b) He pretended to be a policeman.
c) He pretended to be a teacher.

Read 2 to find out →

5 Demara became famous because of his great work as the ship's doctor and his photo appeared in some newspapers in Canada. The mother of the real Dr Cyr saw the photo. She knew this was not her son, so she told the police and they arrested him.

What happened next?

a) He went to prison.
b) He didn't go to prison.
c) He escaped to Europe.

Read 4 to find out →

6 In 1951 Demara pretended to be Dr Joseph Cyr (a real doctor) so that he could work on a ship. The soldiers loved him! He cured their illnesses, he pulled out bad teeth and he performed difficult operations. He had his greatest moment after a soldier was shot.

What did he do?

a) He jumped into the sea and helped the soldier.
b) He pretended to be the dead soldier.
c) He performed an operation that saved the soldier's life.

Read 3 to find out →

VOCABULARY collocations

4A Match 1–7 with a)–g) to make collocations (words that go together).

1	cure	a)	successful/famous
2	make a	b)	a role/a part in a film
3	save	c)	film/documentary
4	become	d)	a crime/a murder
5	be arrested for	e)	a man's life/money
6	spend	f)	illnesses/people
7	play	g)	six months in prison/time abroad

B Work in pairs. Retell the story of Demara's life using the collocations above.

speakout TIP

Many words come in pairs, e.g. *cure illnesses, become famous*. When you hear or read collocations, write them in your notebook. Think of other words that go with *play* and *make*.

GRAMMAR purpose, cause and result

5A Complete sentences 1–3 with *so, to* or *because*.

Purpose (the reason for an action)

1 He appeared in a 1960 film _____ make some money.

Cause (it makes something happen)

2 Demara didn't go to prison _____ people thought he was a hero.

Result (the consequence of something)

3 She knew this was not her son, _____ she told the police.

B Check your answers in the text in Exercise 2B.

C Look again at the text in Exercise 2B and find more examples of *so, to* or *because*.

➡ page 140 **LANGUAGEBANK**

PRACTICE

6A Underline the correct alternative.

1 I'm doing an English course *so/to/because* improve my speaking.

2 I'll do many jobs in the future *so/to/because* I like to try different things.

3 I'd like to become famous *so/to/because* I'm going to study acting.

4 You need to communicate well *so/to/because* become successful in my job.

5 I'd like to make a film about my life *so/to/because* I've had many great experiences.

6 I'd love to spend time abroad *so/to/because* experience another culture.

7 I'm going to take an exam *so/to/because* I have to study a lot.

8 It's difficult to be an impostor *so/to/because* you can never relax.

B Are any of the sentences true for you? Work in pairs and compare your ideas.

7 Work in pairs and take turns. Student A: make sentences with phrases from A. Use the past simple. Student B: complete Student A's sentence with phrases from B and *so, to* or *because*.

A: *I went to the cinema …*

B: *… to watch a film.*

A: *I studied my notes …*

B: *… because I had an exam.*

A	B
go to the cinema	have an exam
study my notes	become a nurse
want to help people	can't drive
go to the doctor	get a Master's degree
like travelling	invite her to a party
go to university	feel sick
phone my friend	love listening to music
cycle to work	watch a film
buy an iPod	become a pilot

SPEAKING

8A Discuss the questions below.

1 Why do people tell lies about their life?

2 When might you tell a lie?

B Work in pairs. Read the situations below and discuss. Would you tell a lie in these situations? Why/Why not?

1 An employee at your company is bad at her job. She tells you a secret: she used false documents (CV and references) to get her job. The boss asks you about her.

2 Your best friend introduces her new boyfriend to you. You don't like him because he doesn't listen or care about anyone else. Your friend asks for your opinion of him.

3 A friend buys a designer bag for $50 from a man on the street. She says the bag usually costs $300 so she bought it. You know the bag isn't a real designer bag. She asks if you want one.

READING

1 Work in pairs. Discuss the questions.

1 Is there a university in your town? What can you study there?

2 Would you like to study in another country? Why/Why not?

2 Read the text and answer the questions.

1 What do Chinese students think about studying abroad?

2 How many Chinese students are there at UK universities?

It's a different world

There is a Chinese saying about education which says, 'Read 1,000 books and walk 1,000 miles.' And this is exactly what students from the People's Republic of China are doing. There are now more than 66,000 Chinese students at UK universities. So, how do students feel about coming to the UK? 'It's difficult at first,' says Yi Lina, a student at Bristol University. 'Everything is very different: the food, the people. But step by step, it gets easier. You open a bank account, get a mobile phone contract, and start talking to people. It has been a great experience.'

VOCABULARY facilities

3A Match 1–5 with the places in the box.

> study centre   book shop   cafeteria
> stationery shop   main reception
> classroom   photocopying room   library
> accommodation/welfare office
> lecture theatre   registration desk

1 borrow a book

2 buy pens, paper and notebooks

3 register for a new course

4 buy a snack

5 find information about where you are staying

B Work in pairs and take turns. Student A: say a place. Student B: say what you can do there.

A: What can you do in a photocopying room?
B: You can make photocopies.

C Discuss. Which of these facilities can you find in your language school/university? Where are they? Which of them do you often/never use?

FUNCTION finding out information

4A Make questions with the prompts below.

a) where / register for my course   _I_

Where do I register for my course?

b) where / the study centre   ___

c) what time / the library open   ___

d) can / help / find my classroom   ___

e) where / use the internet   ___

f) where / buy a notebook   ___

g) where / get a new student card   ___

h) can / tell me / where / go (for information about …) ___

B ▶ 7.3 Listen to the situations. Number the questions above in the order you hear them.

5 Listen again. Are the statements true (T) or false (F)?

1 The registration desk is in the main reception.
2 The study centre is next to the cafeteria.
3 There is internet in the library.
4 The library is open from ten until five every day.
5 You can get a new student card from the main reception.
6 Room 301 is on the third floor on the right.
7 The stationery shop is upstairs.
8 The welfare office is next to the stationery shop.

6A Complete the phrases with the words in the box.

> can excuse have need help time kind

Getting attention
1 _____ me, ...
Could you 2_____ me?
Can you tell me where/what ... ?

Asking for information
Where 3_____ I get/find/buy ... ?
When can I use/start ... ?
What 4_____ is the library open?
What time do the lessons start?
Can I ... ?
Do I 5_____ to ... ?
Is it free/open/near?
I 6_____ to find out about/speak to ...

Thanking someone
Thank you so much.
That's very 7_____.

B Read audio script 7.3 on page 173 to check your answers.

➡ page 140 **LANGUAGEBANK**

7 Find and correct the mistakes. There are two mistakes in each conversation.

1 A: Excuse to me, where's the book shop?
   B: There's one around corner.
2 A: What time do the swimming pool open?
   B: During the week it opens on eight o'clock. At the weekend it opens at nine.
3 A: Can tell me where to get a student card, please?
   B: You need going to reception.
4 A: Where I can get a coffee?
   B: There's a cafeteria over there, next the library.

8 Work in pairs. Student A: turn to page 165. Student B: turn to page 166.

LEARN TO check information

9A ▶ 7.4 Read and listen to the different ways of checking information in bold below.

Extract 1
B: Do you know where the main reception is?
A: **Sorry?**
B: The main reception.
A: Oh, yes.

Extract 2
C: It's next to the cafeteria.
A: **The cafeteria? Where's that?**

Extract 3
A: Do I have to pay?
D: No.
A: **So it's free for students.**
D: Yes, that's right.

Extract 4
E: It's open every day, from 9a.m. until 6p.m.
A: **Did you say 'every day'?**
E: Yes, that's right. Every day, from nine in the morning until six in the evening.

Extract 5
A: I need to find out about my accommodation. Can you tell me where to go?
I: Accommodation? I think you have to go to the welfare office.

B What are the speakers doing in each conversation?
a) Repeating the key words/phrases as a question
b) Asking a checking question/asking for repetition
c) Rephrasing

C ▶ 7.5 Listen and repeat the phrases in bold in Exercise 9A. How does the intonation change?

10 Work in pairs. Role-play the situation below. Student A: you are a student. You have lost your bag. Student B: you work at the reception desk.

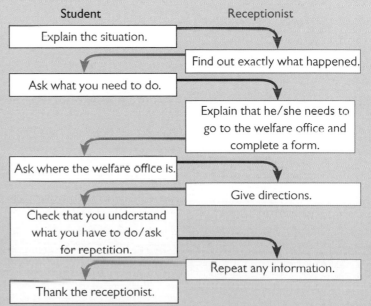

Student	Receptionist
Explain the situation.	
	Find out exactly what happened.
Ask what you need to do.	
	Explain that he/she needs to go to the welfare office and complete a form.
Ask where the welfare office is.	
	Give directions.
Check that you understand what you have to do/ask for repetition.	
	Repeat any information.
Thank the receptionist.	

DVD PREVIEW

1 Work in pairs. Discuss. Have you ever tried to communicate with people who can't speak your language? Where were you? What happened?

2A Read the programme information. Where do the family move to? Why?

BBC My Family And Other Animals

My Family And Other Animals is a BBC film based on Gerald Durrell's book. It tells the story of the Durrells, a rather unusual family: Gerry – a twelve-year old who loves animals, his sister Margot, his brother Leslie, his eldest brother, the intellectual Lawrence and their mother. One wet grey day in the 1930s the family decide to escape the English weather. They sell their house and move to the sunny island of Corfu in Greece. Here they experience a new life of freedom and adventure. But the beginning isn't easy, so they are delighted when they make a new friend, Spiro.

B Look at the photo and read the programme information again. Who are the people in the photo?

▶ DVD VIEW

3 Watch the DVD. Then number the scenes in the correct order.

a) The family are at home in London. It's August, but they do not feel well. __1__

b) The family look for a house to live in, but they cannot find one with a bathroom. ___

c) They meet Spiro and he finds them a beautiful house (villa). ___

d) They decide to look by themselves, so they try to get a taxi. ___

e) They arrive on a boat and the customs officer checks their suitcases. ___

4A Match the people in the box with sentences 1–9 below.

| Mother   Lawrence   Spiro   Gerry   Leslie |

1 'It's August. We need sunshine … Why don't we pack up and go?' *Lawrence*

2 'I'm a writer. That one's very good.'

3 'It's our bed linen. You silly man.'

4 'You've shown us ten houses, and none of them has a bathroom.'

5 'They must have bathrooms. We'll find a place ourselves.'

6 'We don't actually speak Greek.

7 'You need someone who talks your language?'

8 'All the English tourists, they ask for me when they come to the island … There. Villa with bathrooms.'

9 'We'll take it.'

B Watch the DVD again to check.

5 Work in pairs and discuss the questions.

1 Which character do you like best? Why?

2 Where do tourists like to go when they visit your country? What problems do they have?

speakout a new experience

6A ▶ 7.6 **Listen to Agata talking about when she moved to the USA. Answer the questions.**

1 What was the problem?

2 How did she feel?

3 What happened in the end?

B Listen again and tick the key phrases you hear.

keyphrases

It was my first day at …

The biggest problem was …

I felt very nervous/shy/excited when …

I couldn't …

I didn't know …

I wasn't …

Luckily, I met/made friends …

In the end …

7A Talk about a new experience (e.g. when you moved to a new place/started a new course/job). Before you speak, think about the questions below. Make some notes.

1 Where were you?

2 How did you feel?

3 Did you have any problems?

4 What did you do about them?

5 Did you meet anyone who helped you?

6 What happened in the end?

B Work in groups and take turns. Tell each other about your experiences.

writeback a blog/diary

8A Read part of a web diary about Sadie's first year at university and answer the questions.

1 Is she enjoying university life?

2 Did she have any problems? What were they?

So far … so good

I moved to Leeds in July to go to Leeds University and I am really enjoying the experience so far. It's been a fantastic year. I've really enjoyed living somewhere new. Although I miss my family and friends at home. I've met lots of people and I love living in the big city. There is always so much to see and do. It's very different to living at home. When I first arrived, I used to get lost all the time. Now, I've bought a bicycle, and I cycle everywhere.

B Write a blog/diary about your new experience. Use the questions in Exercise 7A and the structure below to help you.

One thing that has really changed in my life is _____. I decided to _____ so that/to _____. Before that, I used to _____.
At first, _____, because _____, but _____. In the end _____.

VERBS + PREPOSITIONS

1A Complete the phrases with a suitable preposition.

1 What do you dream _____ doing in the future?

2 Would you like to travel _____ the world? Which countries would you like to visit?

3 Have you ever given _____ a hobby? Why?

4 Would you ever move _____ a different town? Why/Why not?

5 Are you thinking _____ making any changes to your life at the moment? What are they?

6 Would you like to go _____ to your last school for a day?

B Work in pairs and take turns. Ask and answer the questions.

USED TO

2A Make questions with the prompts. Begin with *Did you use to … ?*

When you were a child:

1 you / work / hard / school?

2 you / eat / fast food?

3 you / spend / time / grandparents?

4 you / get / ill / often?

5 you / have / special friend?

6 you / play any sport?

7 you / travel to school / public transport?

8 you / live / different place?

B Choose two or three of the questions above and write two more related questions.

C Work in pairs and take turns. Ask and answer the questions.

A: *Did you use to work hard at school?*

B: *Yes, I did.*

A: *What subjects did you use to enjoy?*

B: *I used to enjoy art and drama.*

A: *Really? Did you use to get good exam results?*

B: *Well, most of the time …*

COLLOCATIONS

3A Underline the correct alternative in sentences 1–8 below.

1 The doctor *cured/cared* me.

2 This hero *rescued/saved* my life!

3 Sometimes businesses can *become/develop* very successful.

4 My friend Jack *spends/goes* most of his time watching TV.

5 She lost her job after being arrested *by/for* a crime.

6 The criminal *spent/passed* ten months in prison.

7 I *played/was* the role of Hamlet.

8 I would like to *build/make* a film.

B Work in pairs. Add another sentence to sentences 1–8 above.

The doctor cured me. Then I married him!

PURPOSE, CAUSE AND RESULT

4A Match 1–8 with a)–h) to make sentences.

1 I went to the library last week

2 I helped my friend

3 I wanted to eat out

4 I studied

5 I put my feet up and watched TV so

6 I called some old friends to

7 I went to bed late because

8 I went to a meeting

a) to improve my English.

b) I was at a party.

c) to discuss business.

d) hear their news.

e) I could relax.

f) to find a book.

g) because she had a problem.

h) so I went to a restaurant.

B Work in pairs. Choose four phrases from 1–8 above. Make questions to ask what your partner did last week.

A: *Did you go to the library?*

B: *Yes, I did.*

A: *Why?*

B: *To find a book.*

FINDING OUT INFORMATION

5A Put the sentences in the correct order to complete the conversations.

Conservation 1

a) Excuse me, could you help me? _1_

b) Thank you. And what's your surname? __

c) Do you have a registration form? __

d) Your course? OK. Do you have a registration form? __

e) I need to find out about my course. __

f) Sorry? __

g) Oh, yes. In my bag. Here it is. __

h) It's Gorski. __

i) Yes, of course. What can I do for you? __

Conversation 2

a) To the reception? __

b) The swimming pool opens at eight o'clock. __

c) OK, thanks. Is it free for students? __

d) Yes, that's right. __

e) Thanks very much. __

f) No, it's not free, but it's cheaper if you have a student card. __

g) Yes, show your card to the reception when you come in. __

h) Eight. OK. So, do I have to bring my student card? __

i) Excuse me, could you tell me what time the swimming pool opens? __

B Work in pairs and practise the conversations.

BBC VIDEO PODCAST

Download the video podcast and view people describing their lives and how they have changed over time.

Authentic BBC interviews

www.pearsonlongman.com/speakout

SPEAKING
> Talk about a product that people should invest in
> Talk about why you should earn more cash
> Present a business idea

LISTENING
> Listen to a radio programme about great investments
> Listen to a discussion about salaries
> Watch an extract from a BBC documentary about Google

READING
> Understand a web debate
> Read an article about shopping tips

WRITING
> Write a description of a product
> Write an idea for a business investment

BBC CONTENT
▯ Video podcast: How do you feel about shopping?
◉ DVD: The Money Programme: The World According To Google

UNIT
8

money

> **GRAMMAR** | relative clauses   ▶ **VOCABULARY** | money   ▶ **HOW TO** | describe objects, places, things

How do you spend your **money?**

1. Do you usually pay by **cash** or **credit card** when you buy things?

2. Do you ever **lend** money to family or friends? Why/Why not?

3. Have you ever **borrowed** a lot of money? What for?

4. How many **notes** or **coins** do you have in your pocket at the moment?

5. In your country, how much do you **tip** waiters?

6. Which three people do you think **earn** the most money in your country?

7. Have you ever **invested** money **in** something?

8. Who pays the **bills** where you live?

9. Which of your **possessions** is **worth** the most to you?

10. Have you ever had a **money-making** idea?

VOCABULARY money

1A Read the money questionnaire. What do you think the words in bold mean? Which things can you see in the photos?

B Work in pairs. Ask and answer the questions.

➡ page 158 **PHOTOBANK**

LISTENING

2A Discuss the questions.

1 Why do you think the money-making objects below were successful?

2 When do you think they were invented?

B Work in pairs. Discuss. Which of the objects in photos A–D do these sentences describe?

1 One of these appeared in a 1950s film.

2 It is made of rubber.

3 Its name came from a film.

4 It is sold in thirty-seven languages.

5 The US army gives it to soldiers to improve their concentration.

6 750 million people have played it.

7 A company called Apple invented them.

8 In many countries there are more of these than people.

C ▶ 8.1 Listen to a radio programme to check.

3A Work in pairs. Are the sentences true (T) or false (F)?

1 *Chicle* comes from Central and South America. *T*

2 We know that US soldiers were the first people to eat chewing gum.

3 The first mobile phone was invented in 1954.

4 The UK has more mobile phones than people.

5 The name iPod comes from a film called *2001: A Space Odyssey.*

6 The iPod reached the public in 2001.

7 Parker Brothers did not invest in Monopoly immediately.

8 Parker Brothers invented the name 'Monopoly'.

B Listen again to check.

4 Work in pairs. Discuss the questions.

1 Which do you think was the best moneymaker?

2 What other good moneymakers can you think of?

GRAMMAR relative clauses

5 Read sentences 1–5 and complete the rules below.

1 Chewing gum is a sweet which is made of rubber.

2 Mobile phones are phones that you can carry around in your pocket.

3 Charles Darrow made games with a friend who worked in a printing company.

4 Vinnie Chieco was the man that gave the iPod its name.

5 In Monopoly, you buy streets where you can build houses and hotels.

Rules:

Relative clauses tell you:

• which thing, person or place we are talking about.

• what a thing, person or place is or does.

Use ¹ _which_ or ² _____ for things.

Use ³ _____ or ⁴ _____ for people.

Use ⁵ _____ for places.

▶ page 142 **LANGUAGEBANK**

PRACTICE

6A Read sentences 1–3 below. Which things in the box do they describe?

> ~~casino~~ inventor library wallet
> DVD player investor bank credit card

1 It's a place where you go to win money. _casino_

2 It's a thing that you use when you want to pay without cash.

3 It's a person who creates new things.

B Use the prompts below to write definitions for the other things in the box above.

1 place / people look after / your money

2 thing / use / carry / money and credit cards

3 person / gives money / to a product or business (to make more money)

4 place / you go / borrow books

5 thing / use / watch films

C Work in pairs. Student A: turn to page 164. Student B: turn to page 167.

SPEAKING

7 Work in pairs. Look at the famous products below and discuss the questions.

1 Which of these things do you have or use?

2 Who uses them? Why do you think they are popular?

3 Which do you think will still be popular in the future?

WRITING adding emphasis

8A Work in pairs. Read the advertisement below. Look at the words in bold and answer the questions.

1 What type of word comes after them?

2 Which one is the strongest?

3 Which is the weakest?

> ### PENTICAN XP6 LAPTOP COMPUTER
>
> \>\> The laptop is **fairly** new – only used for six months.
>
> \>\> It is in **really** good condition and **very** easy to use.
>
> \>\> It has all the features that you need, including 30GB hard drive and 14 inch screen (see below for more details).
>
> \>\> This is an **extremely** good deal for students or business people who travel and want a light laptop.

B Choose one of the products in Exercise 7 and write an advertisement for it. Include the words in bold from Exercise 8A.

▶ **GRAMMAR** | *too much/many, enough, very*   ▶ **VOCABULARY** | multi-word verbs   ▶ **HOW TO** | talk about quantity

READING

1A Read the text and look at the cartoon. What's the problem?

Violinists in a German orchestra are asking for more money because they play more notes than other musicians. Sixteen violinists, who play in the Beethoven Orchestra in Bonn, say that musicians who play other instruments like the flute or the horn have an easier job. The orchestra's director, Laurentius Bonitz, said the violinists' request was stupid. 'You cannot compare the work of a musician with other jobs,' he said.

B Read the messages below and answer the questions.

Who thinks they should get more money because:

1 they make people happy?

2 they do more than one job?

3 they save the company time or spend more time in the office?

4 they save the company space?

A I send the funniest jokes around the office via email, so I make everyone very happy. The company should give back something in return for this service – for example, enough money for me to buy a big car and go on holiday once a month.

B Where I work, too many people spend hours in the kitchen making coffee, and they never take back their cups at the end of the day. I always do this, so I do my job AND the cleaner's job. I should get a double salary.

C Non-smokers like me, or people who give up smoking at work, should be paid more because we don't leave the office every half an hour for a cigarette.

D When the new boss took over, I showed her how to do her job. This means everyone is happy because she is doing her job properly. My company should pay me for this.

E My boss always has stupid ideas and suggestions for me. I don't say they're stupid – I'm too nice to say that. I usually give in and tell him that I agree. This saves time discussing everything. But I never do the things he suggests. This saves time correcting everything later. I'm not paid enough for being so intelligent.

F I'm only 5 foot 5 inches tall, whereas most of my colleagues are over 6 foot. Therefore I take up less office space than other employees. I think I deserve a bigger salary for this.

C Discuss. Which of these people deserves more money? Why/Why not?

VOCABULARY multi-word verbs

2A Underline the multi-word verbs with *give* or *take* in the messages in Exercise 1B.

B Complete the multi-word verbs.

1 give ___up___ (something): stop doing something (a habit)

2 give _____ : agree to do something you don't want to do

3 give _____ (something): return something to someone or give something to someone because they have done something for you

4 take _____ (something): use or fill an amount of time or space

5 take _____ (something): return something to its correct place

6 take _____ (something): become the boss or take control of something

C ▶ 8.2 Listen to check. Which words are stressed in the multi-word verbs?

3A Think of an example of:

1 a habit or activity you **gave up**

2 a thing you must **give back**

3 an activity that **takes up** a lot of your time

4 a thing you **took back** to a shop (or another place) because you didn't want it

5 a time you **gave in**

6 a thing you would like to **take over** (e.g. a company)

B Work in pairs and take turns. Compare the examples and ask and answer questions about them.

A: *I gave up chocolate.*

B: *Really? When?*

A: *A year ago. It was really difficult.*

🗣 **speakout TIP**

A multi-word verb is a verb + preposition/ adverb, e.g. *wake up*. Multi-word verbs are very common in English. They often have a different meaning from the individual words in them. Always write down multi-word verbs in an example sentence: *I usually wake up at 7.30a.m.* Write down any multi-verbs that you know. Ask your partner to think of an example.

GRAMMAR *too much/many, enough, very*

4A Match sentences 1–6 with sentences a)–f) below that have a similar meaning.

1 I always eat **too much**.
2 **Too many** people spend hours in the kitchen.
3 The company should give … **enough** money for me to buy a big car.
4 I'm **not** paid **enough**.
5 I'm **too** nice to say that.
6 I make everyone **very** happy.

a) I make everyone **really** happy.
b) I eat **more than I should**.
c) **More people than necessary** spend time in the kitchen.
d) They should give me **the right amount** to buy a big car.
e) I'm **so** nice **that I wouldn't** say that.
f) I should earn **more**.

B Look at the cartoons below. Underline the correct alternative to complete the rule.

> Rules:
> 1 Use *too much/too many* with countable nouns.
> 2 Use *too much/too many* with uncountable nouns.

▶ page 142 **LANGUAGEBANK**

PRACTICE

5 Underline the correct alternative.

1 I don't have *enough time/ time enough/ very many time* to do the things I enjoy.
2 I drink *too many/ much/ too much* coffee.
3 I do some *too/ enough/ very* difficult tasks in my work.
4 I am sometimes *very/ enough/ too* busy to study English.
5 I spend *very much/ too many/ too much* hours online.
6 I sleep *very much hours/ enough/ too many* at the weekends.

6A Complete the sentences so they are true for you.

1 I worry too much about …
2 One thing that is too difficult for me is …
3 One thing that makes me very happy is …
4 I don't have enough time to …
5 These days too many people …

B Work in pairs and compare your sentences.

SPEAKING

7A ▶ 8.3 Listen to two people talking about which professions should earn the most money. Which four professions do you think they talk about? Listen and check.

B Read sentences 1–6 below. Which professions are they talking about?

1 They earn too much money.
2 They earn enough money in one week to buy a house.
3 They don't earn enough.
4 They work very hard.
5 They work too hard.
6 (I think) they get too many holidays.

C Listen again to check.

8A Work in pairs. What do the people in photos A–F below do? Who should earn the most money? Why?

I think security guards should earn more than footballers because their job is more important.

B Compare your ideas with other students.

9A Think of three reasons why you or people in your (future) profession should get more money.

B Work in pairs and compare your ideas.

VOCABULARY shopping

1 Work in pairs. Look at the word web below. What do you think the words mean? Add words to each category.

supermarket

markets

shops   **other places/ways to buy things**

butcher

shopping online

shopping

customer

label

people/services   **product**

customer service

brand

2 Work in pairs. Discuss the questions.

1 Do you like shopping? Why/Why not?

2 Where do you usually go shopping?

3 What's the most expensive thing you bought recently? Where did you buy it?

READING

3A Look at the title of the article below. What do you think it says about the things in the box? Read the article to check.

shopping in markets   where to find cheaper brands   food labels   shopping when you are hungry   shopping online   shopping with children

Dos and don'ts for shoppers

- **DO** go to markets early in the morning for the freshest fruit and vegetables. Ask to taste things before you buy.

- **DO** look on the lower and higher shelves in supermarkets. The most expensive brands are always at eye level.

- **DO** read the label when you buy food. The ingredients are listed in order of quantity (the largest quantity comes first).

- **DON'T** go shopping for food if you are hungry. Hungry people always buy too much!

- **DON'T** buy everything online. There's no customer service when things go wrong and there might be extra costs like taxes and credit card handling charges.

- **DON'T** take the children! If you buy only five percent of everything they ask for, you will waste lots of money.

B Work in pairs. Discuss. Which of the things in the article do you usually do? Which three pieces of advice do you think are the most useful? Can you think of any other advice for shoppers?

FUNCTION buying things

4A ▶ 8.4 **Listen to five conversations in shops. What are the people buying? Circle the correct answer.**

1. a) food
   b) we don't know
   c) books
2. a) a carpet
   b) a computer
   c) clothes
3. a) clothes
   b) hair products
   c) we don't know
4. a) a musical instrument
   b) a mobile phone
   c) cleaning products
5. a) a candle
   b) a credit card
   c) we don't know

B Complete the phrases below with the words in the box.

for	here	of	enter	on	cash	me

Customer
Excuse ¹_____.
I'm just looking.
Do you sell … ?
Do you have one ²_____ these in red/blue/a larger size?
Can I try it/this ³_____?
Where's the fitting room?
It doesn't fit/It fits. I'll take it.

Shop assistant
Can I help (you)?
Are you looking ⁴_____ anything in particular?
Who's next, please?
Are you paying by ⁵_____ or credit card?
Can you just sign ⁶_____, please?
Can you ⁷_____ your PIN, please?

C Listen again to check.

5 ▶ 8.5 **Listen to these questions.** Notice how *Do you … ?* and *Can I … ?* are pronounced. Listen again and repeat the questions.

6 Work in pairs. Look at audio script 8.4 on page 173 and practise the conversations.

▸ page 142 **LANGUAGEBANK**

7 Work in pairs. Use the prompts to practise the conversation.

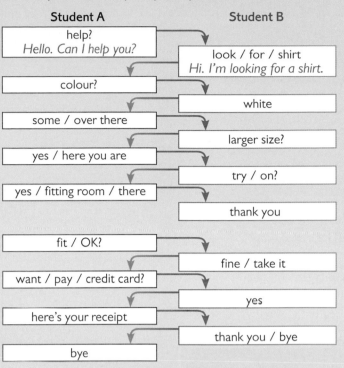

8 Work in pairs. Student A: turn to page 163. Student B: turn to page 166. Role-play the situations.

LEARN TO describe things

9A Look at the phrases in bold. Which are used for countable nouns and which for uncountable nouns?

1. A: Hi there. Are you looking for anything in particular?
   B: Yeah, do you sell **those things that** soldiers wear? Er … it's like a jacket.

2. A: Hello. I was wondering if you've got any of **that stuff you use for** clean**ing** swimming pools.
   B: Um … yeah, we usually sell a liquid cleaner.

B Put the phrases in bold in the correct place in the conversation.

1. It's a type of
   A: What are you looking for?
   B: Pen. You use it to write on walls.

2. It's a kind of
   A: Are you looking for anything in particular?
   B: Yes. Oil that you use for cooking.

SPEAKING

10A Think of an example of a type of clothing, a type of food and something you use in the house.

B Work in pairs and take turns. Student A: describe your things. Student B: guess what they are.
A: It's a type of clothing that you wear around your neck when it's cold.
B: A scarf!

DVD PREVIEW

1 Work in pairs and discuss the questions.

1 Do you use the internet? Why/Why not?

2 Which websites do you visit most regularly?

2A Read the programme information. Why is Google special?

BBC The Money Programme: The World According To Google

The programme tells the story of the internet **search engine** Google. In less than ten years it has **revolutionised** the way people use the internet. It is used by more than 400 million people a month and it has turned its **founders**, who invented the **software**, from students into **multibillionaires**. *The Money Programme* does its own search on this **extraordinary** money-making machine and finds out how it has changed the lives of millions of people.

B Match the words/phrases in bold with 1–6 below.

1 the program a computer uses to do a job

2 strange, unusual or surprising

3 a computer program that helps you find information on the internet

4 the people who start an organisation

5 people who have billions of pounds (or dollars)

6 completely changed the way in which people do something

▶ DVD VIEW

3 Complete the sentences about Google. Watch the DVD to check.

1 Google's founders were two computer science _____, Larry Page and Sergey Brin.

2 They met on a day out from Sergey's _____.

3 Sergey was acting as a _____.

4 They developed a piece of _____ which they believed could revolutionise searching the internet.

5 Google started as a student project but became one of the most _____ companies ever.

4 Watch the DVD again. Are the following statements true (T) or false (F)?

1 At first Larry and Sergey thought their software might not be successful.

2 Google's offices are similar to other big companies' offices.

3 Google became a successful business when it started using a special system of advertising.

4 Companies who advertise on Google choose some key words. When people type these words into the search engine, the advertisement appears.

5 Work in pairs. Discuss. Can you think of any other successful internet companies? What do you know about them?

speakout a money-making idea

6A ▶ 8.6 Listen to someone talking about a money-making idea. Underline the correct alternatives to complete the summary.

The Very Special [1] *Bake/Cake* Company will make cakes for [2] *children/adults*. It plans to sell the cakes at local [3] *markets/parties*, in shops, and on the internet. It [4] *needs/doesn't need* a lot of money to start the business, but it does need a beautiful [5] *website/kitchen*.

B Listen again and use the key phrases to complete sentences 1–5.

keyphrases

Our business is called …

Our idea is to …

We hope to make money by …

To be successful, we need to …

We plan to …

1 go to markets and give people a free taste.

2 make delicious birthday cakes for children.

3 The Very Special Cake Company.

4 advertise.

5 selling the cakes at local markets, in shops and on the internet.

7A Work in groups. Choose a hobby/interest you have and think about how you could make money from it. Answer the questions.

What is the name of business?

What is the product/idea?

How will the business make money?

Who will you sell to?

What will you need to start/be successful?

B Prepare to present your ideas to the class. First practise your presentation. Use the notes in Exercise 7A to help you practise.

C Take turns to present your ideas to the class. Which group has the best idea? Which idea do you think could be the most successful? Why?

writeback a website entry

8A Read an advertisement for a competition and one of the entries. What is different about the business idea?

Calling all entrepreneurs

If you have a good business idea, and would like some help, or investment from us, write and tell us about it. The winner of the 'Entrepreneur of the Year Award' will be given up to €10,000 to help start their business.

We plan to open a clothes shop called 'One World'. Our idea is to import handmade clothes from India and sell them in shops and on the internet. Our business will be different because we will pay fair prices to the people making the clothes in their own country. We need €10,000 to open the shop and build the website.

B Write an entry for the competition. Explain what your idea is, how it is different from other ideas and what you would do with the money. Use the model above to help you.

MONEY

1A Complete the poem.

Brenda Bones was poor and thin
Until her famous lottery win.
She won a million! She paid her
¹b _ _ _ _ !
She bought a big house in the hills.
And after a year of complete rest
Then she decided to ²in_ _ _ _
In a super-size hot air balloon
And flew from Cairo to Cameroon
Forgetting the money she gave or
³l _ _t,
Till every penny of her million was spent.
Then one sad day the balloon crashed
And Brenda Bones ran out of ⁴c_ _ _.
She ⁵borr _ _ ed some ⁶c_ _ ns and took a train
And walked until she was home again.
She had no money, she had no car
So she got a job in a little bar
And told long stories about her trips
And all the customers gave her
⁷t_ _ _.
It took her years to finally learn it
But money's better when you
⁸e_ _ _ it!

B Work in pairs and compare your answers. Then read the poem aloud.

RELATIVE CLAUSES

2A Complete the sentences with *that*, *where* or *who*.

1 Monday is the day of the week
  that
  ⟨ I like best.
2 Pasta is the food I eat most often.
3 My mother is the person has helped me the most.
4 The town I grew up is really beautiful.
5 My brother and sister are the only people understand me.
6 The restaurant I usually have lunch is expensive.

B Make the sentences true for you.

C Work in pairs and compare your ideas.

A: *Sunday is the day of the week that I like best.*
B: *Really? Why?*
A: *Because I can relax.*

MULTI-WORD VERBS

3 Work in pairs and take turns. Ask the questions and complete the responses using the correct multi-word verb.

1 A: Are you still fighting with your boss about your salary?
   B: No. I _gave in_ .
2 A: Do you still smoke?
   B: No. I _____ _____.
3 A: Do you still have her book?
   B: No. I _____ it _____.
4 A: Do you still have all those guitars in your living room?
   B: No. They _____ _____ too much space.
5 A: Did you keep the car your company lent you?
   B: No. They _____ it _____.
6 A: Did he join another company?
   B: No, he _____ _____ this one!

TOO MUCH/MANY, ENOUGH, VERY

4 Look at the pictures. What's the problem in each situation. Make as many sentences as you can using *too*, *very*, *(not) enough*, or *too much/many*.

BUYING THINGS

5A Put the words in the correct order to make conversations.

Conversation 1
A: I / you / help / can?
B: looking / just / I'm

Conversation 2
A: I / help / can?
B: tools / you / gardening / do / sell?
A: just / I'll / check

Conversation 3
A: you / particular / looking / are / anything / in / for?
B: you / these / do / red / have / of / in / one?

Conversation 4
A: it / is / how?
B: doesn't / it / fit
   have / do / in / size / bigger / one / you / a / of / these?
A: look / I'll / a / have
   you / here / are
B: Thanks.
   OK / fits / it

Conversation 5
A: next / who's?
   are / or / credit / paying by / you / card / cash?
B: card, / credit / please
A: here / just / you / please / can / sign?

Conversation 6
A: me / excuse
   this / try / can / I /on?
B: certainly / sir / yes
A: room / where's / fitting / the?
B: left / it's / the / on

B Work in pairs. Practise the conversations.

UNIT 9

UNIT 9

nature

▶ **GRAMMAR** | comparatives/superlatives   ▶ **VOCABULARY** | nature   ▶ **HOW TO** | talk about the environment

VOCABULARY nature

1A Work in pairs. Discuss. Have you ever:
- swum in an ocean, a river or a lake?
- walked in a desert or a rain forest?
- climbed a mountain?

B Work in pairs. Think of an example for each thing in the box.

> ocean lake desert river waterfall
> mountain range rain forest

a mountain range – The Andes

▶ page 158 **PHOTOBANK**

rain forest

desert

LISTENING

2A Work in pairs. How many problems can you think of that are related to the environment?

The rain forest is getting smaller.

B ▶ 9.1 Listen to a programme about the environment. Does it mention your ideas?

3A Listen again. Find and correct the five mistakes in the factfile below.

Face the facts

The planet is in trouble. Let's look at why.

Population

There are more than six billion people on the planet, and by 2050, there might be more than fifteen billion. A big **population** means big problems for the planet.

Water

Many people in the world can't get enough water. In Gambia, Africa one person uses four and a half litres of water a day. But in the USA, it's 6,000 litres. And the deserts are getting smaller.

Animals

People **destroy** the rain forest to make more space for businesses, roads and farms. In the last ten years, we have destroyed more than 150,000 square kilometres – that's an area larger than Greece! Animals and plants will become **extinct**.

Weather

The world is getting warmer. The ice in Greenland is **melting** fast, and on Mount Everest there is more snow every year. **Sea levels** are rising. Soon some of the world's most important cities might be under water.

B Complete the sentences with the words in bold from Exercise 3A.

1 When all the animals of a species die, the species becomes _____.

2 If there is more water in the sea, the _____ go up.

3 The number of people in a place is its _____.

4 When you damage something very badly so now it doesn't exist, you _____ it.

5 The ice is _____ because of the heat.

GRAMMAR comparatives/superlatives

4A Read sentences 1)–4) and complete the rule.

1 People are living long**er** and health**ier** lives **than** before.

2 It gets **more** difficult to find clean water.

3 There are **more** people on the earth.

4 There is **less** space than before.

> **Rule:**
> Use comparatives to compare two things, people or situations.
> With short adjectives, add _____ or _____ to the end of the adjective (+ *than*).
> With longer adjectives use _____ + adjective.
> We also use _____ / _____ + noun to compare things.

B Read sentences a)–c) and complete the rule.

a) It has **the** high**est** number of plant species in the world.

b) **The most important** cities might be under water.

c) **The least important** problem is …

> **Rule:**
> Use *the* + superlative to say which is the biggest, the best, etc. in a group.
> With short adjectives: use *the* and add _____ to the end of the adjective.
> With longer adjectives use *the* + _____/least + adjective.

C Look at audio script 9.1 on page 174 and underline more examples of comparatives and superlatives.

▶ page 144 **LANGUAGEBANK**

waterfall

lake

ocean

PRACTICE

5A Complete the table.

adjective	comparative	superlative
long	*longer*	*the longest*
high	_____	_____
healthy	_____	_____
difficult	_____	_____

B ▶ 9.2 Listen and check your answers.

C ▶ 9.3 Listen and repeat. Underline the stressed syllables.

1 It's the most beautiful place I've ever been to.

2 It's hotter than I expected.

3 The food is cheaper than at home.

4 It's more dangerous than I thought.

6A Complete the questions. Use the comparative or superlative form of the adjective in brackets.

1 What is _____ building in your town? (beautiful)

2 Is your country _____ it used to be? (warm)

3 Where is _____ place you have been to? (nice)

4 Do you think living by the coast is _____ living in the city? Why?/Why not? (healthy)

5 What's _____ away from home you've been? (far)

6 Is your country _____ other countries near it? (big)

7 Are people who live in the country _____ people who live in the city? Why/Why not? (friendly)

8 What is _____ place you have been to? (polluted)

B Work in pairs and take turns. Ask and answer the questions.

SPEAKING

7A Work in pairs. Read *The Great Green Survey*. What can you do to protect the environment? Write two more questions.

> ### THE GREAT GREEN SURVEY
> 1 DO YOU RECYCLE? WHY/WHY NOT?
> 2 DO YOU USUALLY WALK OR TAKE THE CAR?
> 3 DO YOU GROW YOUR OWN FOOD?
> 4 DO YOU THINK NUCLEAR ENERGY IS A GOOD OR A BAD IDEA?
> 5 _____
> 6 _____

B Work in groups. Ask and answer the questions. Who is the 'greenest' person in your class?

WRITING similar sounding words

8A Underline the correct alternative.

1 Is this *you're/your* umbrella?

2 What are you going to *where/wear* today?

3 I bought *too/two/to* tickets for the concert.

4 I'm going to *write/right* an article about it.

5 I can't *sea/see* why it's so difficult.

6 I can't help. It's *there/their/they're* problem.

B Find and correct six spelling mistakes.

> I think everyone should recycle. I've done this since I was a child and it's not difficult. Children need to be educated about the write way to look after the world we live in. I use a bicycle to get to work every day, and I get very angry when I sea people use a car to drive round the corner to the shops. Their are lots of small things we can do to help the environment like turning off the television when your not watching it, using plastic bags for you're rubbish, and recycling, two.

C Choose one of the topics in Exercise 7A and write your own comment.

▶ **GRAMMAR** | articles   ▶ **VOCABULARY** | the outdoors   ▶ **HOW TO** | talk about nature

VOCABULARY the outdoors

1 Work in groups. Discuss the questions.

1 Do you like wild places?

2 Have you ever slept outdoors or been out in the wild?

3 Which wild places would you like to visit?

2A Work in pairs and read sentences 1–8. What do you think the words in bold mean?

1 I'd like to live in a **rural area** when I'm older; it's nicer than the city.

2 The north of my country is an area of **natural beauty**; tourists often visit it.

3 Where I live there is a lot of **beautiful scenery**; it's good for walking.

4 I went camping in a **national park**; it was very quiet and peaceful.

5 We visited the **wildlife centre**; there were lots of unusual birds.

6 I'd like to visit a **tropical rain forest** and see the trees and insects.

7 My country has interesting **geographical features**, like volcanoes and forests.

8 I like being out in the **fresh air**; it's nice to be out of the city.

B Discuss. Which sentences are true for you?

C ▶ 9.4 Listen and underline the stressed parts of the words in bold.

D Listen and repeat the sentences.

READING

3A Look at the picture and the titles of the stories. What do you think happened?

B Read the texts to find out.

4 Answer the questions.

1 In the first story, what was in the tree?

2 Why was Frances screaming?

3 Why was she disappointed with her trip to Bolivia?

4 Why does Mike say is it difficult for tourists to see wildlife?

5 What frightened Mike?

6 What happened at the end of the second story?

5A Work in pairs. Look at words/phrases 1–6. What do you think they mean? Use a dictionary to check your ideas.

1 disturb (paragraph 1)

2 hit (paragraph 1)

3 pull off (paragraph 2)

4 shake (paragraph 2 and 4)

5 attack (paragraph 4)

6 disappear (paragraph 4)

B Use the pictures and words above to retell the stories.

Bee attack!

1 I was on a three-day jungle trip in Bolivia. I really wanted to see amazing wild animals like in the Tarzan films. On the first day we went out and the guide started telling us about the trees and the insects. He went up to one of the trees and said there was a bees' nest inside. He said it was important not to disturb them. Then he hit the tree with his stick six or seven times!

2 Immediately hundreds of small black bees flew out of the tree. In a second there were bees in my hair, inside my jacket and on my arms and legs. I just ran screaming and pulling off my jacket and trying to shake them from my hair. I didn't stop for about five minutes! Fortunately I was OK, but we didn't see any interesting animals on the whole trip; only insects!

(Frances Eales)

A surprise meeting

3 Before I became a BBC TV presenter, I worked as a biologist in tropical rain forests. I spent years living out of a rucksack – looking for places with large numbers of rare animals. When tourists come to the Amazon, they usually don't see much wildlife. Tropical birds and mammals are very shy and difficult to see. But when you live for months in these places, the animals sometimes give you a wonderful surprise.

4 On one occasion I went off the path because I needed the toilet – and there in front of me was a jaguar! South America's biggest cat often attacks people. Fortunately, this one didn't want to have me for lunch. In a couple of seconds the jaguar disappeared into the rain forest, leaving me shaking with amazement . . . and fear!

(Mike Dilger)

GRAMMAR articles

6 Read the rules and put examples 1–5 in the correct place.

1 there in front of me was a jaguar
2 the jaguar disappeared
3 Tropical birds are shy
4 the Amazon
5 I worked as a biologist

Rules:

1 Use *a/an* before singular nouns:
I lived out of a rucksack.
Use *a/an* the first time we mention the thing/person:
a) _____

Use *a/an* before job titles (in general):
b) _____

2 Use *the* before nouns when there's only one:
the moon
Use *the* before the names of some places:
c) _____

Use *the* if we have already mentioned the thing/person (the listener knows which one):
d) _____

Use *the* in some phrases with prepositions:
on the first day, in the wild, on the left

3 Use no article before most cities, countries and continents:
I was on a trip in Bolivia.
Use no article before plural nouns:
hundreds of black bees
Use no article to talk about general types or groups of things:
e) _____

Use no article in some phrases with prepositions:
for lunch, for months, on one occasion, at night, in class

➤ page 144 **LANGUAGEBANK**

PRACTICE

7 Find and correct the mistakes below. There is one mistake in each sentence.

1 I always wanted to be ^*a* presenter of nature programmes.
2 I was one of many tourists in the South America.
3 A guide met us at the airport. The next day, same guide took us hunting.
4 On second day the guide took us to a river.
5 I sometimes make a programmes in Britain.
6 In my job, I can explain natural world to millions of people.
7 Generally I hate the insects, but especially bees.
8 I carried rucksack for many years.

8 Complete the text with *a*, *the* or – (no article).

When I was ten my father took me camping for the first time in ¹_____ Michigan, USA. He wanted to teach me about wild animals, insects and trees.

We enjoyed the first two days together walking and fishing. Then ²_____ my uncles came with ³_____ bows and arrows to go hunting.

One evening we were sitting by the fire when ⁴_____ bird flew over us. Immediately my uncles jumped up and fired their arrows at ⁵_____ bird. All of them missed. But suddenly the arrows were flying down at us from ⁶_____ sky. There were arrows everywhere – they looked like rain! We ran to escape them and fortunately no one was injured.

That day I didn't learn anything about ⁷_____ animals or insects or trees, but I learnt ⁸_____ great lesson about gravity!

SPEAKING

9A Work in pairs. Read two comments about country life and city life. Which is closer to your opinion?

> I can't stand the countryside or wild places. There are too many flies and animals that either want to eat you or your food. Even worse: there are no cinemas, no supermarkets, and you can't get a good coffee!

> I get out of the city whenever I can. I love the peace and quiet of the countryside, and the people are much nicer there. I love the wild: animals, trees, mountains, forests – these are the best things in life.

B Are you a 'country person' or a 'city person'? Think about the good and bad things about life in the country and life in the city.

C Work in pairs. Explain which you prefer.

▶ FUNCTION | making guesses   **▶ VOCABULARY** | animals   **▶ LEARN TO** | give yourself time to think

VOCABULARY animals

1A Work in pairs. Look at the word webs. How many animals can you add to each category?

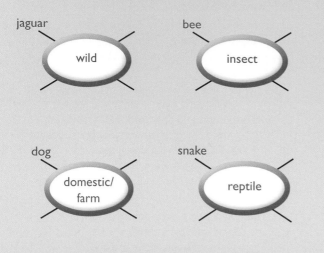

jaguar — wild

bee — insect

dog — domestic/farm

snake — reptile

B Work in pairs and take turns. Student A: say a letter. Student B: say an animal that begins with it.

➡ page 159 **PHOTOBANK**

speakout TIP

Get a study buddy. *Buddy* = 'friend' in US English. Review vocabulary and take turns to test each other.

LISTENING

2 Work in pairs. Discuss the questions.

1 What can humans do better than animals?

2 What can animals do better than humans?

3A Work in pairs and do the *Man or beast?* quiz.

B Compare your answers with other students.

4 ▶ 9.5 Listen to three people discussing the questions in the quiz. How many did you get correct?

5A Match the animals/people in the quiz with sentences 1–8.

1 They lay their eggs where they were born. *sea turtles*

2 They go from Canada to Mexico every year.

3 They can eat electric wires.

4 They can survive in water for three days.

5 They sleep eighteen hours a day for the first few months of their life.

6 They sleep between fifteen and eighteen hours a day for their whole life.

7 They remember friendly faces.

8 They hide their food and remember where it is.

B Listen again to check.

MAN OR BEAST?

We can't fly like birds so we invented the plane. We can't swim like fish so we invented the boat. We can't run like cheetahs so we invented the car. Man is good at inventions but we can't beat the beasts at everything. Do the quiz to find out which is better: man or beast?.

1 Who has the best sense of direction?
a) a monarch butterfly
b) a sea turtle
c) a New York taxi driver

2 Who is the best athlete?
a) a lion
b) a rat
c) a triathlete

3 Who sleeps the most?
a) a black bear
b) a sloth
c) a human baby

4 Who has the best memory?
a) an elephant
b) a jay (a bird)
c) a university professor

FUNCTION making guesses

6A ▶ 9.6 Listen to the first part again and number the phrases in the order that you hear them.

a) It could be …   ____

b) It might be …   ____

c) Maybe …   ____

d) It can't be …   ____

e) Perhaps …   ____

f) It's definitely not …   ____

g) It must be …   ____

B Complete the table with the phrases from Exercise 6A.

It's possible	It's not possible	It's certain
_____	_____	_____
_____	_____	
_____		
_____		

C Answer the questions.

1 Which are the 'silent' letters (letters which are not pronounced) in *could* and *might*?

2 How do you say *must* when you are speaking quickly?

D ▶ 9.7 Listen and repeat.

▶ page 144 **LANGUAGEBANK**

7A Underline the correct alternative.

1 What's the world's biggest fish?

It *could be/can't be* a whale because whales aren't fish.

2 What's the world's fastest bird?

It *is definitely not/might be* a penguin. They can't fly.

3 What is the largest bird?

It *must be/can't be* an ostrich because they are often taller than humans.

4 What's the longest land animal?

Perhaps it's/It can't be a crocodile because some snakes are much longer.

5 What's the world's fastest land animal?

Maybe it's/It can't be a cheetah because they can run at 100 km/h.

6 Which animal causes the most deaths?

It could be/It's definitely not a shark because they only kill a few people every year.

7 Which animal has the largest brain?

It *can't be/must be* a whale because they are very large and intelligent.

8 Which animal lives the longest?

It *can't be/might be* a tortoise because they can live to 150 years old.

B Work in pairs and answer the questions. Then check your answers on page 164.

LEARN TO give yourself time to think

8 Look at the extracts from audio script 9.5. Underline four phrases that give you time to think.

A: The best sense of direction? Perhaps it's the butterfly.

B: Er, I'm not sure.

A: It's hard to say. Well, it could be sea turtles …

B: Um, it might be, but I think it's the butterfly. It can't be the taxi driver, can it?

B: Who sleeps the most? Let me think.

A: Who has the best memory? That's a good question.

9A Find and correct the mistakes in each conversation.

1 A: The world's fastest animal? Er, let me to think.

B: Well, I'm not much sure, but I think it's the cheetah.

2 A: The animal that lives the longest? Um, that's good question.

B: It's hard say, but it could be the tortoise.

B Work in pairs and practise the conversations.

SPEAKING

10A Look at photos A–E below. Which animal/animal parts are shown? Why do you think the parts are special?

A: *What do you think A is?*

B: *I don't know. It could be …*

B Compare your ideas with other students. Check your answers on page 164.

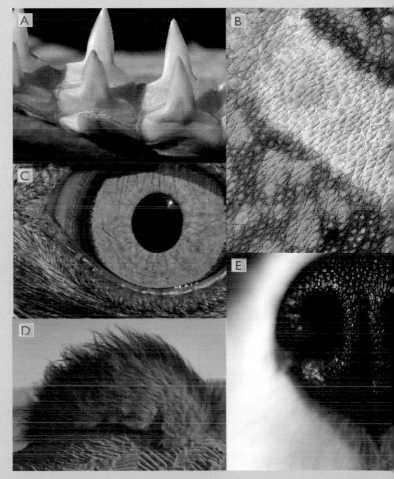

▶ DVD PREVIEW

1A Work in groups. Discuss the questions.

1 What part of the world do you think the picture shows?

2 Why do you think some people like going to places like this?

B Read about the programme information. What does Joanna Lumley do? Where does she go? Why?

BBC Joanna Lumley In The Land Of The Northern Lights

Actress Joanna Lumley grew up in hot Malaysia. During her childhood she dreamed of being somewhere cold, and of seeing the amazing Northern Lights of Norway. Many years later she got the chance. This BBC documentary programme follows her journey. She travels by plane, boat, train, sled and car to get to the far north, where she hopes her dream will come true. Will she see the lights?

▶ DVD VIEW

2A Read sentences 1–5. Which word from the box do you think completes each sentence?

lights books dogs people snow

1 As a child, Joanna never saw _____.

2 She feels as if she's in another world because there are no _____.

3 She brings essential things, for example, _____.

4 After the train journey she meets a guide and his _____.

5 At night, she goes to see the _____.

B Watch the DVD to check your answers.

3A Read sentences a)–f). Match the words in bold to words in the box below with a similar meaning.

amazing   difficult to find   necessary not definitely good or bad   hot and wet climate happy to wait (maybe for a long time)

a) As a little girl I lived in the steamy heat of **tropical** Malaysia.

b) The weather near Tromsø is **uncertain**.

c) And if we're very lucky we might see the **elusive** Northern Lights.

d) This is the most **astonishing** thing I have ever, ever seen.

e) I pack up things that are going to be **essential** on every trip.

f) You just have to be **patient**.

B Watch the DVD again and number the sentences in the order you hear them.

4 Work in pairs and discuss the questions.

1 Would you like to do what Joanna Lumley did?

2 Is there anywhere you have wanted to visit 'all your life'? Where? Why?

speakout an amazing place

5A ▶ 9.8 Listen to a woman talking about a natural place she visited and answer the questions.

1 Where is the place?

2 What is special about it?

B Listen again and tick the key phrases you hear.

keyphrases

What did you think of it?

It was amazing/frightening/wonderful!

The first thing you notice is … (how big it is)

How did you get there?

The best thing about it was … (the silence)

How long did the journey take?

The journey took two hours/two weeks.

Would you like to go back?

6 Answer the questions.

1 What's the highest place you've ever been to?

2 What's the wildest place you've ever been to?

3 What's the most beautiful place you've ever been to?

4 What's the longest walk you've ever done?

5 What's the coldest place you've visited?

6 What's the hottest place you've visited?

7A Work in pairs and compare your answers. Use the key phrases to talk about your experiences.

B Work with other students and tell them about your experiences. Decide which places are the most interesting, the most exciting and the most relaxing?

C Tell the class about your partner's experiences.

writeback a travel blog

8A Read a travel blog. Which country does Matt recommend? Why?

> For an out-of-this-world experience, go to Namibia's Etosha National Park. I went there last month with two old friends and had an amazing time. We hired a car – a Land Cruiser, which was great for the less-than-perfect roads – and just drove around for a week. The wildlife was incredible. We saw elephants drinking by a pool, a lion chasing a deer, two giraffes eating the leaves of a tall tree, and many types of bird. At night we stayed in a tent in one of the many campsites in the area. It was wonderful to wake up to the sound of silence! After a week we went to Windhoek, Namibia's capital, but I would love to go back to Etosha one day.

B Choose a place you have visited. Write about your experience. Use these questions to help you.

1 Where did you go?

2 When?

3 Who with?

4 Why was it an amazing experience?

5 Would you like to go again?

NATURE

1A Do the geography quiz.

THE GEOGRAPHY QUIZ

1 Which mountains are higher?
  a) The Andes
  b) The Rockies

2 Which country has a longer coastline?
  a) Russia
  b) Canada

3 Which lake is larger?
  a) Lake Toba
  b) Lake Michigan

4 Which river is shorter?
  a) the Amazon
  b) the Nile

5 Which is the deepest ocean?
  a) The Pacific
  b) The Atlantic

6 Which is the highest waterfall?
  a) Niagara Falls
  b) Angel Falls

B Work in pairs and compare your answers. Then check the key on page 164.

COMPARATIVES AND SUPERLATIVES

2A What are the comparative/superlative forms of the adjectives in the box?

> hot good lovely cheap
> high boring healthy long
> exciting fast old cold

B Work in pairs and take turns. Student A: say an adjective. Student B: say the comparative/superlative form.

A: big

B: bigger, the biggest

B: expensive

A: more expensive, the most expensive

3A Complete the questions with the correct form of the adjective in brackets.

1 Who is _____ student in the class? (organised)
2 Who studies _____? (hard)
3 Who has _____ hair? (long)
4 Who is _____? (young)
5 Who is _____? (tall)
6 Who has read _____ books this month? (most)
7 Who drives _____ car? (fast)
8 Who lives _____ from the school? (far)

B Work in groups and take turns. Ask and answer the questions.

ARTICLES

4 Add *a/an/the* to the sentences where necessary.

1 Excuse me, where's nearest bank?
2 This city is big, but it doesn't have airport.
3 Cigarettes are bad for you.
4 Hi. Would you like drink?
5 Where's money I lent you?
6 I love ice cream. It's my favourite food.
7 She goes to small school in the centre of London.
8 We missed the bus and waited an hour for next one.
9 My sister is working in United States at the moment.
10 Is there internet café near here?

5 Underline the correct alternative to complete the sentences.

1 I want to be a vet because I like *the animals/an animals/animals*.
2 She looked up and saw an eagle in *the sky/a sky/sky*.
3 He graduated and became *the journalist/a journalist/journalist*.
4 A lion attacked us. Immediately, Jan, our guide, shot *the lion/a lion/lion*.
5 They spent some time in *the Argentina/an Argentina/Argentina*.
6 We went on holiday but it rained on *the first day/a first day/first day*.

ANIMALS

6A Find the names of nine animals in the word square.

c	r	o	c	o	d	i	l	e	e
h	o	a	o	b	o	c	d	t	f
i	t	g	w	h	l	l	j	u	k
m	b	l	m	n	p	i	g	r	o
p	i	p	q	r	h	s	t	t	u
a	t	v	w	w	i	x	y	l	z
n	a	b	h	s	n	a	k	e	c
z	d	e	a	f	f	h	i	j	a
e	a	g	l	e	d	i	o	e	n
e	e	y	e	l	i	p	m	s	o

B Work in pairs and take turns. Student A: describe one of the animals in the word square. Student B: guess which animal it is.

MAKING GUESSES

7A Work in pairs. Guess the countries. Use *must be, may/might be* or *can't be.*

Picture A can't be …

B Check your answers on page 165.

SPEAKING

> ❯ Discuss qualities of different places
> ❯ Decide on the punishments to fit the crimes
> ❯ Talk about an important issue

LISTENING

> ❯ Listen to conversations about different cities
> ❯ Watch an extract from a BBC documentary about the world's oldest rock band

READING

> ❯ Read an article about crime and punishment

WRITING

> ❯ Use formal expressions to write a letter
> ❯ Write an email of complaint
> ❯ Write about an issue

BBC CONTENT

> 🔲 Video podcast: How do you feel about city life?
> ⦿ DVD: Power To The People: The Zimmers Go To Hollywood

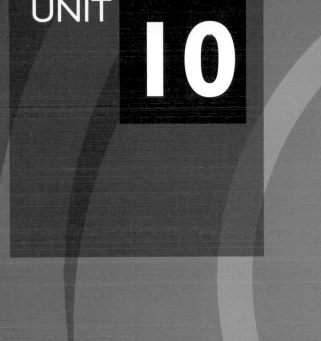

UNIT

10

society

▶ **GRAMMAR** | uses of *like*   ▶ **VOCABULARY** | describing a city   ▶ **HOW TO** | talk about where you live

Copenhagen

Tokyo

SPEAKING

1A Work in pairs. Discuss. Which do you think are the world's ten best cities to live in? Why?

B Read the text. What were the results of the survey? Look at page 165 to find out.

The world's best cities

In 2008 *Monocle Magazine* looked at cities around the world to find the ten best cities to live in. They asked people what is important in a city. The survey came up with some surprising results ...

VOCABULARY describing a city

2A Read sentences 1–12 below. Are they positive (+) or negative (–)?

1 It has clean, safe streets.
2 The public transport system is terrible.
3 There's a lot of traffic.
4 It has beautiful buildings.
5 The people are friendly and polite.
6 There's a lot of crime.
7 It's very polluted..
8 There are nice parks and green spaces.
9 It has good shopping/nightlife.
10 There are lots of things to see and do.
11 It's expensive to live there.
12 It's very crowded.

B Read the positive (+) sentences again. Which three are the most important for a city?

C Work in pairs and compare your ideas.

Dubai

Munich

Sydney

LISTENING

3A ▶ 10.1 Listen to the conversations and look at the photos. Which city does each speaker talk about? What do they think about it?

B Listen again. Which city has these things?

1 perfect weather   *Sydney*
2 fast, cheap public transport
3 cafés where you can sit outside
4 good shops and nightclubs
5 cheap restaurants selling local food
6 lots of cheap taxis
7 a terrible public transport system

4 Read audio script 10.1 on page 174. Underline phrases from Exercise 2 which the speakers use to describe the cities.

GRAMMAR uses of *like*

5A Match questions 1–5 with answers a)–e).

1 What's Sydney like?
2 What's the weather like?
3 Do you like living in Tokyo?
4 What's the public transport like?
5 And what do you like best about living in Tokyo?

a) Yes, Tokyo is a great city to live in.
b) Sydney is one of the best cities in the world.
c) The weather is fantastic.
d) The food, definitely. I love Japanese food!
e) The metro system is fantastic.

B Match questions 1–5 above with the rules below.

Rules:

1 Use *like* (verb) to talk about something you enjoy/think is nice.

2 Use *be like* to describe or give your opinion about something. *Question 1*

⫸ page 146 **LANGUAGEBANK**

PRACTICE

6A Complete the conversations using questions with *like*.

1 A: I've never been to **Madrid**. What's _____?
   B: It's a lovely city. There's a great atmosphere and the people are really friendly.
2 A: Do _____ living in **Moscow**?
   B: I love it! It's one of the best cities in the world.
3 A: _____ your **new** flat _____?
   B: It's very small, but it's near the city centre.
4 A: What _____ best about living in **Rome**?
   B: The food. I love Italian food!

B ▶ 10.2 Listen to check. Then listen again and repeat the questions.

C Rewrite the questions by changing or removing the words in bold.

D Work in pairs and take turns. Ask and answer the questions.
A: I've never been to Poznan. What's it like?
B: It's a small city, so there isn't a lot of traffic.

SPEAKING

7A Choose two cities you know well. Write down three positive things and one negative thing for each city.

B Work in groups and take turns. Describe the cities and say why you like/don't like them. Which of the cities should be in the top ten places to live? Why?

WRITING using formal expressions

8A Work in pairs. Discuss. Is parking a problem in your town/city? Why/Why not?

B Read two letters about plans to build a new car park. Who agrees with the plans, Edith Grove or Greg?

Dear Sir,

I am writing about the plans to build a new car park near the South Stadium. At the moment this area is a beautiful park – a place where people can walk and have a break, and where children can ride bicycles and enjoy themselves. **In addition to this**, it is a place where old people like myself can meet and talk to others. If you build a car park here it will destroy all this, and it will also increase pollution. Please help us to save this special place.

I look forward to hearing from you.

Yours faithfully

Edith Grove

Hi John,

Just a quick note to support the plans to build a new car park near the stadium. I drive into work every day and it sometimes takes me thirty minutes or more to find a parking space. Also, the car parks near my work are very expensive so sometimes I have to walk three miles to my office. I think it's very important to provide enough cheap parking; without this, many people will stop coming to the city. Speak to you soon.

Best wishes,

Greg

C Look at the formal expressions in bold in the first letter. Find informal expressions with a similar meaning in the second letter.

formal	informal
Dear ...	*Hi*
I am writing	
In addition to this	
I look forward to hearing from you	
Yours faithfully	

D Write a letter to the mayor about an issue in your town/city. Use formal expressions. Include these things:
• the reason for your letter
• a short description of the problem
• what you would like the mayor to do

SPEAKING

1A Match photos A–E below with the crimes in the box.

> graffiti murder drink driving
> credit card fraud speeding

B Work in pairs. Which crimes are the most serious? Number them in order.

C Discuss. Are any of these crimes a problem in your town/city?

READING

2A Read the introduction to an article and answer the questions.

1 What did the man do wrong?
2 What was his punishment?
3 What is *alternative sentencing*?

Make the punishment fit the crime

A man is caught stealing books from a bookshop. The judge asks why he did it, and the **thief** says he loves books. What is the man's punishment? A **prison sentence**? A big **fine**? No. The man is sent to read stories and books to hospital patients. He enjoys the job and continues to do it for many years!

Welcome to the new world of alternative sentencing programmes. Instead of traditional punishments, criminals get the punishments that fit their crimes.

B Work in pairs. Discuss. What alternative sentences can you think of for the crimes in Exercise 1?
For drink driving, you should wear a sign saying 'Don't drink and drive!'
For graffiti, you should …

C Read the rest of the article. Does it mention any of your ideas?

What other examples of alternative sentencing are there? Two boys were caught **writing graffiti** on a wall. The normal punishment for this is a fine, but in this case the boys were told to do **community service**. They cleaned seventy walls in three weeks.

A **shoplifter** was caught **shoplifting** three times in one year in a small town in the United States. What was her punishment? She was sent to speak to shop owners. She gave advice on how to stop shoplifters. In one month she spoke to the owners of forty shops. She told them all about shoplifting and the techniques that shoplifters use. It was a great service to the community because after that shoplifting almost disappeared from the town.

What about more serious crimes? Is alternative sentencing possible for crimes like **theft** or credit card **fraud**? It depends on many things. Who are the criminals? Are they young? Is this their first crime? Can they change their way of life? One recent story suggests it is possible.

A thief stole a lot of camping equipment. He loved hiking, mountain climbing and other sports. Instead of going to prison, he was told to keep all the equipment and to take groups of schoolchildren and their teachers camping and hiking every weekend. He loved it, the children loved it, and now it's his job.

D Work in pairs. Discuss the advantages and disadvantages of the alternative sentencing programme. Student A: you think it is a good idea. Student B: you think it is a bad idea.
A: *I think it's a great idea because …*
B: *I don't think it's a very good idea because …*

VOCABULARY crime and punishment

3A Match the words in bold from the text in Exercise 2 with definitions 1–9 below.

1 a person who steals things *thief*
2 time that is spent in prison
3 writing or drawing on public walls, doors, etc.
4 doing unpaid work to help your town/city
5 stealing things
6 a person who steals things from shops
7 cheating someone to make money from them
8 stealing things from a shop
9 an amount of money that you have to pay

B Put the words in the correct place in the table.

criminal	crime	punishment
thief		

> **speakout TIP**
>
> Sometimes words have the same stem, e.g. *shoplifter/shoplifting*. It is a good idea to write these words together. Write them in your vocabulary notebook.

▶ page 159 **PHOTOBANK**

GRAMMAR present/past passive

4A Complete the tables with the passive form.

Present	
active	passive
The police **catch** a man stealing books from a bookshop.	A man _____ caught stealing books from a bookshop.

Past	
active	passive
The judge **sent** the man to read stories.	The man _____ sent to read stories.

B Read the sentences again. Which say <u>who</u> does the actions, the active or the passive? Complete the rule below.

> **Rule:**
>
> Use the passive to talk about what happens to things/people when we don't know who/what caused the action (or it's not important).
>
> Form the passive with: subject + verb _____ (in the present, past or other tense) + past participle.

C Find five more examples of the passive in the article.

▶ page 146 **LANGUAGEBANK**

PRACTICE

5A Make passive sentences with the prompts and the verb in brackets. Use the present simple or the past simple.

1 When I was a child I / many stories (tell)
When I was a child I was told many stories.

2 I / Jim by my friends (call)
3 I / that I am like my father (tell)
4 When I was younger I / by many teachers (help)
5 On my last birthday I / to Disneyland (take)
6 Last Christmas I / an iPod (give)
7 I / every month by my company (pay)
8 I / as captain of my football team when I was at school (choose)

B Change the sentences so they are true for you. Then work in pairs and compare your sentences.

I am called Nico by my friends.

SPEAKING

6A Work in pairs. Complete the stories with the active or passive form of the past simple.

Story 1

Two boys aged nine and eleven [1]_____ (arrest) for robbing a sweet shop. They used a 'gun' which was actually a water pistol with black tape around it. When the shop assistant [2]_____ (start) laughing, the boys ran away, but they [3]_____ (stop) five minutes later by the police. The police arrested them, but said that the gun didn't have any water in it!

Story 2

A woman [4]_____ (send) to prison for internet fraud. Leila Krieff had a website called heroesfund.com, which [5]_____ (ask) the public to send money for ex-soldiers. But Krieff didn't give the money to the 'heroes'. Instead, she [6]_____ (buy) two homes, a Porsche, a Mercedes and a boat.

Story 3

Tony and Gretel Rivera were arrested for art theft. Between 1999 and 2007 they [7]_____ (steal) hundreds of paintings from art galleries in the USA. One painting [8]_____ (take) by the Riveras from a gallery in Santa Fe. The Riveras [9]_____ (catch) when they tried to sell the painting to Joachim Cohen in California. Cohen recognised it immediately; he owned the art gallery in Santa Fe.

B Work in pairs. Think of alternative punishments for crimes in stories 1–3. Present your ideas to the class.

> **FUNCTION** | complaining   > **VOCABULARY** | problems   > **LEARN TO** | sound firm but polite

VOCABULARY problems

1A Work in pairs. Look at phrases 1–8 below. What do the words in bold mean? Which things can you see in photos A–E?

1 public transport **delays**
2 **litter** on the streets
3 bad **service** in a restaurant or shop
4 **faulty** equipment
5 someone speaking **loudly** on a mobile phone
6 computers **crashing**
7 getting **stuck in a traffic jam**
8 receiving **spam** in your inbox

B Discuss. Which of the things in Exercise 1A annoy you the most? What other things annoy you?
I can't stand people eating in the street.

FUNCTION complaining

2A ▶ 10.3 Listen to three people complaining and answer the questions.

1 Where are they?
2 What problems do they describe?

B Listen again and answer the questions.

Conversation 1
1 What does the receptionist offer to do?
2 Does she sound rude or polite?

Conversation 2
3 How long did the man wait for a table?
4 How long did he wait for his meal?
5 What reason did the manager give?

Conversation 3
6 How long has the woman waited?
7 Why is she surprised?

3A Read sentences 1–6 below. Are they complaints (C) or responses (R)?

1 There's a problem with the air conditioning. *C*
2 We'll look into it right away.
3 I'm sorry, but there's nothing we can do at the moment.
4 It doesn't work.
5 I'm really sorry about that.
6 I've been here for over an hour.

B Read audio script 10.3 on page 175 to check your answers.

▶ page 146 **LANGUAGEBANK**

4 Match complaints 1–4 with responses a)–d).

1 I bought this digital camera here last week but there's a problem with it.
2 I had an appointment with Doctor Shipson at 3.00p.m., but I've been here for over two hours.
3 Excuse me, the lights in my room don't work.
4 We were told there's a flight delay of over six hours. Is this right?

a) I'm really sorry about that. He's very busy at the moment.
b) I'm sorry, but there's nothing we can do at the moment. There's a problem with the electricity.
c) I'm afraid that's right. The plane has a faulty engine.
d) OK, can you leave it here? I'll look into it right away.

LEARN TO sound firm but polite

5A Read phrases 1–3 below. When do we use them?

1 Could you help me?

2 I'm afraid I have a complaint.

3 Excuse me, could I speak to the manager?

B ▶10.4 Listen to the pronunciation of the phrases. Underline the stressed words. Then listen and repeat.

speakout TIP

When we want to criticise or complain we usually use a phrase to introduce the complaint. This helps the listener to prepare for what we are going to say. Is this the same in your language? How do you say the phrases in Exercise 5A in your language?

6 There are words missing from conversations 1–3. Complete the conversations with the words in the box.

could   into   doesn't   speak   ago   afraid   problem

Conversation 1

A: Excuse me, could I to the manager?

B: Yes, one moment, please.

A: There's a with the TV in my room. It work.

C: OK, I'll send someone up to have a look at it.

Conversation 2

A: Excuse me, I ordered room service over an hour. Can you look it, please?

B: Yes, of course.

A: Thank you.

Conversation 3

A: You help me? I'm I have a complaint.

B: What's the problem?

A: This soup is cold.

B: I'm sorry, sir. I'll take it back to the kitchen.

7 Work in pairs. Student A: turn to page 165. Student B: turn to page 166. Role-play the situations.

SPEAKING

8A Read sentences 1–6 about the Noparlo School of English. Which problems are the most annoying?

1 Lessons are delayed because the teacher is always late.

2 The equipment in the Self Access Centre is faulty.

3 The classrooms are full of litter.

4 Students use their mobile phones in class.

5 The heating doesn't work and it is winter.

6 The school food is terrible.

B Work in pairs. Student A: turn to page 161. Student B: turn to page 166.

WRITING

9A Read an email that a student wrote to the director of the Noparlo School and discuss. What is wrong with the email?

To	ripoff@noparlo.co.uk
From	kszabo@whiner.com

<u>Hey</u> Mr Ripoff,

I <u>want</u> to complain about my course at the Noparlo School of English. Firstly, I was very mad about the classes. The teacher was always late. Secondly, your advertisement said there was a Self Access Centre with modern equipment, but a lot of the equipment was rubbish. Finally, the classrooms were dirty and full of litter. Give me a refund for the last two weeks of my course.

Write back to me now.

Goodbye!

Katya Szabo

B The words underlined in the email are too direct. Work in pairs and underline five more words/phrases that are too direct.

C Replace the underlined words/phrases with the words/phrases in the box.

would like   Yours sincerely   Dear
disappointed with   faulty
I look forward to hearing from you soon
I would like to receive

D Write an email to the director of the Noparlo School of English. Complain about problems 4, 5 and 6 in Exercise 8A.

DVD PREVIEW

1 Work in pairs. Discuss. What sort of life would you like when you are older? What problems do you think other people sometimes have?

2 Read the programme information and answer the questions.

1 Who are The Zimmers?
2 What makes The Zimmers different to other rock groups?
3 How did they become famous?
4 Why are they going to America?

BBC Power To The People: The Zimmers Go To Hollywood.

Power To The People is a BBC documentary series. For this episode, film-maker Tim Samuels wanted to make a film about what it's like being old in Britain. So he found a group of people who had something to say, and they started a rock band. 'The Zimmers*' were born. With a combined age of over 3,000, they are the world's oldest rock band. They went to the famous Abbey Road studios to record a version of The Who's song, *My Generation*. It became an instant success on YouTube. Now, they're off to Hollywood to appear on America's biggest chat show. Tim Samuels follows them in the studio and on their travels.

*** A zimmer frame** – a frame that helps people to walk

▶ DVD VIEW

3 Watch the DVD and undeline the correct alternative to complete 1–3.

1 Three years ago *Alf/Joan/Winnie* fell and injured herself. The only time she leaves her home is when she needs to go to the doctor or the dentist.

2 *Alf/Joan/Winnie* is ninety-nine years old. She lives in care homes, but she can't find one she likes. She left her last home because she was bored.

3 *Alf/Joan/Winnie* likes to meet his friends and play bingo. Now the bingo club is closing and he is worried he will lose his friends.

4 Watch the DVD again. Match the numbers in the box to the facts they refer to.

~~40~~	16	3,000	2 million	82	90

1 the number of people in The Zimmers *40*
2 the combined age of all the people in the band
3 Joan's age
4 the number of times Winnie has moved care homes
5 Alf's age
6 the number of people who watched the video in the first few days

5 Work in pairs. Discuss the questions.

1 How do you think the Zimmers changed Alf, Joan and Winnie's lives?

2 Do you think it was a good idea to form a rock band? Do you think it will change things for older people?

3 Is there a problem with how old people live in your country? What would help the situation?

speakout an issue

6A ▶ **10.5 Listen to two people talking about issues that concern them. Tick the issues that they talk about.**

| smoking   drugs/alcohol   crime   fast food   technology |
| buildings in your town/city   traffic   litter   supermarket |
| food   cost of living   green issues   public transport |

B What is the problem? Listen again and complete the summaries.

1 She doesn't understand why the supermarket buys ¹_____ from ²_____ when they could buy them from the UK.

2 He is angry that the trains are ³_____. He thinks the service should be ⁴_____.

C Read audio script 10.5 on page 175 to check. Underline the key phrases in the audio script.

keyphrases

One thing that really annoys me ...

I don't understand why ...

I get fed up with ...

I just think ...

And another thing is ...

I think ... should ... / it should be ...

D Work in pairs. Choose an issue you feel strongly about from the box in Exercise 6A (or choose another one). Answer the questions.

1 What is the problem?

2 Why is it a problem? What has caused it?

3 Why do you feel strongly about it?

4 What do you think people should do to change the situation?

E Work in groups and take turns to talk about the problem. Do you agree/disagree with other people's ideas?

writeback a web comment

7A Read the website comment below and answer the questions.

1 What is the problem?

2 How does the writer feel about the problem?

3 How do you feel about it?

One thing that makes me really angry is when people throw rubbish on the streets and on the beaches. The problem is that nobody comes to clear it away. I go out every morning and collect litter that has been left on the beach. Nobody pays me for this. I do it because I love the beaches here. Every year there is more and more litter, and the beaches get dirtier and dirtier. I just don't understand it. I think people who drop litter should pay a fine, and the police should make them come with me in the mornings, and clear all the litter away.

Sabrina, UK

B Write about an issue you feel strongly about. Use the prompts below.

One thing that makes me really angry is _____. The problem is _____. I don't understand _____ _____. I think _____ should _____.

DESCRIBING A CITY

1A Complete the phrases.

1 a lot of tr _ _ _ _ _
2 beautiful bu _ _ _ _ _ _ _
3 friendly, po _ _ _ _ people
4 a good public tr _ _ _ _ _ _ _ system
5 a lot of cr _ _ _
6 clean, safe st _ _ _ _ _
7 good ni _ _ _ _ _ _ _
8 it's ex _ _ _ _ _ _ _ to live there

B Work in pairs and take turns to describe a place you know. Use the phrases above to describe it.

USES OF *LIKE*

2A There is one extra word in questions 1–6 below. Find the word and cross it out.

1 What's ~~do~~ the weather like today?
2 What food do you to like most?
3 What's your capital city it like?
4 What do you like about where do you live?
5 What's about the food in your country like?
6 What like are the people like where you live?

B Work in pairs. Ask and answer the questions.

CRIME AND PUNISHMENT

3 Reorder the letters in the underlined words to complete the sentences.

1 He was given a <u>ironps teennecs</u> for committing the crime.
2 The graffiti artist had to do <u>icymountm viceers</u>.
3 The <u>filterposh</u> was caught in a shop.
4 Unfortunately <u>fehtt</u> is very common in my city.
5 Credit card <u>dufar</u> is a modern crime.
6 He received a <u>nife</u> for parking his car in the wrong place.
7 How did they catch the <u>hefit</u>?
8 She was found <u>wingrit ragffti</u> on a wall.

PRESENT/PAST PASSIVE

4A Match 1–6 with a)–f) to make sentences.

1 The television was
2 The American Constitution
3 Penicillin was discovered
4 The first aeroplanes
5 Surfing was first
6 The Statue of Liberty and the Eiffel Tower were

a) built by French architects.
b) invented by John Logie Baird.
c) practised by Australian sportsmen.
d) was written in 1787.
e) were built by the Wright brothers and Alberto Santos Dumont.
f) by Ian Fleming.

B Work in pairs. Discuss. Do you think the sentences are true (T) or false (F)?

A: *I don't think that penicillin was discovered by Ian Fleming.*

B: *No, he wrote …*

COMPLAINING

5A Underline the correct alternative to complete the conversations.

Conversation 1
A: Hello. Could I speak to Mike Jones?
B: Yes, I'll get him.
A: Hi, Mike. I'm [1]*afraid/frightened* there's a problem with the computer. It's crashed.
B: OK, just bring it over and we'll look [2]*up to/into* it right away.

Conversation 2
A: Excuse me. I'm afraid I [3]*have/make* a complaint.
B: Oh really. What's the matter?
A: It's this remote control I bought from you. It [4]*doesn't/isn't* work.
B: Oh yes, this part's faulty. Would you like another one?

B Work in pairs. Practise the conversations.

6 Work in pairs and role-play the situations. Student A: you are a customer. Read the situation and make complaints. Student B: you are the manager. Try to help the customer.

Situation 1
You are in Yumi Yumi, Europe's most expensive noodle bar. You have just found a hair in your noodles.

Situation 2
You are in the reception of the five-star La Plaza Mayor Hotel. An hour ago you saw a mouse in your room. You called reception but nobody came.

Situation 3
You are in a first class seat on a flight from New York to Paris. Your personal TV doesn't work, there's a strange smell in the cabin and you are cold.

BBC VIDEO PODCAST

Download the podcast and view people describing the advantages and disadvantages of living in a city.

Authentic BBC interviews

www.pearsonlongman.com/speakout

UNIT 11

UNIT 11

SPEAKING
> Talk about things you've done
> Talk about future consequences
> Give your opinion
> Talk about technology you couldn't live without

LISTENING
> Listen to people talking about how they keep in touch
> Listen to a discussion about the internet
> Watch an extract from a BBC documentary about giving up television

READING
> Read an article about computer games

WRITING
> Improve your use of pronouns
> Write your opinion

BBC CONTENT
▣ Video podcast: How do you feel about technology?
◉ DVD: Panorama: Is TV Bad For My Kids?

technology

VOCABULARY communication

1A Discuss. What types of communication can you see in the photos?

B Work in pairs. Complete the table. How often do you and your partner do these things? Write often (O), sometimes (S) or never (N) next to each thing.

use your mobile (phone)		
write a blog		
send a fax/postcard		
check your email		
send an SMS (text message)		
'chat' online		
update your webpage		
use an internet phone (e.g. Skype)		

LISTENING

2A Work in pairs. What are the positive (+) and negative (−) points about the things in the box.

> social networking sites   blogs   text messages
> internet phones

B ▶ 11.1 Listen to four people talking about how they keep in touch. Match each speaker to the type of communication in Exercise 2A.

Speaker 1 _____

Speaker 2 _____

Speaker 3 _____

Speaker 4 _____

3A Read sentences 1–8. Which speaker said them? Listen again to check.

1 It's a great way to tell people about your travel experiences. *Speaker 3*

2 I get really annoyed when you're talking to someone though, and they are texting someone else.

3 The only problem is that I keep looking at the website when I should be working.

4 And sometimes it [the computer] crashes during the phone call.

5 You can post photos or send jokes and funny videos.

6 I text most of the time because it's quick and cheap.

7 The only problem we have is when we can't find an internet café.

8 I use Skype to keep in touch with my family.

B Works in pairs. Discuss. Are the comments positive (+) or negative (−)? Which do you agree with?

GRAMMAR present perfect

4A Read sentences 1–3 and match them with sentences a)–c) below.

1 I haven't learnt how to do it myself **yet**.

2 I've **just** started to use the networking sites.

3 We've been to so many places **already**.

a) I started a few days ago.

b) We didn't think it was possible to travel so much.

c) But I hope to learn soon.

B Complete the rules with *just, yet* and *already*.

Rules:

1 Use _____ in negative sentences or questions, for something you expected to happen before now.

2 Use _____ for something that happened a short time ago.

3 Use _____ for something which happened before now, or earlier than expected.

▐▐▐▶ page 148 **LANGUAGEBANK**

PRACTICE

5A Make sentences with the prompts. Use the present perfect.

1 just / buy / new / I / car
I've just bought a new car.

2 sport / not / do / yet / I / week / this / any

3 have a baby / just / my best friend

4 already / have a holiday / I / this year

5 I / my studies / finish / yet / not

6 new / James Bond / see / film / already / I

7 move / I / house / just

8 I / English course / already / next / pay for / my

B Make the sentences true for you.
I haven't bought a new car recently.

C Work in pairs and compare your answers.

6 Look at the cartoon and the 'Things to do' list. What things has the man already done? What hasn't he done yet?

Things to do:
go to the supermarket ✓
clean the floor
do the washing ✓
iron shirts ✓
cook dinner
water the plants

SPEAKING

7A Work in pairs. Look at the things in the box below and answer the questions.

find a job   travel abroad   start an exercise programme
write a blog   learn a language   learn to play the guitar
learn to drive   create my own webpage

1 Which of these have you done already?

2 Which haven't you done yet, but would like to do?

3 Which have you just done?

B Write a list of five things you want/need to do this week.

C Work in pairs and take turns. Look at your partner's list and ask questions to find out what he/she has done already, and what he/she hasn't done yet.
A: I need to organise my holiday.
B: OK. Have you already decided where to go?
A: Yes. But I haven't booked the tickets yet.

speakout TIP

Every month write a list of five things you want to do to improve your English, e.g. *watch a film in English, read an English newspaper, write an email, etc.* Check your list at the end of the month to see how many of the things you have done.

WRITING pronouns

8A Read the travel blog. Match the pronouns in bold to the things they refer to in the box.

Milan   the course   my new friends (x2)   Laura (x2)
my new friends' and my   the city centre

It's big, beautiful and busy, … it – Milan

Mark's blog   August | Milan

I've just arrived in Milan. **It**'s big, beautiful and busy and the people are so friendly. I've only been here for one week and I've made lots of new friends already. Most of **them** are students too, and **they**'re new to Milan. **Our** course hasn't started yet, but I'm really looking forward to **it**.
I'm going to share a flat with another student, Laura. I haven't met **her** yet, but **she** sounds nice on the phone. The flat is near the city centre and there are lots of bars and restaurants near **there**, so it should be good for going out at night. More news in September.

B Underline the correct alternative.

Use pronouns (*it, them, they, etc.*) *to avoid repetition of words/to write longer sentences.*

C Rewrite this travel blog. Replace the underlined words with pronouns.

Alecia and I have finally arrived in Bucharest, and <u>Alecia and I</u> love <u>Bucharest</u>. We thought we should update you on <u>Alecia's and my</u> tour. Last month we were in Hungary. We had a really good time <u>in Hungary</u>. We met a man called George, who was very friendly. <u>George</u> took us to some wonderful lakes and castles, and we really enjoyed <u>the lakes and castles</u>. The other news is that we have decided to stay <u>in Bucharest</u> for at least two years. We think <u>living in Bucharest</u> will be a wonderful experience for <u>Alecia and I</u>.

▶ **GRAMMAR** | first conditional + *when* ▶ **VOCABULARY** | feelings ▶ **HOW TO** | talk about your future

SPEAKING

1A Work in pairs. Discuss. What do you think of computer games? Do you like them? Why/Why not?

B Do you agree with the opinions below?

> I play computer games all the time. They don't make you violent in real life.
> *Jack, 11*

> Computer games make you feel better. If I'm angry, I shoot lots of aliens in a game. It doesn't hurt anyone.
> *Freya, 17*

> With computer games you can do things that are not possible in the real world, so it's fun.
> *Euan, 26*

> Some people spend too much time in virtual worlds. It's very worrying. People should go out more, play sports and talk to each other.
> *Matthew, 46*

> Only old people don't understand about computer games. In the future everyone will play them.
> *Sophie, 22*

C Complete the sentence and make it true for you.

I think computer games are … because …

READING

2A Read the introduction to an article and answer the questions.
1 What do you think *The Sims* is?
2 What do you think the journalist will see and do?

B Read the rest of the article to check your answers.

C Work in pairs. Answer the questions.
1 What two things does the journalist enjoy doing in the game?
2 What does she find difficult?
3 Do you think computer games like this can be useful for learning?

Meet The Sims

The Sims is the best-selling computer game in history, so when my editor asks me to find out how it works, I decide to try it out. I think, 'It's cheap, it's close. If I go there, I'll meet new people and experience a new culture.' I'm quite **excited**.

Day 1

I choose two characters, Sadie and Troy, and go to Blazing Falls. The brochure says it has miles of beaches and tropical islands. We build a house near the sea. It's a dream. You can walk out of the door straight onto the beach, and when I've finished I sit back with a feeling of real achievement. It's been a good day.

Day 2

After breakfast we go for a walk and look at the different houses. If I visit a house with other players, I'll make some new friends. I walk into a house with twelve people. I've never talked online to strangers before and I feel **nervous**. Some people are playing chess or computer games and others are running around in their swimsuits. I'm not sure what to say, so I type 'hello', and it appears in a big bubble above Sadie's head. No one answers. I feel **uncomfortable** and **lonely**, but if I leave, I won't have a story for my editor. I type 'I'm **confused.** How do I play?' 'What is there to do in this house?' I feel like a new girl at school who nobody wants to talk to. I soon get **bored.** I leave the computer and go and talk to my real friends.

Day 3

I'm **worried** about Sadie. Bad things will happen if she doesn't make friends. So this morning I start with Troy. I send him into a club. He's good-looking, so I hope that when he walks in, people will start talking to him. I'm right. 'What are you looking for?' 'Do you want to dance?' This is much better. There are so many questions, I can't type the answers fast enough. Before I know what's happened, I'm on the dance floor with my new friends. In real life, I haven't been dancing for ages and I'm **amazed** by the good feeling I get.

VOCABULARY feelings

3A Work in pairs. Look at the words in bold in the text in Exercise 2. Match them with definitions 1–8 below.

1 How you feel when you have nothing to do. *bored*

2 How you feel when you don't understand how something works.

3 How you feel when you are alone, and have no friends.

4 How you feel when something special is going to happen, and you are happy.

5 How you feel when you are not relaxed.

6 How you feel when you are very surprised.

7 How you feel when you keep thinking about something bad that might happen, e.g. you might lose your job.

8 How you feel when you worry about something and cannot relax, e.g. before an exam.

B Work in pairs and take turns. Student A: think about the last time you were amazed/ confused/excited/worried, etc. Tell your partner why you felt like that. Student B: ask for more information.

A: *The last time I was really excited was before my birthday party.*

B: *Really. What did you do?*

A: *I had a barbecue in the garden.*

GRAMMAR first conditional + *when*

4 Look at sentences a)–d) and circle the correct alternatives to complete the rules.

a) If I go there, I'll meet new people.

b) If I leave, I **won't** have a story for my editor.

c) **When** he walks in, people **will start** talking to him.

d) Bad things **will happen if** she doesn't make friends.

Rules:

1 In these sentences we are talking about the *present*/*future*.

2 In the *if/when* clause use *the present tense*/*a future form*.

3 In the main clause use *the present tense*/*a future form*.

➡ page 148 **LANGUAGEBANK**

PRACTICE

5A Complete the guide with the correct form of the verb in brackets.

How to look after your Sim

People have needs, and so do The Sims. We need to keep clean, have fun, sleep, relax, talk, eat, exercise and go to the bathroom. If you don't do these things, bad things will happen to your Sim.

- **Keep clean.** If you [1]_____ (not have) showers and wash your hands, your Sim [2]_____ (die) of a disease. Watch out for this!

- **Remember to eat.** When your Sim [3]_____ (be) hungry, he/she [4]_____ (not have) much energy, so buy him/her a pizza or get him/her some dinner.

- **Make friends.** If your Sim [5]_____ (not make) friends, he/she [6]_____ (get) depressed and he/she [7]_____ (not listen) to you.

- **Don't forget to rest.** Your Sim [8]_____ (fall) down and go to sleep on the floor if he/she [9]_____ (not sleep) enough.

- **Think about comfort.** If your Sim [10]_____ (sit) on the sofa, he/she [11]_____ (be) more comfortable.

B Make sentences with the prompts about *The Sims*.

1 If Troy / get / job / policeman / earn lots / money

2 If / earn lots / money / buy nice things / house

3 If / buy / nice things / house / they / have / lot / fun

4 If / have / lot / fun / make / new friends

5 If / make new friends / maybe Troy / find / new girlfriend

6 If / Troy / find / new girlfriend / Sadie / not be happy

7 If / Sadie / not happy / they / fight

8 If / fight / maybe Troy / have to move house

C ▶ 11.2 Listen to check. How is *will* pronounced?

D Listen again and repeat the sentences.

6A Work in pairs. Think of other situations for *The Sims* (e.g. go on holiday/build a house/have a party). Write sentences to talk about the consequences.

If The Sims have a party, they will invite their new friends.

B Compare your ideas with other students.

SPEAKING

7A Make sentences 1–8 true for you.

1 If I move house in the next two years, …

2 When I next go on holiday, …

3 When I get home this evening, …

4 When I go to bed tonight, …

5 If I'm hungry later, …

6 If someone invites me to a party, …

7 If I go out this weekend, …

8 If I lose my mobile phone, …

B Work in pairs and compare your answers.

▶ **FUNCTION** | giving opinions	▶ **VOCABULARY** | internet terms	▶ **LEARN TO** | disagree politely

VOCABULARY internet terms

1 Work in pairs. Look at the internet terms in the box below and answer the questions.

> blog   travel website   search engine   online news
> social networking site   music download site
> video sharing site   photo sharing site   message board

1 Do you use/visit any of these?

2 Which ones do you visit most frequently?

3 Do you think they are useful/not very useful. Why?

READING

2A Look at the cartoon and the title of the text. What do you think *wilfing* is? Read the article to find out.

Stop wilfing!

We've all done it, but now wilfing on the internet is becoming a real problem. Wilfing (short for 'What Was I Looking For') describes what happens when you spend a lot of time on the internet without doing anything in particular. A new report has shown how computer users waste up to two days a month on the internet. Most of the people who were questioned said they were distracted 'all or most of the time' when they work or study online. The study showed that the internet can be bad for relationships too, as people argue with their partners who spend too much time in front of their computer. Luckily, there is a simple answer to the problem. Pete Cohen, who helps internet addicts, says, 'Get off the computer and get on with your life.'

B Answer the questions.

1 How much time do people spend 'wilfing'?

2 What are people trying to do before they get distracted?

3 Why is the internet bad for relationships?

3 Work in pairs and discuss. Student A: you think people spend too much time on the internet. Student B: you think the internet is essential.

FUNCTION giving opinions

4 ▶ 11.3 Listen to three people discussing the internet. Are the statements true (T) or false (F)?

1 The men both use the internet at work.

2 The woman thinks people shouldn't use the internet when they are at work.

3 The men both think that the internet is a waste of time.

5A Look at statements 1–6. Tick the ideas that are mentioned in the recording.

Surfing on the internet is:

1 addictive. Some people can't stop using it.

2 bad for relationships.

3 dangerous. You can meet dangerous people on the internet.

4 good when you want a break from work. It's like having a cup of coffee.

5 causing people to fail their university degrees because they spend too much time on social networking sites when they should be studying.

6 a waste of time.

B Listen again to check.

6A ▶ 11.4 Listen and complete the phrases in the table.

agreeing	disagreeing	giving an opinion
That's _____ _____ true	I totally _____ I'm not _____ about that	I _____ I _____ think

B Add these phrases to the table above.

> in my opinion   definitely   I don't think so

▶ page 148 **LANGUAGEBANK**

7A Find and correct the mistakes in the conversations below. There is a mistake in each response.

1 A: Everyone should learn a second language.

B: I ~~don't~~ think so. It's very useful.

2 A: It's not polite to arrive late for an appointment.

B: That's not true. I always arrive on time.

3 A: It's good to ask as many questions as possible in class.

B: I'm sure about that. Some students ask too many questions.

4 A: It's best to live in a hot sunny country.

B: Definitely not. Everybody loves the sunshine.

5 A: Children should study for exams from the age of six.

B: I am totally disagree. No child under ten should have to study for an exam.

6 A: Everyone loves classical music.

B: I don't think. Most people like pop music.

B Work in pairs. Do you agree with A's opinions? Take turns to give your own opinions.

LEARN TO disagree politely

8A Look at the responses in 1–5 below. Which do you think is more polite? Tick A or B.

1 A: I'm sorry, but I really don't see what the problem is.

B: I really don't see what the problem is.

2 A: I disagree.

B: I'm not sure about that.

3 A: I don't think it's a waste of time at all.

B: It's not a waste of time.

4 A: That's true, but I don't think the problem is the internet.

B: The problem is not using the internet.

5 A: I totally disagree.

B: I'm afraid I totally disagree.

B ▶ 11.5 Listen to check your answers. Notice the intonation. What does the speaker do to sound polite?

C Work in pairs. Practise saying the phrases using polite intonation.

❝ speakout TIP

Use language carefully when you disagree. Don't be too direct. Use phrases like *I'm sorry, but …* , *I'm afraid …* , *I'm not sure …* and *I don't think …*

SPEAKING

9A Read the statements below. Do you agree/disagree? Write your opinion in a few words.

You shouldn't believe what you read on the internet.

The internet has made the world a better place.

A lot of the technology we use is not necessary.

It's better to talk to someone than to send them a text message.

Downloading songs for free is OK.

Online books will mean the end of bookshops.

Everybody in the world should have a computer.

B Work in groups and compare your ideas.

DVD PREVIEW

1 Work in pairs. Discuss. Which of the things in the box do you own? Which do you use every day? Do they save or waste time?

> mobile phone   laptop   MP3 player
> DVD player   digital camera   digital TV

2A Work in pairs. What numbers do you think complete 1–5 in the quiz below? Check the answers on page 166.

Did you know … ?

1 In the USA a child watches TV for an average of _____ hours a day.
2 In the UK, _____ percent of children over 5 years old have a TV in their bedroom.
3 The average person spends _____ years eating and _____ years watching TV.
4 Children under three years old who watch more than _____ hour(s) of TV a day may have problems concentrating at school when they are older.
5 In the USA some families spend only _____ minutes a week having meaningful conversations with their children. Those children spend _____ minutes a week watching TV.

B Discuss. How many hours do you spend watching TV per week? Do you think this is OK/too much/not enough?

3 Read the programme information and answer the questions.

BBC Panorama: Is TV Bad For My Kids?

Panorama is a BBC documentary series that looks at important issues. In this programme Jeremy Vine does an experiment in the UK: for two weeks several families have to live without televisions, computers and video games. Can they survive? What can we learn from the experiment? Watch to find out.

1 What do you think the children will do when their televisions and video games are taken away?
2 How do you think the parents will feel during the experiment?

▶ DVD VIEW

4 Watch the DVD. Were your ideas in Exercise 3 correct?

5 Watch the DVD again. Are the sentences true (T) or false (F)?

1 Children who watch too much TV get fat.
2 The programme *Panorama* went to a secondary school in Manchester.
3 They took the microwaves out of the homes of half the children in the class.
4 They gave the children a camera to record what happened.
5 The parents had to work a lot harder when there were no TVs.
6 After the experiment, the families watched the same amount of TV as before.

6 Work in pairs and answer the questions.

1 Did the parents think the experiment was positive? Why/Why not?
2 What do you think of the experiment? Do you think it was a good idea?

speakout technology

7A ▶ 11.6 Listen to people talking about essential gadgets. Write them in the correct column.

speaker	essential	not essential
I	*mobile phone*	*MP3 player*
2		

B Listen again and tick the key phrases you hear.

keyphrases

That's essential.

I love it.

I use it all the time/every day …

I couldn't live without …

It's good/important because …

I don't go anywhere without it/I take it everywhere.

I need it in case …

I suppose I don't need …

I can live without …

It's very useful.

C Decide which gadgets are essential/not essential for you. Think about why you need them. Make some notes. Use the key phrases to help you.

D Work in groups. Tell your group why you need the gadgets you chose. Which are the most popular?

writeback a web comment

8A Read the comments. Do these people think technology is good or bad? Why?

| people | forum | topic |

> **Is technology a good or a bad thing?**

How have computers, the internet, email and mobile phones changed your life? Have they changed the way we do business? Are there good and bad things about technology? What do you think?

reply> Most people say technology has made our lives very fast and very convenient. But I don't think so. The fact is that it has also made us very lonely. We interact with machines for 8–10 hours a day and spend less than 2–3 hours interacting with other humans.
> Shantanu, USA/India

reply> It seems to me that technology is a good thing. It allows me to find out what is really happening in the world, not just what the media want me to believe. The problem is that some governments want to control what is available on the internet too.
> Jake, UK

B Write your own comment using the structure below.

It seems to me that technology _____.
Most people say _____. But I'm not sure about that/I don't think so. In my opinion, _____.
For example, _____.
The fact is that/The problem is that _____.
Finally, _____. Technology _____ my life.

COMMUNICATION

1A Complete the words.

1 When did you buy your m_b_l_ ph_n_?

2 Do any of your friends have a w_b p_g_?

3 When you travel, do you send p_stc_rds, or write a bl_g?

4 When did you last send a f_x?

5 Do you prefer to speak to someone on the phone or send an S_S (t_xt m_ss_g_)

6 Have you ever tried to ch_t online? What happened?

B Work in pairs and take turns. Ask and answer the questions.

PRESENT PERFECT

2A Write answers to 1–6 in the circle.

1 The name of something you have just bought.

2 The name of something you would like but you haven't bought yet.

3 Somewhere you have already spent a lot of time.

4 Somewhere you haven't been to yet, but you plan to.

5 Something you have just finished (a book/a course, etc.).

6 Something you have done already today.

B Work in pairs and take turns. Look at each of the words/ phrases in your circles. Ask for more information.

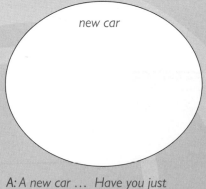

new car

A: *A new car … Have you just bought one?*

B: *That's right.*

A: *What kind of car did you buy?*

B: *A Peugeot.*

FEELINGS

3A Complete the sentence in different ways using the words in the box.

> nervous   lonely   uncomfortable
> bored   confused   worried
> amazed   excited

I feel _____ when …

I feel nervous when I have to do an exam.

B Work in pairs. Discuss. What do you do in each situation to make yourself feel better?

FIRST CONDITIONAL

4A Match 1–6 with a)–f) to make sentences.

1 If you break a mirror,

2 If you walk under a ladder,

3 If you find a penny on the floor,

4 If you eat an apple a day,

5 If you give away a wedding present,

6 If a baby is born at 12 o'clock,

a) it will keep the doctor away.

b) he/she will be very lucky when he/ she grows up.

c) paint might fall on your head.

d) your marriage will fail.

e) you will have seven years' bad luck.

f) you will have good luck all day.

B Work in pairs. Discuss. Do you have the same superstitions in your country? What other superstitions are there?

5A Write down three things that might happen to you in the next six months.

I might find a job abroad.

B Work in pairs. Discuss the possible consequences.

A: *I might find a job abroad.*

B: *What will happen if you do that?*

A: *I'll have to move house.*

GIVING OPINIONS

6A Put the words in the correct order to complete the conversations.

Conversation 1

A: I think video sharing sites are bad for children.

B: totally / disagree / afraid / I / I'm

Conversation 2

A: Nobody should eat meat.

B: not / that / I'm / about / sure

Conversation 3

A: all / drugs / my / be / opinion / should / in / legal

B: I'm sorry, but I don't think that's a good idea.

Conversation 4

A: I really think teachers should be paid more money.

B: right / that's / so / too / think / I

Conversation 5

A: government / do / the / better / next / think / be / you / will?

B: Definitely!

Conversation 6

A: Children under the age of ten shouldn't have a mobile phone.

B: so / think / I / don't

Conversation 7

A: I can never find anything I want to watch on television. It's all rubbish.

B: agree / true / that's / I

Conversation 8

A: Policemen should all carry guns.

B: totally / I / disagree

B Work in pairs and take turns. Practise the conversations. Give your own opinions and remember to use polite intonation.

A: *I think video sharing sites can be dangerous.*

B: *Yes, I agree. Anyone can upload videos of illegal things.*

SPEAKING
> Talk about your favourite film
> Talk about what you would do if you were famous

LISTENING
> Listen to people talking about being famous
> Listen to people making requests
> Watch an extract from a BBC documentary about Lewis Hamilton

READING
> Read a magazine article about film extras
> Read a text about personal concierges

WRITING
> Use paragraphs to write a profile of a famous person
> Write about your childhood ambitions

BBC CONTENT
> Video podcast: Would you like to be famous?
> DVD: Lewis Hamilton: Billion Dollar Man

UNIT 12

fame

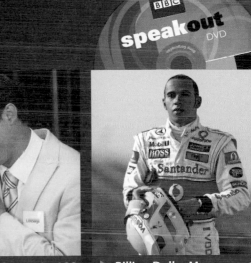

VOCABULARY   film

1 Look at the film posters and match them to the types of film in the box. Which ones fit more than one category?

> an action film   a comedy   a fantasy film
> a science fiction film   a (historical) drama
> a western   a horror film   a thriller
> a musical   a documentary

The Dark Knight is a fantasy film and also an action film.

2 Work in pairs. Discuss the questions.

1 How many of the films in the posters have you seen? What did you think of them?

2 What's your favourite type of film?

READING

3A Do you think statements 1–4 are true (T) or false (F)?

1 An 'extra' appears in films, but doesn't usually speak and isn't usually professional.

2 Film studios cannot use criminals in their films.

3 Film studios have to pay everyone who appears in their film.

4 Actors get more money for speaking roles than non-speaking roles.

B Read the text to find out.

FASCINATING FACTS *about film extras*

Producer Mario Cecchi Gori employed a very large number of **actors** for his 125th film, *The Department Store* (1986). He told everyone it was his last film and used every available actor from his previous 124 films. Some were the **stars** of the film, but most of them had **roles** as extras.

In the western *Man of Conquest* (1939) the Native American actors used sign language. The **studio** said they didn't have speaking roles so they should earn less money than the other actors. The Native Americans told the actors' union that sign language was speaking, and they wanted more money. They got it.

During the filming of *Reds* (1981), director Warren Beatty told the extras about the theories of Marxist John Read, who said that workers were badly treated in capitalist societies. The extras learnt quickly. They had a meeting and refused to go to work the next day because the salary was too low. Beatty agreed to pay more.

The **extras** in *Hell's Highway* (1932) were all ex-criminals. **Director** Fritz Lang used real criminals in his film, *M* (1931). Before filming finished, twenty-four were arrested for various crimes.

The largest number of extras in a film was for *Gandhi* (1982) – 300,000 for the funeral **scene**. People heard about the film through radio and newspaper advertisements, on TV and on the streets. There were 94,560 extras with a contract (they earned 40p each) and more than 200,000 volunteers. The scene was filmed on 31st January, exactly thirty-three years after Gandhi's funeral, and it took two minutes and five seconds of the film.

4 Match the words in bold in Exercise 3 with definitions 1–8 below.

1 a short part of a film, when the events happen in one place

2 a person who controls the artistic part of a film and tells the actors what to do

3 a person who controls the making of a film, e.g. the money involved

4 people who perform in films or plays

5 people who appear in a film, but have small unimportant parts

6 a film company

7 characters in a film

8 very famous actors

5A Think of a film you know and complete phrases 1–6 below.

1 This is a film about …

2 The star(s) of the film is/are …

3 He/She played a/an …

4 Other actors in the film include …

5 The director of the film was …

6 I liked it/didn't like it because …

B Work in pairs and take turns. Describe the film you chose in Exercise 5A.

GRAMMAR reported speech

6 Compare the words spoken to the reported sentences and answer questions 1–2 below.

1 How do the verb forms change?

2 Which verbs do we use to report speech?

direct speech	reported speech
'It's my last film.'	He told everyone it was his last film.
'Sign language is speaking.'	They told the union that sign language was speaking.
'They don't have speaking roles.'	The studio said they didn't have speaking roles.
'They are badly treated.'	He said that workers were badly treated.

⮕ page 150 **LANGUAGEBANK**

PRACTICE

7 Put the paragraph below into reported speech. Begin each sentence with *He told me* or *He said*.

> *'I'm an actor. I can play any role, but I don't like playing criminals. I'm moving to Hollywood and I'm going to be a big star! I'll stay in touch!'*

He told me he was an actor. He said he …

Favourite film quotes

1 Who _____, 'I'm going to make him an offer he can't refuse'?
a) Marlon Brando in *The Godfather Part 1*
b) Harrison Ford in *Star Wars*
c) Julia Roberts in *Pretty Woman*

2 Who _____ a policeman, 'I think this is the beginning of a beautiful friendship'?
a) the boy in *ET: The Extra Terrestrial*
b) Humphrey Bogart in *Casablanca*
c) Hugh Grant in *Notting Hill*

3 Who famously _____, 'I'll be back'?
a) Mr Bean in *Mr Bean's Holiday*
b) Tom Hanks in *Apollo 13*
c) Arnold Schwarzenegger in *Terminator*

4 Who _____ a dog, 'I have a feeling we're not in Kansas any more'?
a) the dog owner in *Amores Perros*
b) Lassie's owner in *Lassie*
c) Dorothy in *The Wizard of Oz*

5 Who _____, 'I am the king of the world'?
a) the leader in *Seven Samurai*
b) Russell Crowe in *Gladiator*
c) Leonardo DiCaprio in *Titanic*

6 Who _____, 'I'm having an old friend for dinner'?
a) Anthony Hopkins in *The Silence of the Lambs*
b) Birgitte Federspiel in *Babette's Feast*
c) Morgan Spurlock in *Super Size Me*

8A Complete the *Favourite film quotes* quiz questions above with *said* or *told*. Then circle the correct answer.

B Check your answers on page 166.

C Work in pairs. Read the quotes again and change them to reported speech.

1 He said he was going to make him an offer he couldn't refuse.

SPEAKING

9A Read the questions and add one or two of your own.

1 What's your favourite film?

2 What type of film is it?

3 Why do you like it?

4 Who's your favourite actor? What films has he/she acted in? Why do you like him/her?

5 Do you have a favourite director? What films has he/she made?

B Work in pairs and take turns. Ask and answer the questions. Make a note of your partner's answers.

C Work with other students. Tell them how your first partner answered the questions in Exercise 9A.

He said Mamma Mia was his favourite film.

She said she liked films by the Japanese director Kurosawa because they told great stories.

▶ **GRAMMAR** | second conditional   ▶ **VOCABULARY** | suffixes   ▶ **HOW TO** | talk about hypothetical situations

VOCABULARY suffixes

1 Work in pairs. What are the positive/negative things about being famous? Use the photos to help you.

2A Discuss. What do you think a 'web celeb' is? Read the article to find out.

The internet has changed the meaning of celebrity. In the past you had to be a successful actor, musician or sportsperson to be famous. Now all you need is the internet. One of the world's first web celebrities was Ghyslain Raza. He filmed himself acting as a Star Wars hero and his friends put the embarrassing video on YouTube. Millions of people watched it and 'the Star Wars Kid' became world famous. Another web celebrity is Gary Brolsma, 'the Numa Numa guy', whose video of himself singing a Romanian pop song has been watched more than thirteen million times. In 1968 artist Andy Warhol said, 'In the future everyone will be famous for fifteen minutes.' With the invention of the internet and YouTube, maybe that time is now.

B Answer the questions.

1 What is different about fame now?

2 What did Ghyslain Raza and Gary Brolsma do to become famous?

3 Have you heard of any other web celebrities?

3A Look at the article in Exercise 2A and find one example of a word with each suffix.

adjective endings		noun endings		
-ful	-ous	-ion	-ity	-er/-or/ -ian (jobs)
successful				

B Complete words 1–8 below and put them in the correct column in the table.

1 celebrat_____   5 adventur_____ (adj)
2 photograph_____   6 help_____ (adj)
3 politic_____   7 danger_____
4 popular_____   8 wonder_____

C ▶ 12.1 Listen to check your answers. Underline the main stress.

D Can you think of any other words with these suffixes?

LISTENING

4A Work in pairs. Discuss. Would you like to be famous? Why/Why not? What would you like to be famous for?

B ▶ 12.2 Listen to eight people answering the last question. Put the number of the speaker next to the thing they mention.

an artist / an actress   a singer/dancer   a musician
successful in business   a politician/president   a model
a footballer/sportsperson   a writer   a scientist/inventor

5A Listen again and complete the sentences.

1 If I had more _____, I would love to paint.

2 If I could have a painting in a _____, I'd be really happy.

3 If I was a politician, I would try to _____ the world.

4 Imagine if you scored a goal for your country in the _____ Cup, that would be such a good feeling.

5 I'd love to _____. If I could be famous for anything, I think I'd be a singer.

6 I'd like to be remembered as a great _____.

7 If I was famous, I would be _____, live in a big house, and have all those clothes.

8 If I invented something that made people's _____ better, that would be good.

9 If I was famous, I wouldn't be _____.

B Work in pairs. Discuss. Do you agree with any of the speakers?

A: I think I'd like to be a model.

B: Really? I wouldn't ...

GRAMMAR second conditional

6A Look at Exercise 5A and complete the table.

If clause: If + ¹_____ tense	main clause: ² _____ (+ infinitive)
If I ³_____ more time, If I was famous, If I ⁵_____ a politician,	I would love to paint. I ⁴_____ be happy. I would try to change the world.

B Underline the correct alternative to complete the rules.

Rules:

1 Use the second conditional for *real/imaginary* situations in the present.

If I was famous (but I'm not …), I would …

2 Use the second conditional for *likely (probable)/unlikely (impossible)* situations in the future

If I didn't have to work tomorrow (but I do), I would …

➡ page 150 **LANGUAGEBANK**

PRACTICE

7 Underline the correct alternative.

1 If I did more sport, I *would feel/felt* fitter.

2 If I *had/would have* the day off, I would stay in bed.

3 If I *didn't/wouldn't* work or study, I would be bored.

4 I would read more if I *didn't have/wouldn't have* a TV.

5 I *would use/used* my bicycle more if I didn't have a car.

8A Use the prompts to make questions in the second conditional.

1 If / win / lottery / what / do?

If you won the lottery, what would you do?

2 If / can / have dinner / with any two living people / who / choose?

3 If / have / no money / what / do?

4 If / have / more time / what / do?

5 If / could change / one thing / about yourself / what / change?

B Work in pairs. Ask and answer the questions.

WRITING paragraphs

9A Put sentences a)–d) in the correct paragraphs to complete the profile of Albert Schweitzer.

a) He was born in 1875 in France and he spent his childhood in a village, Gunsbach, where his father taught him music.

b) In 1913 Schweitzer and his wife left for Lambaréné in Gabon, Africa, to start a hospital.

c) Albert Schweitzer was a theologian, a musician, a philosopher and a doctor who dedicated his life to helping the sick.

d) As a young man, Schweitzer became a world famous musician.

1 _____. He won the Nobel Peace Prize in 1953 for his work for humanity.

2 _____. After school, he studied theology at the University of Strasbourg, but he continued to play the organ.

3 _____. He gave many performances and wrote books about the life of Bach. But at the age of thirty he decided to dedicate his life to helping people, so he studied to become a doctor.

4 _____. At the beginning they had very little, but Schweitzer made money by performing music in Europe and writing books. In the 1960s the hospital had more than seventy buildings and when Schweitzer won the Nobel Peace Prize, he gave the $33,000 prize money to the hospital. Albert Schweitzer died in 1965, and was buried in Lambaréné.

B Choose the correct heading for each paragraph.

Achievements and later life

Rise to fame

Childhood and education

Introduction

C Research the life of a famous person you admire or read the profile on page 167. Write the profile of this person using paragraphs.

speakout TIP

Each paragraph should have a different topic. The first sentence of each paragraph (the topic sentence) should introduce that paragraph. Plan the topic of the paragraph before you start writing.

▶ **FUNCTION** | requests and offers ▶ **VOCABULARY** | collocations ▶ **LEARN TO** | ask for more time

VOCABULARY collocations

1A Work in pairs. Complete phrases 1–6 with the verbs in the box.

| ~~get~~ recommend book organise |
| rent invite |

1 _get_ tickets for a concert
2 _____ a car for the day
3 _____ a table for two
4 _____ someone to dinner
5 _____ somewhere good to visit
6 _____ a private tour

B Look at photos A–C. Which of the things in Exercise 1A can you see?

C Work in pairs. Discuss. How often do you do the things in Exercise 1A?

I sometimes get tickets for a concert. The last concert I saw was …

READING

2A Read the definition. Discuss. What other things do you think a personal concierge does to help rich and famous clients?

> **Personal concierge** *(n)* someone who organises things for (usually rich) clients e.g. booking tables in restaurants, buying tickets for concerts, etc.

B Read the text to find out.

He can book you a table at the world's top restaurants, get you the best seats for *The Lion King*, find you a private plane for the next day or organise a red carpet for you at the Oscars. He's a personal concierge and he can get you anything you want … if you have enough money!

The concierges we spoke to have done some amazing things for their clients: one got twenty tickets for a Rolling Stones concert an hour before it started; he also flew some of Madonna's favourite tea to London and found some rare birds for Jennifer Lopez. Another concierge asked former US President, Bill Clinton, to have dinner with his client. Clinton said 'yes'!

FUNCTION requests and offers

3A ▶ 12.3 Listen to a personal concierge talking to four clients. What does each client want?

B Listen again. Complete the sentences with one word.

1 I'd _____ to go on a private tour …
2 Would it be _____ to book a ticket … ?
3 _____ you like me to get a ticket … ?
4 Would you be _____ to organise it?
5 Do you _____ me to get a … ?
6 _____ you recommend somewhere?
7 _____ I book it?

C Look at sentences 1–7 again and answer the questions.
a) Which phrases are requests (R) and which are offers (O)?
b) Which request says what we want to do?
c) Which two requests ask if something is possible?
d) Which request asks for someone's opinion?

▸ page 150 **LANGUAGEBANK**

4A Put the words in the correct order to make questions or sentences.

1 food / to / like / I'd / local / try / some
2 recommend / nightclub / a / could / good / you?
3 book / be / tickets / would / to / three / you / able?
4 car / rent / would / be / it / to / a / possible?
5 I / ticket / buy / shall / your?
6 table / book / want / you / to / do / a / me?
7 to / the / like / manager / me / you / call / would?

B Match questions 1–7 above with responses a)–g).

a) Yes, I'll print out some information for you about the daily rates.
b) There are some excellent restaurants in this area.
c) There's a famous one that opens at midnight.
d) Certainly. I'll just call the box office.
e) Yes, for six people, please.
f) No, don't worry – I'll speak to him myself.
g) Yes, please. I'll pay you back later.

5A Complete the sentences in any way you choose. You can use the picture below to help you.

1 Could you recommend a _____?
2 Would you be able to _____ for me?
3 Would it be possible to _____?
4 I'd like to try _____.

THE NEW MUSEUM OF ART

B Work in pairs and take turns. Student A: read your sentence. Student B: respond.

A: Could you recommend a good café?
B: Yes, go to The Café on the Bridge. It serves great coffee! Do you want me to take you there?

ask for more time

6A Look at the extracts from audio script 12.3 on page 176. Underline three more phrases to ask for more time.

Extract 1
A: Right, let me see if I have a number ... <u>hang on</u> ... ah, here it is.

Extract 2
A: OK. Just a moment. I'll call Mr Branson.

D: We told our friends this weekend. Would you be able to organise it for us?
A: Yes, of course. Can you give me a moment? I'll make a few calls.

Extract 3
E: And can you give us directions?
A: Have you got your laptop with you?
E: Yes.
A: Hold on. I'll email you a map.

B Are the phrases formal or informal? Which expression do you think is the most formal?

7A Complete B's responses with one word.

Conversation 1
A: Can you get me a meeting with <u>Mr Scorsese</u>?
B: Hang. I'll call him on his mobile.

Conversation 2
A: I'd like to rent <u>Buckingham Palace</u> for my birthday party.
B: Can you give a moment? I need to make a call.

Conversation 3
A: Would it be possible to get <u>tennis</u> lessons with <u>Mr Federer</u>?
B: A moment. I'll speak to him.

Conversation 4
A: Would I be able to bring my <u>pet tiger</u> on the plane?
B: Hold. I'll call the airline.

B ▶ 12.4 Listen to the answers and repeat.

C Work in pairs. Prepare to read the conversations above. Change the underlined words. Plan what you are going to say.

Can you get me a meeting with <u>Mr Clooney</u>?

8 Work in pairs. Student A: look at page 165. Student B: look at page 167. Read your roles.

9A Write out one of your conversations. Try to use phrases for making requests and offers and asking for time.

B Act out your conversation in front of other students.

DVD PREVIEW

1 Work in groups and discuss the questions.

1 Is Formula 1 popular in your country? Why/Why not? Who are the best-known drivers?

2 What type of person do you think can become a Formula 1 driver?

2A Read the programme information and answer the questions.

1 How old was Lewis Hamilton when he became a Formula 1 driver?

2 Do you think Lewis is happy with his life?

BBC Lewis Hamilton: Billion Dollar Man

Billion Dollar Man is a BBC documentary about Formula 1 driver Lewis Hamilton, who **is** now **a celebrity**. He started life as an **ordinary** British boy – he wasn't from a rich or amazingly talented family – but Lewis and his father were always **ambitious**. Lewis first found fame and glory by winning competitions with electric cars and then go-karts. His **progression** was fast: in his early twenties he became a Formula 1 driver. Though young, he has already had a big **impact** on the sport. He has a great **attitude**: he always wants to win, but he is always smiling and polite. For this reason, **sponsors** love him and want to invest money in him. Lewis says his life now is a dream come true.

B Match the words in bold with definitions 1–7 below.

1 normal, common

2 people or companies that pay to use someone in their advertisements

3 wanting to be successful

4 development

5 feelings and opinions that you have about something

6 a famous person

7 effect or influence that someone has

► DVD VIEW

3 Watch the DVD and answer the questions.

1 What type of people are usually involved in Formula 1?

2 What was he doing when he first appeared in a competition on TV? How old was he?

3 What was his ambition when he was a teenager? Why?

4 Read the things people say about Lewis Hamilton. Watch the DVD again. Number a)–f) in the order you hear them.

a) 'Someone who's preparing for those very same championships is Lewis Hamilton, who is only seven years old.' ___

b) 'He's my new hero. He really is. He's a hero for loads of people.' ___

c) 'I feel so passionate about his story, his progression and the impact he's made on Formula 1.' ___

d) 'Before I was just a driver but now it seems to change absolutely everything, and it's just an unreal feeling.' ___

e) 'Lewis Hamilton has won four British go-karting championships. Now he says he wants to be world Formula 1 champion by the time he's twenty.' ___

f) 'Everybody's talking about Lewis Hamilton. Everybody wants to talk to me about Lewis Hamilton. I want to talk to them about Lewis Hamilton.' ___

5 Discuss. Why do you think people say Lewis Hamilton is 'a hero'? Does he seem like a hero to you?

speakout dreams and ambitions

6A ▶ 12.5 Listen to Rhodri talking about his dreams and ambitions. Tick the questions he answers.

1 Where did you grow up?

2 When you were younger, did you dream of doing a particular job?

3 What/Who inspired you to do this?

4 Did you have a teacher/someone to help you to learn a special skill?

5 Have you achieved any of your dreams? What did you do?

B Work in pairs and try to remember how Rhodri answers the questions.

C You are going to talk about the dreams and ambitions you had when you were younger. First, think about your answers to the questions in Exercise 6A. Then look at the key phrases. Underline any phrases you want to use.

keyphrases

I always wanted to be a …

As a child I always used to …

It started with … / My dream began …

I thought it would be nice to …

I spent a lot of time …

As I grew up, I realised …

I changed my mind …

In the end, I decided to …

D Work in pairs and take turns to talk about your childhood dreams/ambitions. Have they changed now that you are older? If so, how?

writeback a web comment

7 Read the BBC website and answer the questions.

1 What did Damien want to be as a child.

2 What does he want to do now?

	Search

REFLECTIONS | CHILDHOOD AMBITIONS

How have your childhood ambitions changed? We asked people the following questions: what were your childhood ambitions? What do you do now? And what do you hope to become in the future?

Damien (31), Slovenia:

As a child, I always wanted to be a teacher. Now, I have achieved that dream. I teach Geography, History, Art and Sociology to 12–15-year-old students at a secondary school here in Ljubljana. I love working with children. It's much better than an office job. But now I'm planning a career change. I'm going back to college and I'm going to study to become a lawyer. I'd like to work in international law.

---

8 Write a comment for the website about your childhood ambitions using the model. Answer the questions below.

1 What were your childhood ambitions?

2 What do you do now?

3 What do you hope to become in the future?

FILM

1A Complete the text with the words in the box.

> role   actors   extras   director
> thriller   star   scene

My favourite film this year was *Zero Game*, the latest ¹_____ by ²_____ Xi Dong. It has several well-known Chinese ³_____ and one real ⁴_____, Li Mu Bai, who plays the ⁵_____ of the policeman who has to catch a thief, Jun Fat. Li Mu Bai is brilliant. In the best ⁶_____, he chases Jun Fat across the city on a motorbike, watched by thousands of ⁷_____.

B Work in pairs and take turns. Describe your favourite film of the year. Use the words in the box in Exercise 1A to help you.

REPORTED SPEECH

2A Put the last lines from films into reported speech.

1 'I'm too old for this.' (*Lethal Weapon*)

   He said he …

   _____

2 'It's a strange world … ' (*Blue Velvet*)

   He said it …

   _____

3 'Where we're going, we don't need roads.' (*Back to the Future*)

   He said where they were going …

   _____

4 'I can see now.' (*City Lights*)

   He said …

   _____

5 'It's too bad she won't live, but then again who does?' (*Blade Runner*)

   He said it was too bad she …

   _____

B Work in pairs. Discuss. Which is the best line?

SUFFIXES

3A Complete the questions with the correct suffix.

1 What is the most danger___ thing you have ever done?

2 Have you been anywhere wonder___ recently? Where did you go?

3 When was the last time you had a family celebrat___? What was the reason?

4 Have you ever met someone fam___? Who?

5 Which would you prefer to be: a politic___ or a music___? Why?

6 Are you success___ in your work/studies? Why/Why not?

B Work in pairs and take turns. Ask and answer the questions.

SECOND CONDITIONAL

4 Complete the sentences with the correct form of the verb in brackets.

1 If I _____ (not have to) work tonight, I _____ (take) you out.

2 She _____ (be) very upset if I _____ (lose) her scarf.

3 If you _____ (be able to) do any job in the world, what _____ you _____ (choose)?

4 If I _____ (live) on a desert island, I _____ (be) perfectly happy.

5 You _____ (not say) that if you _____ (know) more about it.

6 They _____ (be) ideal partners if they _____ (not argue) so much.

5 Work in pairs. Play the consequences game. Student A: read and complete the first phrase. Student B: add another sentence, starting with the last consequence.

A: If I lived in Italy, I would eat more pasta.

B: If I ate more pasta, I would get fat.

1 If I lived until I was 200 years old, …

2 If I met a good-looking man/woman this evening, …

3 If I lived in a bigger house, …

4 If I had more time, …

5 If I had to get a new job, …

6 If I was a famous film star, …

REQUESTS AND OFFERS

6A Underline the correct alternative to complete the requests and offers.

1 Would it be possible *to see/see/seeing* the exhibition?

2 Would you like *buy/me buy/me to buy* a ticket for you?

3 Would you be *able for/able to/able* arrange dinner?

4 Could you *recommend/to recommend/recommending* a bar?

5 Shall *to call/I call/I call you* a taxi?

6 Do you want *to get/me to get/me get* you a seat?

7 I'd *like to visit/like visit/like for visit* the museum.

B Imagine your wildest dreams have come true! You have $50 million and a personal concierge. What would you like? Think of three things or choose from the box.

> go shopping alone at midnight
> buy a private island
> hold a peace conference
> buy a painting   meet your hero
> buy a famous building
> fly into space

C Work in pairs and take turns. Student A: act out the role of client. Student B: act out the role of concierge.

A: What can I do for you, sir?

B: I'd like to buy a private island.

A: Whereabouts, sir?

B: In the Caribbean, I think.

BBC VIDEO PODCAST

Download the podcast and view people talking about fame and which famous people they'd like to meet.

Authentic BBC interviews

www.pearsonlongman.com/speakout

IRREGULAR VERBS

Verb	Past simple	Past participle
be	was	been
beat	beat	beaten
become	became	become
begin	began	begun
bite	bit	bitten
blow	blew	blown
break	broke	broken
bring	brought	brought
build	built	built
burn	burned/burnt	burned/burnt
buy	bought	bought
catch	caught	caught
choose	chose	chosen
come	came	come
cost	cost	cost
cut	cut	cut
deal	dealt	dealt
do	did	done
draw	drew	drawn
dream	dreamed/dreamt	dreamed/dreamt
drink	drank	drunk
drive	drove	driven
eat	ate	eaten
fall	fell	fallen
feel	felt	felt
fight	fought	fought
find	found	found
fly	flew	flown
forget	forgot	forgotten
forgive	forgave	forgiven
freeze	froze	frozen
get	got	got
give	gave	given
go	went	gone
grow	grew	grown
hang	hung	hung
have	had	had
hear	heard	heard
hide	hid	hidden
hit	hit	hit
hold	held	held
hurt	hurt	hurt
keep	kept	kept
know	knew	known
learn	learned/learnt	learned/learnt

Verb	Past simple	Past participle
leave	left	left
lend	lent	lent
let	let	let
lie	lay	lain
lose	lost	lost
make	made	made
mean	meant	meant
meet	met	met
pay	paid	paid
put	put	put
read	read	read
ride	rode	ridden
ring	rang	rung
run	ran	run
say	said	said
see	saw	seen
sell	sold	sold
send	sent	sent
set	set	set
shake	shook	shaken
shine	shone	shone
show	showed	shown
shut	shut	shut
sing	sang	sung
sit	sat	sat
sleep	slept	slept
smell	smelled/smelt	smelled/smelt
speak	spoke	spoken
spend	spent	spent
spell	spelt	spelt
spill	spilled/spilt	spilled/spilt
stand	stood	stood
steal	stole	stolen
swim	swam	swum
take	took	taken
teach	taught	taught
tear	tore	torn
tell	told	told
think	thought	thought
throw	threw	thrown
understand	understood	understood
wake	woke	woken
wear	wore	worn
win	won	won
write	wrote	written

GRAMMAR

1.1 question forms

Yes/No questions are questions that only require a yes or no answer.

For questions in the present and past simple, put the auxiliary *do/does/did* before the subject.

A: Does he live here? B: Yes, he does.

For questions with *be*, put *be* before the subject.

A: Is he married? B: No, he isn't.

Wh- questions are questions which ask for more than a Yes/No answer. Use the same word order as Yes/No questions.

question word	auxiliary do/does/did	subject	infinitive
Where	does	he	live?
When	do	you	see your parents?
Why	did	they	phone me?

question word	be	subject	adj/noun/verb + -ing, etc.
Why	are	you	sad?
What	is	he	doing?

Use *who* for people. **Who** is your boss?

Use *where* for places. **Where** is the bathroom?

Use *what* or *which* for things. **What** music do you like? **Which** do you prefer, football or rugby?

Use *when* for time. **When** do you want to meet?

Use *how often* for frequency. **How often** do you go to English lessons?

Use *how long* for length of time/distance. **How long** does the lesson last?

Use *how much/many* for quantity. **How much** does this cost? **How many** brothers do you have?

Use *why* for reasons. **Why** are you studying English?

Use *what time* for a time. **What time** do you start work?

Note: *Which* has a limited number of possible answers **Which** do you want, the red or the blue jumper?

What has a large number of possible answers.

What music do you like?

1.2 past simple

Past simple regular verbs			
+	I/you/he/she/it/we/they	worked	in a restaurant
–		didn't work	
?	Did	work	in a restaurant?

Past simple irregular verbs			
+	I/you/he/she/it/we/they	went	out
–		didn't go	
?	Did	go	out?

Use the past simple to talk about finished actions in the past.

In negatives and questions use the auxiliary *did +* infinitive.

Do not use *did* in negatives and questions with the verb *be*. *I wasn't very happy.* NOT *I didn't be happy.*

Spellings: regular past simple verbs		
verbs ending in:	rule	example
	+ -ed	start – started
-e	+ -d	live – lived
-y	-y + -i + -ed	marry – married
consonant-vowel-consonant	double the consonant + -ed	stop – stopped

Form the past simple with regular verbs by adding -ed.

Many common verbs have an irregular past simple form. Look at the list on page 127.

Use the past simple to talk about finished actions in the past.

1.3 making conversation

starting		ending
This is my friend (name).	Did you have a good weekend?	It was nice to meet you.
Hi. Nice to meet you.	Did you watch the match last night?	It was nice to meet you, too.
Nice day, isn't it?	How do you know (name)?	I hope we meet again soon.
Would you like a drink?	So, what do you do?	See you soon.
Where exactly do you come from?		I'll probably see you on (day/date).
So, do you work here?		Yes, let's keep in touch.

PRACTICE

I.I

A Complete the questions. How many can you answer?

I _____ states are there in the USA?

2 _____ was the first person to walk on the moon?

3 _____ is the largest island in the Mediterranean Sea?

4 _____ is H_2O?

5 _____ did the Berlin Wall come down?

6 _____ is Lake Wanaka?

7 _____ country is famous for the Samba?

8 _____ long is the River Nile?

B Match questions 1–8 with answers a)–h).

a) Brazil

b) Neil Armstrong

c) 9th November 1989

d) in New Zealand

e) 50

f) water

g) 6,695 km

h) Sicily

C Find and correct the mistakes. There is a mistake in each sentence.

I How much this cost?

2 You have any brothers or sisters?

3 What time starts the film?

4 How often do you playing football?

5 Who your new teacher is?

6 Do want you to come and have a pizza?

7 Why don't you liking grammar?

8 Where you go on holiday last year?

I.2

A Complete the story with the correct form of the verbs in the box. Use the past simple.

> ask (x2)   email   say   get (x2)   arrive   see   know   fall   decide

A single father-of-two [1] _asked_ his American girlfriend to marry him only four minutes after he [2] _____ her for the first time.

Carl Dockings, 36, from Wales, met Danielle on the internet.

'We [3] _____ on so well. We always [4] _____ what the other was thinking.' He said they [5] _____ and talked in chat rooms. They [6] _____ in love even before exchanging pictures.

After ten months Carl [7] _____ to fly 4,000 miles to meet Danielle in person. He [8] _____ the important question at Chicago's O'Hare Airport soon after he [9] _____.

The 26-year-old [10] _____ 'yes' and the couple [11] _____ married four months later.

They now live in his home city with their daughter Isabel.

B Put the verbs In brackets Into the correct form of the past simple.

I My grandfather _____ (teach) me how to paint.

2 Where _____ you _____ (grow up)?

3 We _____ (meet) in Ireland last year.

4 At first we _____ (not get on) very well.

5 I _____ (leave) college and _____ (get) a job in an office.

6 I _____ (live) in the USA, so we _____ (not see) each other for six months.

7 _____ you_____ (enjoy) the concert last night?

8 They _____ (not have) children.

9 My sister _____ (finish) her degree last year.

10 She _____ (study) Russian.

I.3

A Find and correct the mistakes. There is a mistake or missing word in each sentence.

I This is ~~the~~ /friend, Sara. *(my)*

2 Hi. Nice to know you.

3 Do you like a drink?

4 It was nice meet you.

5 Did you have good weekend?

6 How you know Pieter?

B Put the words in the correct order to make sentences.

I keep / touch / let's / in

2 you / I'll / Saturday / probably / on / see

3 do / what / so / you / do?

4 we / meet / I / again / hope / soon

5 come / where / do / from / exactly / you?

6 soon / see / you

GRAMMAR

2.1 present simple and continuous

	present simple	present continuous
+	I work at home. He watches TV.	I'm working at home. He is watching TV.
–	She doesn't study now. We don't text in class.	She isn't studying now. We're not texting in class.
?	Does he live with you? Where do the workers have lunch?	Is he living with you? Where are the workers having lunch?

Spelling with –ing forms		
verbs ending in:	rule	example
-e	~~-e~~ + -ing	take – taking
vowel + consonant	double the consonant +-ing	run – running
-ie	~~-ie~~ + -y	die – dying
-y	+ -ing	study – studying

Use the present simple to describe something that is always or generally true.

It is common to use these words with the present simple: *sometimes, usually, every day, often*.

I usually get up at 7a.m.

Use the present continuous to talk about:

• an activity happening right now, at the time of speaking.
• a temporary activity happening around now (maybe at the moment, but maybe not).

Form the present continuous with the verb *be* + the *ing* form of the verb.

It is common to use these words with the present continuous: *now, at the moment, currently, this month*.

I'm living with my parents at the moment.

Some verbs are not usually used with continuous tenses: *be, know, like, love, understand, want*, etc. These are called 'state verbs'.

I want to go to bed now. NOT *I ~~am wanting~~ to go to bed now.*

2.2 adverbs of frequency

Use adverbs of frequency to say how frequently you do something. Some of the most common are: *never, rarely, occasionally, sometimes, often, usually, always*.

There are several adverbial phrases of frequency, e.g. *hardly ever, once in while, every day/month/year*.

With *be* put the adverb **after** the verb.

*I **am always** here.   They **were usually** early.*

We usually put the adverb **before** other verbs.

*I **sometimes spoke** to him.   We **hardly ever ate** there.*

With auxiliary or modal verbs, we usually put the adverb **after** the auxiliary or modal.

I can help. → *I can **always** help*

She doesn't stay here. → *She doesn't **usually** stay here.*

We haven't visited them. → *We have **never** visited them.*

Adverbs of frequency can also go at the beginning, middle or end of a sentence.

***Occasionally** I go dancing.*
*I **occasionally** go dancing.*
*I go dancing **occasionally**.*

Always and *never* do not normally go at the beginning or end of sentences.

Once in while and *every day/month/year* usually go at the beginning or end of sentences.

There are other phrases to show how frequently something happens:

every day = one time per day   *I have a shower every day.*

once a week = one time per week   *She writes to me once a week.*

twice a week = two times per week   *They go shopping twice a week.*

2.3 expressing likes/dislikes

There are a number of verbs and other phrases to show likes and dislikes. After these verbs and phrases, we usually use the *-ing* form.

positive
I **like** sing**ing**/meat.
I **absolutely love** swimm**ing**/tennis.
I'm **keen on** runn**ing**/beach holidays.

negative
I **can't stand** smok**ing**/computers.
I **don't like** work**ing**/rock music.
I **hate** watch**ing** TV/films.
I'm **not very keen on** work**ing**/fruit.

Note: We can also use *like* + infinitive.
Like + infinitive means 'do as a habit' or 'choose to do'.

*I **like** to go to bed early.*

Note: I don't mind means 'It's OK for me. I don't like it or dislike it'.

*I **don't mind** sleep**ing** on the floor.*

PRACTICE

2.1

A Complete the conversations with the correct form of the verbs in the box. Use the present simple or present continuous.

eat	be	wait	know	work	wear	play

1 A: It takes him ten minutes to get to work.

  B: I know. His house _____ far from the office.

2 A: Isn't your son an actor?

  B: Yes, but at the moment he _____ in a restaurant.

3 A: What is all that noise? I'm trying to work!

  B: I _____ with the children.

4 A: What _____ you _____ about the new software program?

  B: The new software program? Absolutely nothing.

5 A: Why _____ that jacket in the office? It's really warm!

  B: Because I'm cold!

6 A: Would you like some beef?

  B: No thanks. I _____ meat. I'm a vegetarian.

7 A: Why are you standing there?

  B: I _____ for a taxi.

B Find and correct the mistakes. There is a mistake in five of the sentences.

1 John works in sales and he is going to the office every day at 8a.m.

2 The new employee says she's eighteen, but I'm not believing it.

3 At the moment I'm doing a task for my boss.

4 Don't buy a bottle of wine for her. She isn't drinking alcohol.

5 I can't speak Chinese, but my friend teaches me.

6 Excuse me, is anybody sitting here?

7 I'm taking art classes this term.

8 Hey! What do you do with that knife?!

2.2

A Put the words in the correct order to make sentences.

1 I / dinner / at / weekend / cook / sometimes / the

  I sometimes cook dinner at the weekend.

2 once / I / while / go / in / swimming / a

3 I / money / waste / never / my

4 Najim / often / tennis / play / doesn't

5 Akiko and Toshi / evening / stay / usually / the / home / at / in

6 why / late / are / always / you?

7 I / work / Fridays / rarely / late / on

8 Mary / ever / hardly / deals / with / customers

9 occasionally / a / team / work / I / in

B Underline the correct alternative.

1 *Always/Usually/Hardly ever* our IT consultant deals with these problems; it's his job.

2 I get up early *never/rarely/every day* and go to work at 6a.m.

3 You *sometimes/every week/once in a while* need to risk your life in this job.

4 We *often/never/rarely* see each other – maybe once a year.

5 We *occasionally/always/rarely* work under pressure; we never have a chance to relax.

6 *Often/Hardly ever/Once in a while* I speak to my boss – maybe once a month.

7 We have a summer party *every year/always/never*.

8 I deal with customers *rarely/often/occasionally*, but only if my boss is out.

2.3

A Complete the sentences with one word.

1 I like _____ to music while I study. It helps me concentrate.

2 I _____ mind getting up early for my job. It's no problem for me.

3 Stefania is keen _____ travelling so she's studying tourism.

4 Mick _____ like talking to customers. He says it's boring.

5 Lorenzo absolutely _____ dancing. He's really good at samba.

6 I can't _____ working at the weekend.

GRAMMAR

3.1 present continuous/*be going to* for future

Present continuous				
+	I	'm	spending	the day with my grandmother on Saturday
–	We	're not	playing	football this evening
? What	are	you	doing	at the weekend?

It is common to use the present continuous to talk about things happening now or temporary situations. It is also possible to use the present continuous to talk about definite future plans and arrangements.

It is common to use an expression of future time with the present continuous, e.g. *this weekend, tomorrow morning, later.*

Be going to				
+	I	'm going to	take	some time off work
–	They	're not going to	win	
? Is	it	going to	rain?	

Use *be going to* + infinitive to talk about future plans and predictions.

Usually, we can use both the present continuous and *be going to* to talk about plans.

I*'m meeting* my girlfriend later.

I*'m going to meet* my girlfriend later.

But there is a small difference:

For plans which involve other people and have a fixed time and place, the present continuous is more common.

We're having a barbecue on Saturday. (We have invited people, bought food and drink, etc.)

For plans which do not involve other people, *be going to* is more common.

I*'m going to stay in* and read a book.

When *be going to* is followed by the verb *go*, it is possible to omit *go to*.

I*'m going to* (go to) *the cinema.*

3.2 questions without auxiliaries

subject	verb		answer
Who	sent	the present?	David.
What	causes	this problem?	The water pipes.
Whose guitar	cost	$300?	Mine.
Which footballers	played	for that team?	Beckham and Cole.

When *who, what, which* or *whose* is the **subject** of the sentence, do not use an auxiliary verb (*do, did,* etc.). The verb is in the third person.

Who ate all the pies?

Which students forgot their homework?

When *who, what, which* or *whose* is the **object** of the sentence, use an auxiliary verb as usual.

What **do** you do?

Whose book **did** you use?

3.3 making a phone call

Caller	
start the call	Hello, this is Andy. Hello, it's Wendy. (NOT ~~I am Wendy.~~)
ask to speak to someone	Can I speak to … ?
when the person you want isn't there	Can I leave a message?
finish the call	See you soon. Goodbye.

Receiver	
start the call	Hello. Paul speaking*
find out who is speaking	Who's calling (please)?
when the person the caller wants isn't there	I'm afraid she's not here at the moment. Can I take a message? I'll ask her to call you back.
finish the call	Thanks for calling.

*We say this when we answer the phone at work.

PRACTICE

3.1

A Match prompts 1–4 with pictures A–D.

1 play / football
2 stay home / watch TV
3 go / cinema
4 have / meeting

B Look at the pictures and make sentences with the prompts. Use the present continuous.

Next week

This evening

Saturday

Next weekend

C Put the verbs in brackets into the correct form of the present continuous or *be going to*.

A: What ^{1}_____ you _____ (do) tonight?

B: I ^{2}_____ (go) John's house party.

A: Really? We ^{3}_____ (be) there, too.

B: Great! ^{4}_____ you _____ (take) any food or drink?

A: Yes, we ^{5}_____ (bring) some food, but we ^{6}_____ (not bring) drink.

B: What type of music ^{7}_____ he _____ (have)?

A: He's got a DJ and he ^{8}_____ (play) dance music.

B: It sounds great. How ^{9}_____ you _____ (get) there?

A: We ^{10}_____ (drive). Do you want a lift?

3.2

A Find and correct the mistakes. There is a mistake in five of the questions.

1 Do you like reading?
2 Who does read the most in your family?
3 Who be your favourite writer?
4 Which books have become famous recently?
5 What did be your favourite book when you were a child?
6 Who did write it?
7 How often you read on the internet?
8 Where and when do you like to read?

B Make questions with the prompts. Use the past simple. One question needs an auxiliary verb.

1 What colour / be / The Beatles' / submarine?
2 Who / write / *Stairway to Heaven*?
3 Whose / home / be / Graceland?
4 Which country / Diego Rivera / come from?
5 Who / paint / the *Mona Lisa*?
6 Which painter / invent / Cubism?

3.3

A Put the words in the correct order to make a phone conversation.

A: speaking / David

B: it's / Johnson / hello / Mark

A: can / Mr / help / how / I / you / Johnson?

B: to / like / Sara / please / I'd / to / speak / Torres

A: the / afraid / here / I'm / she's / moment / not / at

B: a / leave / I / can / message?

A: course / of / yes

B: you / me / her / can / ask / call / to / back?

A: problem / no

B: number / 0276 765356 / is / my

A: repeat / you / that / can / please?

B: 0276 765356

A: calling / thanks / OK / for

B: Bye

A: Bye

GRAMMAR

4.1 present perfect + *ever/never*

Present perfect: positive and negative

+	I/You/We/They	have ('ve)	finished	the project
	He/She/It	has ('s)		
−	I/You/We/They	haven't/(have never)	visited	Mexico
	He/She/It	hasn't/(has never)		

Present perfect: questions / **Short answers**

Have	I/you/we/they	(ever) played	chess?	Yes	I/you/we/they	have
				No		haven't
Has	he/she/it			Yes	he/she/it	has
				No		hasn't

Form the present perfect with *have/has* + past participle.

The past participle is verb + *-ed* for regular verbs. For a list of irregular verbs, see page 127.

Use the present perfect to talk about past experiences without saying an exact time.
I've been to Warsaw.

When we want to say an exact time, we use the past simple.
I went to Warsaw in 2007.

Use *ever* with the present perfect to mean 'during your life until now'. *Never* is the negative of *ever*.

*Have you **ever** visited Madrid?*

*She's **never** been to a nightclub.*

Spoken grammar 1: When we are asked a *Have you ever ... ?* question, we often reply: *No, never* instead of *No, I haven't*.

A: Have you ever been to the Maldives?

B: No, never.

Spoken grammar 2: When we want to repeat the same *Have you ever ... ?* question, we usually say *Have you?*

A: Have you ever been to Zurich?

B: No, have you?

4.2 *can, have to, must*

Use modal verbs *can/can't, have to/don't have to, must/mustn't* to talk about present obligation.

Use *can* to talk about something which is possible/allowed.
*You **can** use dictionaries during the exam.*

Use *can't* to talk about something which is not possible/allowed.
*You **can't** park here.*

Use *must/mustn't/have to* to talk about rules or things that are necessary.
*We **have to** study for our exam.*

*You **must** return the books to the library before Friday.*

*You **mustn't** chew gum in the classroom.*

Use *don't have to* to talk about something that is not necessary (but it is possible/allowed).

*We **don't have to** be there until eight o'clock.* (But we can get there earlier if we want to.)

Use *he/she has to* in the positive, and *he/she doesn't have to* in the negative.

*She **has to** pay for the exam.*

*He **doesn't have to** do any extra work.*

4.3 giving/responding to advice

phrases for giving advice	example
I think you should ...	I think you should study more.
You should ...	You should hear her play the trumpet.
You shouldn't ...	You shouldn't be late all the time.
Why don't you ... ?	Why don't you finish your homework later?
I (don't) think it's a good idea to ...	I think it's a good idea to take some lessons.
Find/Write/Do ...	Find a cheap hotel on the internet.

phrases for responding to advice
That's a good idea.
I suppose so.
You're right.
I'm not sure that's a good idea.

PRACTICE

4.1

A Find and correct the mistakes. There is one mistake in each sentence.

1 Have you ever saw the film *Titanic*?
2 Two days ago she's been to a museum.
3 Unfortunately, we have ever won the lottery.
4 Has ever she visited you?
5 I haven't meet your brother.
6 In 2006 they've travelled to Geneva.
7 Have you seen that TV programme last Wednesday?
8 He never has played a musical instrument.

B Complete the conversations with the correct form of the verbs in the box. Use the past simple or present perfect.

make   eat   visit   hear   do   work

Conversation 1

A: _____ (ever) business in China?

B: Yes, I have. I did business there in 2006.

Conversation 2

A: Peter Duvall is a diplomat, isn't he?

B: Yes, he _____ all over the world.

Conversation 3

A: She loves travelling, doesn't she?

B: Yes, she _____ fifteen countries last year.

Conversation 4

A: _____ many speeches?

B: No, he hasn't. That's why I'm worried.

Conversation 5

A: Is Coldplay's new CD good?

B: I don't know. I _____ it.

Conversation 6

A: Have you ever tried sushi?

B: Yes, we _____ some yesterday!

4.2

A Underline the correct alternative.

1 We *have to/has to* get up early to catch the train.
2 Children *can't/can* stay with their parents if they are very quiet.
3 I'm afraid I *can't/must* leave work early. It's not allowed.
4 They *have to/don't have to* put a notice on the door so you know which room to go to.
5 You *can/don't have to* park your car here. It's free on Saturdays.
6 You *mustn't/have to* smoke in the office. It's against the law.
7 You *can't/have to* leave your coat on the floor. Hang it up!
8 We *must/don't have to* worry about transport. A taxi will take us to the airport.

B Complete the sentences with *can/can't, have to/don't have to* or *must/mustn't*.

1 You _____ leave the room when you have finished the exam. (it's allowed)
2 We _____ book a table. That restaurant is never busy on Mondays. (it's not necessary)
3 You _____ log in using your PIN number. (it's necessary)
4 You _____ eat as much as you like. (it's allowed)
5 Sadie _____ bring extra clothes. I have got lots here. (it's not necessary)
6 You _____ wear jeans in the nightclub. (it's not allowed)
7 Harry _____ work on his pronunciation. (it's necessary)
8 You _____ do that. It's illegal! (it's not allowed)

4.3

A Put the words in the correct order to make sentences.

a) a / idea / that's / good
b) think / I / out / after / lesson / go / should / the / we
c) not / I'm / sure / I / much money / haven't got / because
d) for / we / a / out / meal / why / go / don't?
e) OK / to / Butler's café / let's / coffee / a / for / go

B Put sentences a)–e) in the correct order to make a conversation.

GRAMMAR

5.1 past simple and past continuous

	past simple	past continuous
+	I watched a film yesterday.	I was watching a film yesterday.
–	He didn't play here.	He wasn't playing here.
?	Did you talk to John?	Were you talking to John?

Use the past simple to talk about completed actions.

*I **ate** a salad last night.*

Use the past continuous to talk about actions in progress at a particular time.

*At 8a.m. yesterday I **was travelling** to work.*

It is common to use the past simple and the past continuous together to tell stories. The past continuous describes an action that starts first, but is interrupted by a second action. Use the past simple for the second (usually short) action.

*What **were you doing** when the bus **crashed**?*
*I **was sleeping** when the thief **entered** the house.*

It is common to use *when* or *while* to link the two actions. Use *while* before the continuous action.

***While** I was sleeping, it started to rain.*

Use *when* before the continuous action or the short action.

***When** we **were talking**, the bus appeared.*
*We **were talking** when the bus **appeared**.*

Do NOT use *while* before the short action.

I was sleeping while it started to rain.

I was sleeping → → → → → → → → → → → →
11p.m.   the thief entered (3a.m.)
past ▬▬▬▬▬|▬▬▬▬▬▬▬▬▬|▬▬▬ present

5.2 verb patterns

Sometimes we use two verbs together.

*I **love playing** football.*

After some verbs put the second verb in the infinitive with *to*.

*She decided **to go** to Mexico.*
*We need **to make** a phone call.*

After some verbs use the *-ing* form.

*I enjoy runn**ing**.*
*They avoided travell**ing** by bus.*

Some common verb patterns	
verb + *-ing*	verb + infinitive with *to*
enjoy	choose
finish	hope
avoid	expect
imagine	would like
stop	decide
like	seem
don't mind	want
spend (time)	need
	help
	promise

Many verbs that show preference (things that we like or don't like) are followed by *-ing*, e.g. *like, enjoy, don't mind*.

After some verbs it is possible to use the *-ing* form OR the infinitive with *to*, e.g. *love, hate*.

*I love **dancing**. I love **to dance**.*
*I hate **getting up** early. I hate **to get up** early.*

There is little change in meaning.

5.3 asking for/giving directions

go left

go past the turning

go along the main road

take the first right

keep going until you reach …

at the corner

go through the centre

cross a bridge

go straight on

in front of you

useful questions	directions	saying you understand
Can we walk? Excuse me, can you help me?	It takes about twenty minutes	OK So I need to …
Is this the right way?	Keep going You'll see …	Right
Can you show me on the map?	You can't miss it	
Is it far?		

PRACTICE

5.1

A Complete the story with the correct form of the verbs in brackets. Use the past simple or past continuous.

Alvin Straight, a 73-year-old, ¹ _____ (live) quietly on his farm in Iowa, USA, when he heard the news that his brother Lyle was seriously ill. After ten years with no contact between the brothers, Alvin ² _____ (decide) to visit Lyle. Alvin couldn't drive so he ³ _____ (buy) a lawnmower, which moved at five miles per hour, and ⁴ _____ (begin) the 250-mile-journey.

While he ⁵ _____ (travel), he met many people including a priest and a teenage girl who was running away from her family. He helped them all simply by talking about life. Some of them also ⁶ _____ (help) him. For example, one day when he ⁷ _____ (drive) the lawnmower, it broke down. While two mechanics ⁸ _____ (fix) it, he met a friendly couple and ⁹ _____ (stay) with them.

The journey took him six weeks. And ¹⁰ _____ the story _____ (end) happily? See the 1999 film, *The Straight Story*, to find out!

B Make sentences with the prompts and the correct form of the verbs in the box. Use the past simple or past continuous.

pass	know	like	play	dance	swim	travel
have						

1 He / tennis when he hurt his leg.
2 Sarah / the job because it was boring.
3 While they / they met lots of other tourists.
4 How / you / my name?
5 Who / you / with in that nightclub when I saw you?
6 I / in the sea when I saw the shark.
7 I / my exam?
8 The thief broke in while Jack / breakfast.

5.2

A Complete the sentences with the correct form of the verbs in the box.

live	read	drink	swim	visit	have	play	finish

1 They want _____ the monuments tomorrow morning.
2 I can't imagine _____ in that flat – it's so small!
3 I don't like _____ water from a bottle.
4 They decided _____ football this morning.
5 Would you like _____ dinner in this restaurant?
6 Do you enjoy _____ in the sea?
7 I hope _____ my degree next year.
8 I love _____ books about adventures.

B Find and correct the mistakes. There are eight mistakes in the advertisement.

Mad Dog Tours

Are modern holidays too boring for you?
Would you like doing something more exciting?

Mad Dog Tours is perfect for people who hate spend time asleep on a beach. If you enjoy to travel to strange places, if you don't mind to stay in cheap hotels and want knowing how the local people really live, we promise helping you. Cheap holidays are our speciality. If you choose booking your holiday with *Mad Dog Tours*, you can expect living your dreams!

5.3

A Match 1–10 with a)–j) to make sentences or questions.

1 Excuse me, can
2 Is this the
3 Is
4 Can you show
5 It takes
6 You can't
7 Can we
8 So I
9 You'll see the
10 Keep

a) about an hour.
b) need to go left here.
c) restaurant on your right.
d) it far?
e) right way?
f) going.
g) me on the map?
h) you help me?
i) walk?
j) miss it.

B Underline the correct alternative to complete the conversations.

Conversation 1

A: Excuse me, how do I get to the swimming pool?

B: You need to go ¹*along/at/with* the main road. Keep going until you ²*go/have/reach* the town hall. Then ³*go/make/be* left and it's ⁴*the/in/to* front of you.

Conversation 2

A: Excuse me, is this the right way to the Bach Concert Hall?

B: No, you need to turn around, then ⁵*do/cross/go* the bridge. After that, you ⁶*have/are/take* the first right and go ⁷*at/with/through* the centre of town. The concert hall is at the ⁸*first/corner/cross* of Ducane Road and Bright Street.

6.1 present perfect + *for/since*

Use the present perfect to talk about things that started in the past and are still true now.
We've been married for fourteen years. (We got married fourteen years ago and we are still married now.)

Use *since* to talk about the specific time something started, e.g. *1992, last week, Monday, I was a child*.
We've known each other *since* we were children. (We are friends now.)

He *has played* football since 2002.

Use *for* to talk about a period (length) of time, e.g. *ten years, two months, a long time, an hour, a few weeks*.
I haven't seen him *for* a few weeks.
I've lived in Barcelona *for* twenty-five years.

To ask about the length of time, use *How long have you … ?*
How long have you worked for Dell?

Use the past simple, not the present perfect, for things which happened at a specific time in the past.
I moved to Spain in 2001. NOT *I ~~have moved~~* to Spain in 2001.

6.2 *may, might, will*

Use *may/might* + infinitive to talk about probable situations.

We also use *may/might* + infinitive to talk about future possibilities.
I might go to the party
They *might* not *arrive* today.
We *may have* some problems.

She *may not* like the dress.
Do not use contractions with *might not* and *may not*.

The question form with *might* is rare.

The question form with *may* is used for asking permission. It is a very polite form.
May I sit here? *May I open* the window?

Use *will* + infinitive to talk about a future prediction.

The negative of *will* is *won't* (or *will not*).
I will be home at 9p.m. tonight.
She *won't* come here tomorrow.
Will they *win* the match?

In spoken English use the contracted form of *will* (*'ll*) in positive sentences. Do not use this in questions.
I'll be home at 9p.m. tonight.

It is common to use *think/don't think* + *will*.
I think she*'ll get* the job.
I don't think I'll go to university next year.

6.3 seeing the doctor

Doctor
What's the matter/problem?
How long have you had this problem?
Where does it hurt?
Can I have a look (at …)?
It's nothing to worry about.
I'll give you some pills/antibiotics/medicine.

Patient
I feel sick/terrible.
I can't sleep.
I'm worried about …
It hurts when I walk/talk.
It's very painful.

PRACTICE

6.1

A Underline the correct alternative.

1 I *didn't do/haven't done* much work *for/since* my boss left.

2 I *didn't go/haven't been* to China *for/since* 2002.

3 She *has been/was* a doctor *for/since* more than forty years. She retired in 2006.

4 Hi, Angela. How are you? I *haven't seen/didn't see* you *for/since* ages.

5 I *left/have left* university in 1995. I've worked in this company *for/since* about fifteen years.

6 I *didn't see/haven't seen* Sam yesterday. In fact I *didn't see/haven't seen* him *for/since* Monday.

7 He's really tired. He's been working *for/since* 5.30a.m.

8 She *hasn't driven/didn't drive* a car *for/since* she had the accident.

B Complete the sentences with *for* or *since*. Put the verbs in brackets into the correct form of the present perfect or past simple.

1 I've lived in this city _____ 2007. I _____ (come) here with my family.

2 I _____ (buy) this house in 1999, so I _____ (live) here _____ more than ten years.

3 I _____ (know) Marissa _____ a long time. We _____ (meet) in 1998.

4 They _____ (move) to Australia last December, so they _____ (be) there _____ nearly a year.

5 We _____ (not be) back to Russia _____ 1990.

6 He _____ (not see) his father _____ he left home.

7 I've been learning English _____ I _____ (start) school.

8 She _____ (have) that car _____ ages!

6.2

A Match statements 1–6 with responses a)–f).

1 I'm hungry because I missed breakfast.

2 You eat too much junk food.

3 I'm just going out to get a snack.

4 The film was really good.

5 She looks a bit stressed.

6 We want to visit the museum this afternoon.

a) I won't be long.

b) I think she'll need a holiday soon.

c) We may not have time.

d) You might get fat.

e) I may have an early lunch.

f) I think my father might enjoy it.

B Find and correct the mistakes. There is a mistake in each sentence.

1 I don't will know my exam results until August.

2 Will you to go to university next year?

3 Anna is very busy so she may not comes tonight.

4 The traffic is heavy so they may to be late.

5 Edson mights be the best player we have ever seen.

6 I might go not to the exercise class today.

7 We'll to be back at 6 p.m.

6.3

A Complete the conversation with phrases from the boxes on page 138.

Doctor: Good morning. I'm Dr Gordon. ¹_____ _____ _____?

Patient: ²_____ _____ _____ . I've got a sore throat, and a cough.

Doctor: ³_____ _____ _____ _____ _____ _____ _____?

Patient: About a week.

Doctor: Have you got a temperature?

Patient: Yes, I think so.

Doctor: ⁴_____ _____ _____ _____ _____ at your throat?

Patient: Yes. It's ⁵_____ _____ . ⁶_____ _____ when I talk.

Doctor: Right. ⁷_____ _____ _____ some medicine. Take this for one week, and if you don't feel better, come back to see me again.

Patient: Thank you.

GRAMMAR

7.1 *used to*

		subject	*used to*	infinitive	
+		I, you, he/she/it, we, they	used to	go	to the cinema every Saturday
–			didn't use to never used to	go	on holiday
?	Did	you	use to	work	hard?

Note: Notice the spelling of *use to* in the negative and question form.

We **didn't use** to live in a big house. **NOT** We didn't ~~used~~ to live …

Did you **use** to play a lot of football? **NOT** Did you ~~used~~ to play… ?

Use *used to* to talk about a past habit or situation which is not the same now.

We used to live in London. (But now we live in Warsaw.)

I used to play a lot of tennis. (But I don't play any more.)

It is possible to use the past simple instead of *used to*.

*I **used to go** out a lot. = I **went** out a lot.*

It is not possible to use *used to* to talk about something which happened just once or at a specific time. For this, use the past simple.

We moved in 1992. **NOT** *We ~~used~~ to move in 1992.*

It is not possible to use *used to* to talk about the present.

I usually eat at home. **NOT** *I ~~used~~ to eat at home.*

The negative of *used to* is *didn't use to*. In spoken English, *never used to* is more common.

They never used to worry about money.

We never used to eat chocolate.

7.2 purpose, cause and result

Use *to* + infinitive to talk about the reason or purpose for an action.

*I went to the shop **to buy** some milk.*

Note: It is not possible to say ~~for to buy~~ some milk.

It is also possible to use *in order (not) to* + infinitive.

*He came to class **in order to** learn English.*

*They came back early **in order not to** miss the party.*

It is also possible to use *so that* + subject + verb.

*I'll cook **so that** you can relax.*

Use *because* + subject + verb to talk about a cause.

*I left work **because** I hated the job.*

***Because** we don't eat meat, we buy a lot of fish.*

Use *so* + subject + verb to talk about the result of an action.

*It rained **so** we went inside.*

*I forgot my wallet **so** I didn't have any money.*

7.3 finding out information

getting attention	asking for information	thanking someone
Excuse me, … Could you help me? Can you tell me … ?	Where can I get/find/buy … ? When can I use/start … ? What time is the library open? What time do the lessons start? Can I … ? Do I have to … ? Is it free/open/near? I need to find out about/speak to …	Thank you so much. That's very kind.

PRACTICE

7.1

A Complete the sentences with *used to/didn't use to* and the words in brackets.

1 I _____ (study) hard when I was at school so I always passed my exams.

2 He _____ (smoke) before he got ill, but he had to give up.

3 We _____ (never/argue), but now we argue all the time.

4 They _____ (live) in the city, but now they have moved to the sea.

5 I _____ (not/like) eating mushrooms, but now I love them!

6 _____ you _____ (enjoy) working in an office?

7 She _____ (go out) with Steve, but now she has met someone else.

8 I _____ (do) a lot of cooking, but now I don't have time.

B Look at the pictures. How have things changed? Complete the sentences.

1 He _____ have long hair. Now it's short.

2 He _____ drive a car. He rode a motorbike when he was younger.

3 He _____ wear a leather jacket. Now he wears a suit.

4 He _____ do a lot of sport.

5 He _____ win competitions.

6 He _____ be fat.

7 He _____ work as an actor. Now he's a politician.

8 He _____ not _____ be interested in politics.

7.2

A Complete the sentences with *so*, *to* or *because*.

1 She took the job _____ make some money.

2 The company became successful _____ it had brilliant sales reps.

3 I became a doctor _____ cure people of their illnesses.

4 They treated her badly _____ she left the company.

5 Put the key in your pocket _____ you don't lose it.

6 You need to work hard _____ pass your exams.

7 He spent twenty years in prison _____ he killed a man.

8 I have been at this school for ten years _____ I know all the teachers.

B There are eight words missing from the text. Complete the text with *so*, *to* or *because*.

I usually get a newspaper I want to know what's on TV, but today I read a strange story. An Englishman was feeling terrible he was under pressure at work, he decided to disappear. He went to a beach go swimming (he said). Then he left his clothes there that someone could find them. He also left his wallet with a photo and ID the police knew who it was. The police went to his home speak to him, but he wasn't there. He was in Australia and had a different name! Three years later he was caught when his cousin, who was in Australia attend a conference, recognised him. Where were they? On a beach!

7.3

A Find and correct the mistakes. There is an extra word in each line.

Conversation 1

A: Excuse me. Can you tell me where to can find a post-office?

B: Yes, there's one just behind of you!

Conversation 2

A: I need to be find out about my accommodation.

B: There's an accommodation office on downstairs.

Conversation 3

A: Breakfast is in the restaurant from on 7 o'clock.

B: Sorry? Did you to say 7 o'clock!

Conversation 4

A: Do you is know where the main reception is?

B: Yes, I'll show it you.

A: That's you very kind.

Conversation 5

A: Is it a free to park my car here?

B: No, it's you have to pay.

GRAMMAR

8.1 relative clauses

Use relative clauses to talk about what a person, place, or thing is (or does).

This is the machine **which we used to make the copies.**

He's the man **who helped us.**

Also use relative clauses to explain which one we are talking about.

She's the girl **who has green eyes.**

That's the town **where I was born.**

Use *who* for a person.

He's the doctor **who** *looked after your grandmother.*

Use *where* for a place.

This is the city **where** *she grew up.*

Use *which* for a thing.

This is the knife **which** *the killer used.*

It is possible to use *that* instead of *which* or *who*.

She's the girl **that** *lives next door.*

This is the machine **that** *we used to make the copies.*

When we define something by using a relative clause, we use *the* not *a/an*.

It's **a** *car. We used it at the weekend.*

It's **the** *car* **that** *we used at the weekend.*

8.2 *too much/many, enough, very*

word	use it before	meaning	example
too	adjectives/adverbs	more than is necessary/right	I'm **too tired** to study.
too much	uncountable nouns		There's **too much water.**
too many	countable nouns		There are **too many people** here.
enough	nouns	the correct amount	Is there **enough petrol** for the trip?
not enough	nouns	less than is necessary/right	There **aren't enough chairs.**
very	adjectives/adverbs	emphasis (can be good or bad)	She's **very nice.** He's **very ugly.**

Too is always used to say that something is negative. (more than is necessary/right).

These trousers are **too** *small.* (negative)

Much is used with uncountable nouns, e.g. *rice, water, money, news.* These are called uncountable nouns because we cannot say ~~one rice~~ or ~~two rice~~.

Many is used with countable nouns, e.g. *days, people, dollars, computers.* These are called countable nouns because it is possible to say *one day, two days,* etc.

It is possible to use adjective + *enough* to say something is OK.

The room is **big enough.**

It is possible to use *enough* before a noun.

Do we have **enough chairs?**

Use *very* + adjective with positive or negative ideas.

She's **very nice.** (positive)

This hat is **very expensive.** (negative)

Spoken grammar: We sometimes use *enough* as a noun.

That's enough. You're talking too much, children.

It is common to end a sentence with *enough* when the listener already knows what we are talking about.

A: What about drinks?   *B: We have enough.*

8.3 buying things

customer	assistant
Excuse me.	Can I help (you)?
I'm just looking.	Are you looking for anything in particular?
Do you sell … ?	Who's next, please?
Do you have one of these in red/blue/a larger size?	Are you paying by cash or credit card?
Can I try it/this on?	Can you just sign here, please?
Where's the fitting room?	Can you enter your PIN, please?
It fits./It doesn't fit.	

PRACTICE

8.1

A Rewrite the two sentences as one sentence. Use the prompts and relative clauses.

1 Laguna is a town. I spent my holidays there.
Laguna is the town *where I spent my holidays*.

2 Did you get the present? I sent it to you last week.
Did you get the present _____?

3 Burnham Place is a restaurant. You can watch the chefs make your food there.
Burnham Place is the _____.

4 Geekstore is a shop. It sells cheap iPods and mobiles.
Geekstore _____.

5 Nichola Leeson is an accountant. She helped me complete my tax form.
Nichola Leeson is the _____.

6 Corleone is a town. I learnt how to do business there.
Corleone is the town _____.

7 A man invested the money. He was a criminal.
The man _____.

B Match the endings in the box to 1–6 and write relative clauses. You need to change/cut some words.

> ~~you study there~~   she lends me   it sells insurance
> he borrows $1,000,000 to buy a horse
> she was working as a chef   we went on our honeymoon

1 A school is a place *where you study*.
2 The film is about a man
3 I work for a company
4 I always give back the money
5 What happened to that girl
6 The Bahamas is the place

8.2

A Find and correct the mistakes. There is a mistake in six of the sentences.

1 The film was great. It was too funny!
2 There aren't eggs enough to make a cake.
3 That child eats too much sweets.
4 Do you earn money enough to pay the bills?
5 I spent too many time on the first question.
6 I can't help you because I'm too busy.
7 She's very generous   she always tips the waiters.
8 There isn't enough of time to do this exercise.

B Complete the sentences with *too, too much/many, (not) enough,* or *very.*

1 You spend _____ time on your mobile phone. It's bad for your work.
2 I didn't get _____ money from the bank so I need to go back.
3 He was _____ lazy to study so he failed his exam.
4 I don't know how many coins I have in my collection. There are _____ to count.
5 He did _____ well to give up smoking after ten years.
6 I didn't take the dogs for a walk. It was _____ cold.
7 The sofa takes up _____ space. Let's buy a smaller one.
8 The company agreed to do more work, but this was a mistake. There were _____ employees to do it.

8.3

A Complete the conversation with the words in the box.

> help   fitting   enter   on   fit   size   one   by

A: Hello, can I ¹_____ you?
B: Do you sell jackets?
A: Yes, they're just over there.
B: Can I try this ²_____?
A: Yes, of course. How is it?
B: It doesn't ³_____. Do you have it in a larger ⁴_____?
A: I think so. Just a moment. Yes, here you are.
B: Thanks. And do you have ⁵_____ of these in black?

A: Yes, here it is. Would you like to try it on?
B: Yes, please. Where's the ⁶_____ room?
A: Just over there.
B: It fits. I'll take it.
A: OK. Are you paying ⁷_____ cash or credit card?
B: Credit card.
A: OK, can you ⁸_____ your PIN, please?
B: OK.

GRAMMAR

9.1 comparatives/superlatives

type of adjective	example	comparative		superlative	
one-syllable	cheap	+-er	cheaper	the +-est	the cheapest
some two-syllable	quiet	+-er	quieter	the +-est	the quietest
adjectives: ending in –e ending in –y ending in CVC	safe friendly big	+ -r y+ier double the final consonant +er	safer friendlier bigger	the + -st the + y + -iest the + double the final consonant + -est	the safest the friendliest the biggest
many two-syllable	interesting	more/less + adjective	more/less interesting	the most/least + adjective	the most/least interesting
irregular	good bad far		better worse further		the best the worst the furthest

There are different ways to compare one or more things.

Superiority: *much/a lot more* + adjective + *than*   A is *a lot more* expensive *than* B

Equality: the same as, *as* + adjective + *as*   A is *the same as* B.

Inferiority: *not as/so* + adjective + *as*   A is not *as big as* B

It is possible to use comparatives with nouns.

more/less + noun   He has *more money than* we thought.

It is common to use the superlative with the present perfect. It's the *best* restaurant *I've* ever *been* to!

9.2 articles

the (definite article)	example
to talk about something that has already been mentioned or information that the speaker and the listener already knows	I saw a lion. The lion was sleeping.
to talk about something when there is only one	I looked at the moon.
before some plural place names	the United States
before seas/oceans/rivers	the Atlantic
before the names of some areas	the north west of England
in some phrases with prepositions	in the evening, at the beginning
with superlatives	She is the tallest.

a/an (indefinite article)	example
the first time something is mentioned	I saw a lion yesterday.
before singular nouns	There's a library in the town.
before job titles (in general)	I'm an actor.

no article (zero article)	example
to talk about things or people in general	Dogs are friendly animals.
before plural nouns	I'm taking four classes this term.
before most cities, countries and continents	I live in Germany.
in some phrases with prepositions	on Tuesday, at sea, in hospital, at work.

9.3 making guesses

It is possible	example
It could + infinitive	He could be late because of traffic.
It might + infinitive	It might be John at the door.
Maybe …	Maybe it's an antelope.
Perhaps …	Perhaps she went to bed late last night.

It is not possible	example
It can't be …	It can't be Mary's coat because she didn't come to the party.
It's definitely not …	What's the answer? It's definitely not 'A'.

It is certain	example
It must + infinitive	You must be very happy that you passed

PRACTICE

9.1

A Put the adjectives in brackets into the correct form.

1 Eating at home is _cheaper than_ eating in restaurants. (cheap)

2 People in cities work _____ hours _____ in the past. (long)

3 There is more traffic now, so the streets are _____. (noisy)

4 History is much _____ _____ _____ physics. (interesting)

5 Houses are _____ _____ _____ they were ten years ago. (expensive)

6 Life in the city is _____ _____ _____ it was before. (dangerous)

7 Cairo is even _____ _____ I expected. (hot)

8 South America is _____ _____ _____ Europe. (exciting)

9 I wish it was _____ _____ in this country. I'm freezing! (cold)

B Make superlative sentences with the prompts.

1 This / exciting / holiday / I ever have
This is the most exciting holiday I've ever had.

2 You / good / friend / I ever have

3 That / boring / film / I ever see

4 This / short / day / year

5 That / long / run / I ever do

6 This / old / building / I ever see

7 That / hard / job / ever do

9.2

A Underline the correct alternative.

1 Many people are frightened of *a/an/the/–* spiders.

2 I had a pet cat which I loved, but *a/an/the/–* cat didn't like me!

3 *A/An/The/–* vegetarians are people who don't eat meat.

4 The blue whale is *a/an/the/–* heaviest animal in the world.

5 We heard that there is *a/an/the/–* new gorilla in the zoo.

6 *A/An/The/–* bats drink blood.

7 There is *a/an/the/–* elephant that lived to the age of seventy-eight.

8 The mammal that sleeps *a/an/the/–* longest is the barrow ground squirrel.

9 We saw *a/an/the/–* eagle when we were in Namibia.

10 She used to work at Animals4U before *a/an/the/–* shop closed down.

B There is an article missing (*a, an* or *the*) in each sentence in the text. Complete the text with the missing articles.

I was feeling bored so I went for walk. The trees were green and sky was blue. It was beautiful day. Suddenly I heard a strange noise, like animal. But I knew it wasn't cat because cats don't sound like that. Sound continued for a minute or more. I went home and switched on TV to watch the local news. The newsreader said, 'Some animals have escaped from city zoo.'

9.3

A Match statements 1–8 with responses a)–h).

1 She didn't come to school today.

2 This letter says I have $500,000,000 in the bank.

3 Who is that man?

4 What's that smell in the kitchen?

5 When is her birthday?

6 I can't find my keys.

7 He's lost his homework.

8 How many people are called Smith?

a) It might be onions. My mother is cooking.

b) I don't know but it's definitely not today.

c) Perhaps the dog ate it again.

d) There must be millions. It's the most common name in the UK.

e) She could be sick.

f) Maybe you left them in the car.

g) It must be a mistake.

h) It can't be David. He's out of the country until next week.

GRAMMAR

10.1 uses of *like*

like (verb)				
+		I	like	living in the city
–		She	doesn't like	
?	Do Where do	you	like	going out in the evening?

Use *like* (verb) to talk about things you like:
What do you like doing in the evening?
I like going out at night.

be like (preposition)				
?	What	is	he/she/it Antigua/ your new house	like?

Use *be like* (prepostion) to ask for a description:
A: *What's it (the city) like?*
B: *It's a big city, with lots of traffic.*

Note: Be careful not to confuse the two forms.
Question: What's it like?
Answer: It's a lovely city. NOT ~~I like it very much.~~

10.2 present/past passive

Use subject + *be* + past participle to form the passive.

Present passive				
	subject	*be*	past participle	
+	I/you/he/she/it/we/they	am	told	that he is the best player
–	Rugby	isn't	played	here
?	Is	this dish	made	with potatoes?

Past passive				
	subject	*be*	past participle	
+	I/you/he/she/it/we/they	was/were	stopped	by a policeman
–	The photo	wasn't	taken	here
?	Was	the dog	killed?	

Use the active voice to talk about the things people do: *John **stole** the camera. Liz **ate** the bread.*

Use the passive voice:

* to talk about what happens to things or people: *The camera **was stolen** by John. The bread **was eaten** by Liz.*

* when the cause of the action is unknown: *Thousands of people **are killed** on the roads every year.* (We don't know who kills them.)

* when the cause of the action is not important: *The cakes **are made** in France.* (It is not important who makes them.)

If we want to say who does/did the action, we use *by*: *The criminal was caught **by** the police. Penicillin was discovered **by** Sir Alexander Fleming.*

10.3 complaining

before making a complaint	complaint	response
Could you help me? I'm afraid I have a complaint. Excuse me, could I speak to the manager?	There's a problem with … It doesn't work. I've been here for over an hour.	We'll look into it right away. I'm sorry but there's nothing we can do at the moment. I'm really sorry about that.

PRACTICE

10.1

A Put the words in the correct order to make questions.

1 like / job / your / what's / new?

2 new / do / my / dress / like / you?

3 like / what / is / tapas?

4 there / the / what's / like / weather?

5 like / in / you / living / the / do / country?

B Match questions 1–5 above with answers a)–e).

a) I love it. It's so peaceful.

b) Yes. It really suits you.

c) It is delicious. It is small dishes of vegetables, fish and meat. You can eat them as a starter.

d) It's great. I really like the people I'm working with.

e) It's terrible. It's windy and wet.

C Find and correct the mistakes. There is a mistake in each line.

1 I like listen to music. My favourite band is Jamiroquia.

2 How is the flat like? Is it modern?

3 Have you seen *Terminator 4*? Did you like?

4 So, you've got a new boss. What's like he?

5 What's like the weather? Is it raining?

6 Are you like speaking English?

10.2

A Underline the correct alternative.

1 Only fresh fish *is serve/is served/is to serve* in this restaurant.

2 Yesterday she *has given/was given/is given* a ten-year prison sentence.

3 Shoplifters *aren't caught/not caught/aren't **catch*** very often.

4 This book *was written/is written/was wrote* by a Frenchman in 1886.

5 At the moment films *are show/were shown/are shown* only on Wednesday evenings.

6 Hundreds of people *arrested/were arrest/are arrested* for drink-driving every day.

7 I made the mistake because I *am not telling/wasn't told/haven't told* what to do.

8 The prisoners *are sent/were send/were sent* home last night.

B Rewrite the sentences in the passive. Add *by* where necessary.

1 The French eat snails.

Snails _____.

2 Dostoyevsky wrote *Crime and Punishment*.

Crime and Punishment _____.

3 A journalist asked me some questions.

I _____.

4 Alejandro Ledesma produces all of our programmes.

All of our programmes _____.

5 Alec Guinness played most of the roles in that film.

Most of the roles in that film _____.

6 Swiss companies make the best chocolate.

The best chocolate _____.

10.3

A Put the words in the correct order to make conversations.

Conversation 1

A: me / excuse / complaint / have / afraid / a / I'm / I

B: what's / problem / the?

A: doesn't / shower / work / the

B: look / away / it / into / we'll / right

Conversation 2

A: me / excuse / you / me / help / could?

B: Yes

A: a / the / with / problem / internet / connection / there's

B: nothing / sorry / can / but / I'm / the / we / at / moment / there's / do

Conversation 3

A: excuse / to / speak / me / could / manager / I / the?

B: Yes

A: an / I've / been / hour / here / over / for

B: sorry / really / I'm / that / about

GRAMMAR

11.1 present perfect + *just/yet/already*

It is common to use the present perfect with *just*, *yet* and *already*.

Use *just* to talk about something which happened very recently. Put *just* before the main verb.

I've **just** passed my driving test!

We've **just** got back from holiday.

Use *yet* in negative sentences and questions to talk about something which hasn't happened, but you expect it to. Put *yet* at the end of the sentence.

A: Are you ready?

B: No, we haven't finished **yet**.

A: Have you booked a table **yet**?

B: No, not **yet**. I'll call the restaurant in a minute.

Use *already* to talk about something which happened, maybe before you expected. Put *already* before the main verb or at the end of the sentence.

I've **already** had four cups of coffee this morning.

He's found a job **already**!

Spoken grammar: It is common to use *not yet* as a short response to a question. It means we expect to do something soon, but we have not done it.

11.2 first conditional + *when*

If/When	+ present	+ will/won't + infinitive
If	you don't study	you won't pass the exam.
When	the film finishes	I'll turn off the TV.

Use *If/When* + present + *will* + infinitive to form the first conditional.

There are two clauses: the *if/when* clause and the main clause. You can reverse the order of the clauses, but the *if/when* clause always uses the present tense.

(*if/when* clause)   (main clause)

If we see Ann, we'**ll ask** her to call you.

NOT ~~If we will see Ann, we'll ask her to call you.~~

(main clause)   (*if/when* clause)

We'**ll** ask Ann to call you **if** we see her.

Use the first conditional to talk about situations in the future and their consequences.

Use *if* for a situation which is likely. Use *when* for a situation which is certain.

If I pass my driving test today, I'll be very surprised. (I'm not sure about this.)

When I pass my driving test, my father will buy me a car. (I'm sure about this.)

It is also possible to use *may/might/could/should* in the main clause instead of *will*.

If it's sunny, we **might** have a picnic later.

When they arrive, they **should** call to tell us.

11.3 giving opinions

agreeing	disagreeing	giving your opinion
That's right	I totally disagree	I think …
That's true	I'm not sure about that	I don't think …
Definitely	I don't think so	In my opinion …

To sound polite, use *I'm afraid* and *I'm sorry, but …* when you disagree.

I'm afraid I totally disagree.

I'm sorry, but it's just not possible.

PRACTICE

11.1

A Underline the correct alternative.

1 We're travelling around the Greek Islands. We've been to fourteen islands *just/yet/already*.

2 I'm leaving this evening, but I haven't packed my bags *just/yet/already*.

3 A: Have you seen Martha?
   B: She's *just/yet/already* left. You might catch her in the lift if you hurry.

4 A: Can you wait a minute, please?
   B: I've *just/yet/already* been here for more than half an hour.

5 A: Do you know if your sister is coming to the party?
   B: I'm not sure. I haven't spoken to her *just/yet/already*.

6 I thought Alf was going away for three weeks, but he's *just/yet/already* come back.

7 Great! I've *just/yet/already* booked the tickets on the internet. Now, we wait for the confirmation.

8 A: Can you call Emily?
   B: I've *just/yet/already* spoken to her. That was her on the phone a minute ago.

B Find and correct the mistakes. There is a mistake in the word order in each conversation.

1 A: Have you read this book?
   B: Yes, I've finished it just.

2 A: Are you ready to go?
   B: No, Imelda hasn't called yet us.

3 A: Let's go to the British Museum.
   B: We've been already there.

4 A: Becky looks tired.
   B: Well, just she's run five miles.

5 A: Are you coming out later?
   B: I'd love to come out, but I haven't finished yet my work.

6 A: There's a film on tonight.
   B: Yes, but already I've seen it three times!

11.2

A Put the verbs in brackets into the correct form.

1 I _____ home when I _____ my studies. (leave/finish)

2 If you _____ the class, I _____ some notes for you. (miss/take)

3 When I _____ Sandra, I _____ her what she thinks. (see/ask)

4 We _____ time for lunch if the train _____ at 12 o'clock. (not have/leave)

5 If I _____ my boss for a pay rise, he _____ it to me. (ask/not give)

6 I _____ dinner if you _____ the shopping. (cook/do)

7 If the weather _____ nice, we _____ out for a walk. (be/go)

8 We _____ on holiday when Al _____ some time off work. (go/get)

B Find and correct the mistakes. There are mistakes in four of the sentences.

1 If you will be in the office tomorrow, we talk about it then.

2 When Brian comes back from holiday, we'll arrange to go out.

3 When I hear from the rest of the team, I'll let you know.

4 We'll ask the doctor when we will get to the hospital.

5 If Theo behaves badly in class, the teacher speak to his parents.

6 They move into the house as soon as Mark will finish building it.

11.3

A There is a word missing in each sentence. Complete the sentences with the missing word.

1 I'm, but I don't think there is enough money for that.

2 I don't we should spend too much time discussing this.

3 I have to say I think right.

4 I'm afraid totally disagree.

5 Make them pay fines? I'm not sure that.

6 In opinion, we should start from the beginning.

B Complete the conversations with the phrases in the box.

> I'm afraid   I think   totally disagree
> my opinion   Definitely   not sure about

A: [1] _____ we should all go home early today.

B: I'm [2] _____ that.

A: It's OK to hunt animals for sport.

B: [3] _____ I [4] _____.

A: In [5] _____, these politicians should go to prison.

B: [6] _____. They're criminals.

GRAMMAR

12.1 reported speech

direct speech	reported speech
present simple →	past simple
'I **play** the guitar.' →	She **said** she **played** the guitar.
present continuous →	past continuous
'They **are** watching a film.' →	He **told** us they **were watching** a film.
will →	would
'I**'ll** call you later.' →	She **said** she **would** call me later.
can →	could
'He **can** work until 9.00.' →	She **told** me he **could** work until 9.00.

When we report speech, the pronouns sometimes change.

'I **eat** meat.' → He said he **ate** meat.

'We**'ll** help you tomorrow.' → They said they **would** help me tomorrow.

Use reported speech to tell someone what another person said.

It is common to change the verb tense/form when we report speech.

It is common to use *say* and *tell* to report speech.

Tell is followed by an object.

He **told me** (that) he was hungry. NOT He ~~told that~~ he was hungry.

Say is not followed by an object.

She said she worked in France. NOT She ~~said me~~ she worked in France.

When the present simple is used to describe a habit, we don't need to change the verb tense in reported speech.

'I get up at 6 a.m.' → She said she **gets up** at 6 a.m.

'We don't eat meat.' → They told us they **don't** eat meat.

12.2 second conditional

If + past simple	+ would/wouldn't + infinitive
If I had more money	I would buy a car.
If I wanted a job	I would look for one.
If I was famous	I wouldn't be happy.

Use *If* + past simple + *would/wouldn't* + infinitive to form the second conditional.

Use the second conditional to talk about an imaginary situation in the present or future and its consequence.

*If I **knew** the way to the museum, I **would tell** you.*
(I don't know the way to the museum.)

*If I **won** the lottery, I **would** never **work** again!*
(I'm very unlikely to win the lottery – it's an imaginary situation).

Would is often contracted (*I'd, you'd, he'd, we'd, they'd*). *Would not* is contracted to *wouldn't*.

*If we had more money, we**'d** buy a bigger house.*

*We **wouldn't** live in the city if we didn't need to.*

It is possible to change the order of the clauses. Notice that there is a comma after the *if* clause in the first example, but no comma in the second example.

If we had children, our lives would be very different.

Our lives would be very different if we had children.

With the verb *be* it is possible to use *were* (instead of *was*)

*If he **was/were** a lawyer, he would tell you what to do.*

Use *If I were you* … to give advice.

If I were you, I'd tell him your plans. NOT *If I ~~was~~ you.*

It is also possible to use *could*.

*If I **could** sing, I would start a band.*

12.3 requests and offers

requests	response	offers
I'd like to …	No problem.	Would you like me to … ?
Would it be possible to … ?	Certainly.	Do you want me to (get a) … ?
Would you be able to … ?	Yes, of course.	Shall I … ?
Could you recommend … ?		

PRACTICE

 12.1

A Rewrite the sentences as reported speech.

1 'My favourite film is about an invisible man.'
She told me _____.

2 'I don't like westerns.'
He said _____.

3 'They can act.'
She told us _____.

4 'The film isn't really about fashion.'
He said _____.

5 'I'm working for a film studio.'
He told me _____.

6 'That director will become famous.'
We told her _____.

7 'I'm writing a thriller.'
She said _____.

8 'The scene reminds me of another film.'
He said _____.

B Rewrite the reported sentences as direct speech.

1 Gianella said she loved chocolate.
'I love chocolate.'

2 He told us he would be at home by six.
'_____.'

3 Marina said she didn't want to do her homework.
'_____.'

4 They told me they were busy.
'_____.'

5 Yannick said he couldn't understand the lecture.
'_____.'

6 I told you I didn't like flying.
'_____.'

7 Xun Li said she was going back to China.
'_____.'

12.2

A Match 1–6 with a)–f) to make sentences.

1 If you went to bed earlier,
2 If she asked Tim to marry her,
3 If we came in the summer,
4 We would visit you tomorrow
5 I'd get there early
6 She would earn more money

a) would we go to the beach?
b) if I were you.
c) you wouldn't feel so tired.
d) if the trains were running.
e) if she worked longer hours.
f) I'm sure he would say 'Yes'.

B Put the verbs in brackets into the correct form.

1 I _____ to the doctor if I _____ you. He can give you some medicine. (go/be)

2 If they _____ ice cream here, _____ you _____ some? (sell/buy)

3 I _____ you if I _____ , but I'm too busy right now. (help/can)

4 If I _____ my phone with me, I _____ him. (have/call)

5 If we _____ more food, I _____ them to stay for dinner. (have/ask)

6 If you _____ nearer to us, we _____ you more often. (live/see)

7 _____ your brother _____ happier if he _____ so hard? (be/not work)

8 If you _____ always _____ such a mess, the kitchen _____ cleaner! (not make/be)

12.3

A There are words missing from the conversations. Complete the conversations with the words in the box.

| want it me shall no of to able could |

Conversation 1

A: You recommend a good coffee shop?
B: Certainly. There's one on Elm Road called Hot Beans.
A: Great.
B: Would you like to show you where it is?
A: Oh yes, please. That's very kind of you.

Conversation 2

A: I'd like eat out tonight.
B: OK. Do you me to choose the restaurant?
A: Yes, why not?
B: OK. And I book a table for two?
A: Er, no – three. I'm inviting Bobby.

Conversation 3

A: Would you be to get me a good plumber?
B: Problem.
A: Would be possible to do it today? I have to travel tomorrow.
B: Yes, course.

1 Match photos A–P to the jobs.

1 accountant
2 architect
3 businessman/woman
4 chef
5 electrician
6 estate agent
7 housewife
8 lawyer
9 PA (personal assistant)
10 plumber
11 receptionist
12 sales assistant
13 scientist
14 soldier
15 TV presenter
16 vet

2 Work in pairs. Discuss. Which jobs do you think are dangerous/ enjoyable/boring? Why?

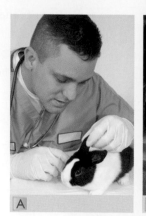
A

B

C

D

E

F

G

H

I

J

K

L

M

N

O

P

1 Match photos A–O to the activities.

collect:

  1 stamps

  2 coins

go to:

  3 a concert

  4 a nightclub

  5 the gym

go to/see:

  6 an exhibition

  7 a show

  8 hang out with friends

  9 join a club

play:

  10 cards

  11 chess

  12 computer games

  13 board games

14 surf the net

15 walk/cycle/skate through a park

2 Work in pairs. Discuss. Which of these have you never done? Which would you like to do?

A

B

C

D

E

F

G

H

I

J

K

L

M

N

O

1 Answer the questions.

1 Where did you go to primary school?

2 Which subjects did you enjoy at secondary school?

3 Have you been to university? What did you/would you like to study?

4 Is the education system in your country similar to the one in England?

18+ College or University	
Secondary school 11–18 years	**16–18 FE College or Sixth Form**
	11–16
Primary school 4–11 years	**7–11 Juniors**
	4–7 Infants

State Education in England

maths

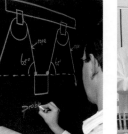

physics

chemistry

biology

geography

history

languages

art

design and technology

PE (Physical Education)

IT (Information Technology)

RE (Religious Education)

drama

TRANSPORT

1 Match photos A–N to the types of transport.

1 aeroplane
2 coach
3 ferry
4 helicopter
5 hot air balloon
6 lorry
7 minibus
8 moped
9 motorbike
10 ship
11 speedboat
12 taxi
13 tram
14 underground

2 Work in pairs. Discuss. Which types of transport do you use regularly? Which do you think are the most enjoyable ways to travel?

TRAVEL ITEMS

1 Match photos A–R to the travel items.

1 alarm clock
2 aspirin
3 binoculars
4 dictionary
5 digital camera
6 first aid kit
7 map
8 money belt
9 notebook
10 rucksack
11 soap
12 souvenirs
13 suitcase
14 sun hat
15 travel guide
16 umbrella
17 walking boots
18 waterproof clothes

2 Work in pairs and take turns.
Student A: describe an item.
Student B: guess the item.

A: *You wear these when it is raining.*

B: *Waterproof clothes.*

1 Which of these foods do you a) never eat b) eat a lot of?

2 Which types of food/drink do you think are a) very good b) very bad for your health?

GRAINS

corn

wheat

oats

MEAT AND FISH/SEAFOOD

chicken

duck

beefsteak

leg of lamb

fish

shrimps

mussels

lobster

DAIRY

milk

cheese

yoghurt

cream

DESSERTS

jelly

cake

biscuits

ice cream

DRINKS

tea

coffee

orange juice

fizzy drink

VEGETABLES

soya

potatoes

carrots

spinach

broccoli

cabbage

lettuce

peas

onion

garlic

cucumbers

courgettes

FRUIT

pineapple

apple

orange

grapes

grapefruit

bananas

kiwi fruit

mango

melon

watermelon

plums

lemon

SPORTS

1A Check the meaning of sports 1–30 below.

1 badminton
2 basketball
3 boxing
4 cricket
5 cycling
6 football
7 golf
8 hockey
9 horse racing
10 horseriding
11 jogging
12 judo
13 karate
14 ping pong/table tennis
15 rollerblading
16 rugby
17 running
18 sailing
19 scuba-diving
20 skateboarding
21 skiing
22 squash
23 snorkelling
24 snowboarding
25 surfing
26 swimming
27 tennis
28 volleyball
29 windsurfing
30 yoga

B Which sports can you see in photos A–M?

2 Work in pairs. Discuss. Which sports are popular in your country? Which have you tried?

net

ball

bat

racket

PHOTO BANK

MONEY

1 Match photos A–H to the words.

1 bank statement
2 cheque
3 notes
4 ATM
5 credit cards
6 coins
7 bill
8 receipt

2 Work in pairs and take turns. Student A: describe an item. Student B: guess the item.

A: This is money made from metal.
B: Coins.

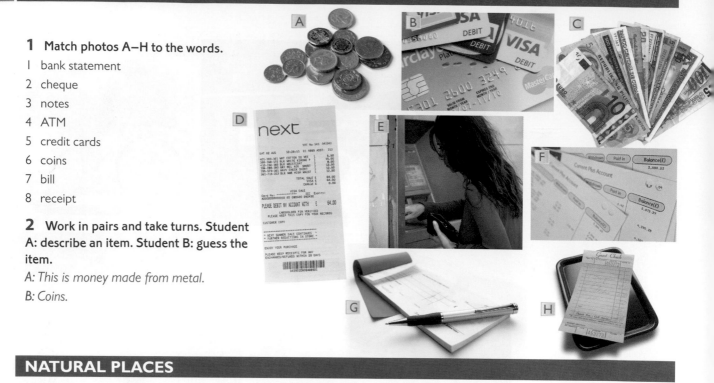

NATURAL PLACES

1 Which do you like to visit on holiday? Which of these do you have in your country? Work in pairs. Discuss.

ocean

lake

river

waterfall

mountain range

desert

glacier

rain forest

coastline

ANIMALS

1 Write the names of the animals in the correct places.

1 bear
2 butterfly
3 camel
4 chimpanzee
5 cow
6 crocodile
7 dolphin
8 eagle
9 elephant
10 fly
11 gorilla
12 leopard
13 lion
14 monkey
15 ostrich
16 penguin
17 pigeon
18 snake
19 spider
20 tiger
21 whale

2 Work in pairs. Discuss. Which do you think are dangerous/beautiful/intelligent?

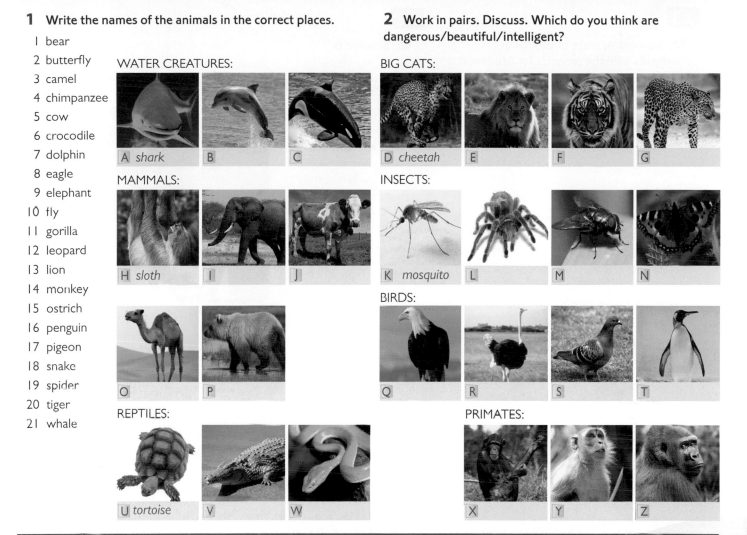

WATER CREATURES:
A *shark*   B   C

BIG CATS:
D *cheetah*   E   F   G

MAMMALS:
H *sloth*   I   J

O   P

INSECTS:
K *mosquito*   L   M   N

BIRDS:
Q   R   S   T

REPTILES:
U *tortoise*   V   W

PRIMATES:
X   Y   Z

CRIME AND PUNISHMENT

1 Which words can you see in the pictures?

People:
1 criminal
2 police officer
3 judge
4 victim

Verbs:
5 steal
6 break in
7 shoot
8 arrest
9 investigate

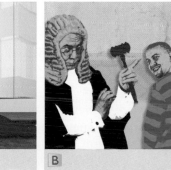

A   B   C   D

2 Can you match any of the people to the verbs.

Criminals steal things.

E   F   G

1.3

4A Student A: make questions or comments with the prompts for Student B. Listen to Student B's responses.

1 would / like / drink?

2 do / work / here?

3 watch / match / last night?

4 how / know / Sam?

5 nice / day?

6 was / nice / meet

B Listen to Student B's questions and comments. Choose the correct response.

1 Hi, Pete. Nice to meet you./Dear Mr Pete. How do you do?

2 Yes, thanks. I didn't do much./Yes, thank you. I am enjoying it.

3 I work in an office./I love my job.

4 I'm coming from Madrid./I come from Madrid.

5 It's nice to meet you again./I'll probably see you tomorrow.

6 Yes, let's keep in touch./It's a nice day.

3.5

4C Answers to quiz

2 Reagan

3 *A Night at the Opera*

4 Raphael

5 Elton

6 One Love

7 Venice

8 Celine

9 Nelly Furtado

4.3

9A Student A: explain your problem. Then listen and respond to the advice.

Your son is eighteen years old and lives at home. He needs to study for his exams but in the evening he goes out with friends until late. He often misses lessons or falls asleep when he is studying. At home you do all the cooking and cleaning and give your son money every week.

B Listen to another student's problem. Give the student some advice.

2.2

4B Student B

Danger rating 6/10

The alarm rings and emergency doctor Mathias Uhl, paramedic Andreas Würtl and helicopter pilot Martin Nussdorfer jump into the helicopter. Perhaps it's a skier with a broken leg, a climber in fog or an avalanche.

Mountain rescue worker, Austria

But it isn't. This time, the alarm is only a test – but accidents can happen at any time and in dangerous places. Bethany Bell met the mountain rescuers and asked them about the job. Nussdorfer says that today the weather is good but 'usually we fly in much worse weather conditions'. These can be very dangerous. Another problem, Würtl says, is that often the people they rescue are frightened.

The mountain rescuers sometimes get angry with the people they rescue. Uhl says, 'These people always risk their lives but they also risk our lives for nothing.'

Uhl, Nussdorfer and Würtl have some great moments and occasionally they get a surprise. Uhl says, 'I remember one time – there were two people on a ski tour in an avalanche. Every bone was broken. Half a year later, this woman comes to us, brings us some wine, says thank you.' The people they rescue, Uhl explains, hardly ever say thank you!

3.3

8 Student A: think about what you are going to say when you receive and make phone calls in these situations. Role-play the situations with Student B.

Answer the phone

1 You work for Nova Restaurant. Take a message.

2 You work for Amber Cinema. Answer the phone and tell a customer the times of the film *The Magic Hat*: 2.30p.m., 5.00p.m., 7.30p.m. and 10.00p.m., with a special extra showing at 12.00p.m. at the weekend.

3 Answer the phone normally. Listen and respond to the invitation.

Make a call

4 You are calling Ripping Yarns, a theatre company. You would like six tickets for *Hamlet* for Friday.

5 You are calling Brandon's Restaurant. You want to change your reservation from 7.30p.m. on Tuesday to 8.00p.m. next Wednesday. There will now be ten people, not five, so you need a bigger table.

6 Ask your partner if he/she wants to go for a snack after class.

5.1

3 Student B: read the text and make notes.

Apollo 13

On 11 April 1970, James Lovell, John Swigert and Fred Haise put on their space suits, sat in Apollo 13 and said goodbye to Earth. The plan was to walk on the moon, do a number of biological experiments and take photos.

But while they were travelling, something went wrong – really wrong. There was an explosion on Apollo 13, which destroyed important equipment. Lovell contacted Earth and said the famous line, 'Houston, we have a problem.'

Apollo 13 started losing oxygen, electricity and water. Back on Earth the NASA engineers told Lovell, Swigert and Haise what to do and the astronauts built important pieces of equipment using just their hands. With only a little oxygen left, it was a race against time. Finally, while the world was watching on TV, they returned home from space and landed safely in the ocean. The story was later made into a film, *Apollo 13*.

5.3

8 Student A: look at the map and ask Student B for directions to:
- a nightclub called Risky Business
- a restaurant called The Waterfall
- the Screen by the Pond cinema
- a pub called The Courier's Rest
- the Museum of Fashion and Design

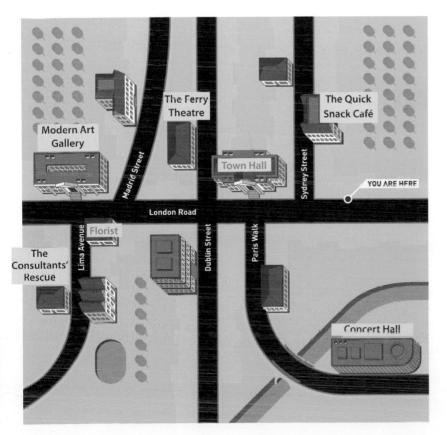

6.3

8A Student A: you are a doctor seeing a patient. Use the prompts to ask questions and make suggestions.
- how long?
- where / hurt?
- when / hurt?
- how / you / hurt?
- take painkillers
- get lots of rest
- don't do sport

Start like this:
Hello. How can I help you?

B Student A: now you are a patient seeing a doctor. Use the prompts to explain your problem.
- you have a bad cough
- you have had the cough for a few months
- you have tried antibiotics
- you don't have a temperature
- you don't feel ill
- you smoke ten cigarettes a day

10.3

8B Student A: you are a student at the Noparlo School of English. You are going to complain to the director of the school. Choose four of the problems in Exercise 8A. Think about what you are going to say. Use these expressions:
'I'm afraid I have a complaint.'
'There's (also) a problem with …'
'Can you look into it?'

1.3

4A Student B: listen to Student A's questions and comments. Choose the correct response.

1 I'd love an orange juice, please./I like orange juice, please.

2 Yes, I'm just visiting./No, I'm just visiting.

3 Yes, it was brilliant./Yes, it's lovely.

4 Yes, I know him well./We work together.

5 Yes, nice to meet you./Yes, it's lovely.

6 It was nice to meet you, too./How do you do?

B Make questions or comments with the prompts for Student A. Listen to Student A's responses.

1 this / friend / Pete

2 have / good / weekend?

3 what / you / do?

4 where / exactly / from?

5 see / soon

6 hope / meet / again / soon

3.3

8 Student B: think about what you are going to say when you make and receive phone calls in these situations. Role-play the situations with Student A.

Make a call

1 You are calling Nova Restaurant. You booked a table for Saturday, but you have to cancel it.

2 You are calling Amber Cinema. Ask what time the film *The Magic Hat* is showing.

3 Invite your partner to a film this evening. Say the name and time of the film.

Answer the phone

4 You work for Ripping Yarns, a theatre company. Answer the phone and confirm a ticket reservation.

5 You work for Brandon's Restaurant. A customer wants to change his/her reservation. Take the message and confirm if it is possible.

6 Answer the phone normally. Listen and respond to the invitation.

2.2

4B Student C

Danger rating 6/10

'Bang!' goes the gun. The gates open and the horses come running out. All eyes are on them. Money, fame and glory are the prizes.

Horse riding looks so beautiful that it is sometimes easy to forget

Jockey, France

how dangerous it is. Life as a jockey is rarely safe and it usually involves a few broken bones. Once in a while jockeys even die during a race.

Jacky Rowland spoke to jockey Eric Legrix in France. As a young man, Legrix was one of the best jockeys of his generation. He knows the sport is dangerous but he never worries. 'We jump out of the gate and we totally forget about our danger. You know you're not on a bicycle or on a motorbike or in a car.'

During his career Legrix has broken many bones, including his fingers and his ribs, and he once fell off his horse and was knocked unconscious. So why do jockeys risk their lives? 'I like to be outside, I like the speed, I like power. In my normal life I have a big motorbike, I have a fast car and we live like this. All jockeys are like that.'

4.3

9A Student B: explain your problem. Then listen and respond to the advice.

Your flatmate loves shopping. Every month she buys new clothes, shoes and designer bags using a credit card. Her room is full of clothes she never wears. She spends more money than she has and borrows money from you to pay her rent. She hasn't paid you back for two months.

B Listen to another student's problem. Give the student some advice.

5.1

3 Student C: read the text and make notes.

Rabbit-Proof Fence

It is Australia in 1931. Three Aborigine girls, Molly, fourteen, her sister Daisy, eight, and their cousin Gracie, ten, were taken from their home by government officials because of their race. They were sent to live in a camp far from home. Life at the camp was terrible, and they hated it.

One night when it was raining, the girls decided to escape. They knew that the rain would hide their footprints in the mud, so they began the long journey home. In the desert they had no food and nowhere to sleep. They didn't have a map either, but while they were walking, they saw the 'rabbit-proof fence', one of the longest fences in the world. It was there to stop rabbits from entering farmland. The girls recognised the fence and walked next to it for 1,200 miles. After nine weeks they got home.

Many years later, Molly's daughter, Doris Pilkington Garimara, wrote a book about the journey and in 2002 the story was made into a film, *Rabbit-Proof Fence*.

5.3

8 Student B: look at the map and ask Student A for directions to:
- The Quick Snack Café
- The Ferry Theatre
- The Concert Hall
- a bar called The Consultants' Rescue
- the Modern Art Gallery

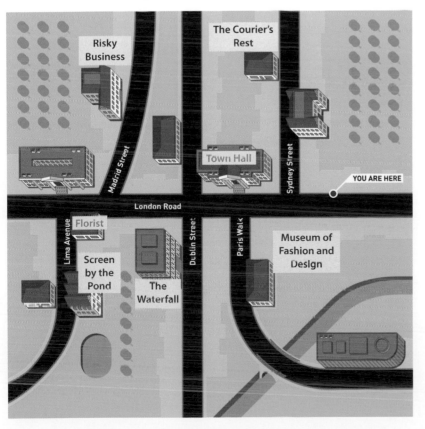

6.3

8A Student B: you are a patient seeing a doctor. Use the prompts to explain your problem.
- your have had the problem for two weeks
- the pain is in your lower back
- it hurts when you move (stand up, sit down, walk, etc.)
- you hurt it playing football

B Student B: now you are a doctor seeing a patient. Use the prompts to ask questions and make suggestions.
- how long?
- a temperature?
- feel ill?
- smoke cigarettes?
- have an X-ray
- give up smoking

Start like this:
Hello. What's the problem?

8.3

8A Student A: you work in a clothes shop. You start the conversation.
1 Offer to help.
2 Ask what colour.
3 Give the customer the shirt and say, 'Here you are. The fitting room is over there.'
4 Ask if it fits OK.
5 Ask how he/she wants to pay.
6 Ask him/her to enter his/her PIN.
7 Say thank you and goodbye.

B Student A: now you are in an electronics shop. Student B starts the conversation.
1 Say you are looking for a camera.
2 Say you need a digital one.
3 Thank him/her.
4 Ask for a cheaper one.
5 Say 'This one is fine.'
6 Say you will pay by cash.
7 Say thank you and goodbye.

9.3

7B Answers

1 whale shark
2 spine-tailed swift
3 ostrich
4 python (a snake)
5 cheetah
6 mosquito (it kills people indirectly, by transmitting malaria)
7 whale
8 tortoise

9.3

10B Answers

A A shark's tooth –

Some types of shark have thousands of teeth. These teeth are extremely hard. A shark can bite through iron.

B A chameleon's skin –

A chameleon's skin can change colour when the chameleon needs to hide.

C An eagle's eye –

Eagles can see fish in the water from hundreds of feet away and an eagle's sight is four times stronger than a human's.

D A camel's hump –

Camels' humps are made of fat and they allow camels to survive in the desert without food or water for up to two weeks.

E A dog's nose –

Dogs have an amazing sense of smell. Many dogs can recognise the smell of their old owners many years after they last saw them.

9.5

1B Answers

1 The Andes are higher than the Rockies.
2 Canada has a longer coastline (151,485 miles) than Russia (23,396 miles).
3 Lake Michigan in the USA is bigger than Lake Toba in Sumatra.
4 The Amazon is shorter, but wider than the Nile.
5 The Pacific is the deepest ocean.
6 Angel Falls in Venezuela, is the highest waterfall.

4.3

9A Student C: explain your problem. Then listen and respond to the advice.

Your friend would like a girlfriend. The problem is he works long hours and is too tired to go out in the evenings. He usually buys a take-away meal and falls asleep watching the TV. He doesn't have any hobbies and is getting fat. You know lots of single women but you don't think they would be interested.

B Listen to another student's problem. Give the student some advice.

8.1

6C Student A: write definitions for the completed words with the prompts.

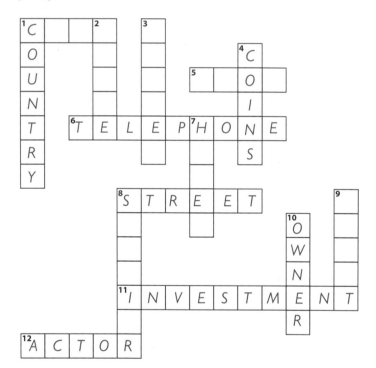

Down

1 place / has its own government   *a place which has its own government*
4 pieces of money / made of metal not paper
10 person / owns something (he/she bought it or was given it)

Across

6 thing / use / call someone
8 place / you find / cars, houses, shops, etc.
11 money / use / start a business and make more money
12 person / acts in / films or theatre

D Ask Student B for definitions for the missing words.

Down: 2, 3, 7, 8 and 9

Across: 1 and 5

10.1

1B Survey results:

People want cities which are safe, not too expensive, have good public transport, nice weather, parks and green spaces, good cafés, etc. The cities which come out top are:

1 Munich
2 Copenhagen
3 Zurich
4 Tokyo
5 Vienna
6 Helsinki
7 Sydney
8 Stockholm
9 Honolulu
10 Madrid

10.3

7A Student A: you are a hotel guest. You start the conversation.

1 Greet the hotel receptionist.
2 Say you have a problem: your fridge doesn't work.
3 Thank the receptionist.

B Student A: now you are a waiter. Listen to what Student B says, then:

1 Ask how you can help.
2 Apologise for the mistake. Say you will bring the right dish.
3 Apologise again.

12.3

8A Student A: you are a concierge. Listen and respond to your client's requests. Ask for more time if necessary. Your client wants to:

• go to the best restaurant in town.
• get tickets to the theatre.

B Student A: now you are a client. Tell the concierge:

• you want to go shopping for clothes. Ask him/her to recommend a good area for shopping.
• visit a film studio and meet some stars. Ask him/her if it's possible.

7.3

8A Student A: you are new to this town/city. Ask your partner questions to find out this information.

1 You want to know what time the shops open.
2 You want to know where the nearest train station is.
3 You need to exchange some money. Find out where to go.

Excuse me, …

B Student A: now answer Student B's questions using the information below.

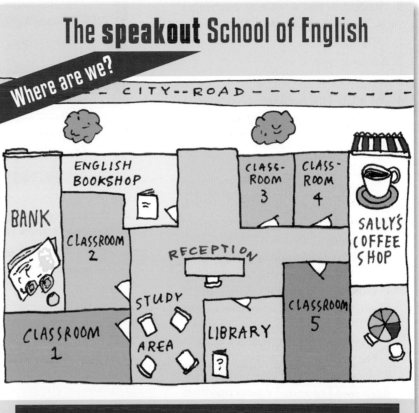

The **speakout** School of English

Where are we?

- - CITY ROAD - - ~ - - ~ - -

BANK
ENGLISH BOOKSHOP
CLASSROOM 2
CLASS-ROOM 3
CLASS-ROOM 4
SALLY'S COFFEE SHOP
RECEPTION
STUDY AREA
CLASSROOM 1
LIBRARY
CLASSROOM 5

We are open:
Mon–Sat: 8a.m.–10p.m.
Sun: 8a.m.–1p.m.

Join the speakout School of English and learn English fast!

9.5

7B
Countries:

A Chile
B France
C Japan
D Australia

8.3

8A **Student B: you are in a clothes shop. Student A starts the conversation.**

1 Ask for a formal shirt.
2 Say you need a white one.
3 Thank him/her for the shirt.
4 Say it fits. Say 'I'll take this one.'
5 Say you want to pay by credit card.
6 Say yes (to enter your PIN).
7 Say thank you and goodbye.

B **Student B: you work in an electronics shop. You start the conversation.**

1 Offer to help.
2 Ask what type.
3 Say 'They are over there.'
4 Ask if it is what he/she is looking for.
5 Say 'There are some cheaper ones over there.'
6 Ask how he/she wants to pay.
7 Say thank you and goodbye.

11.4

2A **Answers**

1 In the USA a child watches TV for an average of **4** hours a day.
2 In some parts of the UK, more than **60%** of primary school children have a TV in their bedroom.
3 The average person spends **3.5** years eating and **12** years watching TV.
4 Children under three years old who watch more than **1** hour of TV a day may have problems concentrating at school when they are older.
5 In the USA some families spend only **3.5** minutes a week having meaningful conversations with their children. Those children spend **1,600** minutes a week watching TV.

12.1

8B **Answers**
1 a 2 b 3 c 4 c 5 c 6 a

7.3

8A **Student B: answer Student A's questions using the information below.**

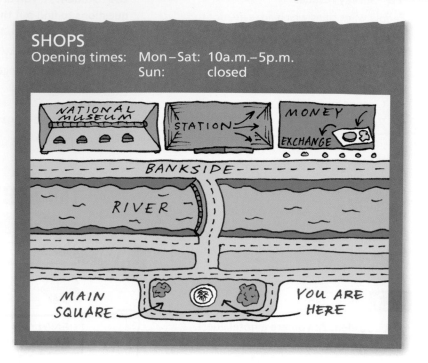

SHOPS
Opening times: Mon–Sat: 10a.m.–5p.m.
                Sun: closed

NATIONAL MUSEUM
STATION
MONEY EXCHANGE
BANKSIDE
RIVER
MAIN SQUARE
YOU ARE HERE

B **You are new to this school. Ask questions to find out this information.**
1 You want to know where the nearest coffee shop to the school is.
2 You want to know where you can buy an English dictionary.
3 You want to know what time the school closes.
Excuse me, …

10.3

7A **Student B: you are a hotel receptionist. Listen to what Student A says, then:**
1 Greet the guest.
2 Apologise. Offer to send someone to the room to look into the problem.
3 Say 'you're welcome' and apologise again.

B **Student B: you are a customer in a restaurant. You start the conversation.**
1 Get the waiter's attention.
2 Say you have a problem: you asked for pasta with chicken. You were given pasta with fish.
3 Thank the waiter.

10.3

8B **Student B: you are the director at the Noparlo School of English. A student is going to complain about some of the problems in Exercise 8A. Apologise to the student and think of reasons for the problems. Use these expressions:**
'I'm really sorry about that.'
'We had a problem with … '
'I'll look into it.'

8.1

6C Student B: write definitions for the completed words with the prompts.

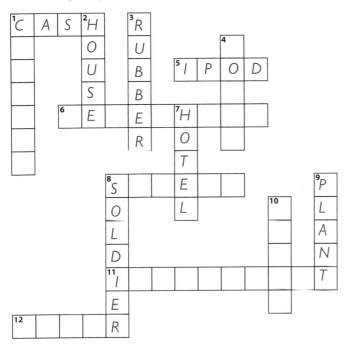

Down

2 place / people live *a place where people live*

3 material / use / make car tyres and chewing gum

7 place / stay when you are travelling

8 person / fight / for his country in wars

9 thing / grows in the earth and is usually green

Across

1 thing / use / pay for something (not a credit card)

5 thing / use / download and listen to music

D Ask Student A for definitions for the missing words.
Down: 1, 4, and 10
Across: 6, 8, 11 and 12

12.3

8A Student B: you are a client. Tell the concierge:

• you want to go to the best restaurant in town. Ask him/her to recommend one.

• you want tickets to the theatre. Ask if he/she can get six seats for tonight.

B Student B: now you are a concierge. Listen and respond to your client's requests. Ask for more time if necessary. Your client wants to:

• go shopping for clothes.

• visit a film studio and meet some stars.

4.3

9A Student D: explain your problem. Then listen and respond to the advice.

You have worked for the same company for five years. You don't enjoy your job very much because you are not very interested in it. You like your colleagues. You have just got a new boss, however, who you don't like. You would like another job, but you are not sure what you can do. Also this job pays you well.

B Listen to another student's problem. Give the student some advice.

12.2

9C Fact file

Birth name:	Nelson Rolihlahla Mandela
Birth place:	Village near Umtata in the Transkei, South Africa
Date:	18 July 1918
Childhood/Education:	Went to a mission school where teacher gave him the English name 'Nelson'. Studied at Fort Hare University and University of Witwatersrand and qualified in law in 1942.
Early career:	Moved to Johannesburg and started a law firm to help fight for the political rights of young black people. Active member of the ANC (African National Congress) party.
Rise to fame:	Arrested in 1962 for political activities. Spent nearly 27 years in prison. Released from prison on 27 February 1990. Became head of ANC. Elected President of South Africa in 1994 (first black man).
Later life:	Nobel Peace Prize 1993. World famous public statesman. Retired from public life in 1999.

AUDIOSCRIPT

UNIT 1 Recording 2

1 How many people are in your family?
2 How often do you see your parents?
3 Do you enjoy spending time with your family?
4 When was your last family celebration?
5 Who do you live with?
6 How often do you eat out with friends?
7 Where does your best friend live?

UNIT 1 Recording 7

I've known Bruno for as long as I can remember. He's one of my best friends because we grew up together. We lived in the same street and went to all the same schools. I think we get on well because we know each other so well. We have a lot of the same friends and we enjoy doing the same things. We both enjoy films, so we watch films together or we go out and have a good time. We don't live in the same town now, so we don't see each other very often. But we keep in touch by email. And when I go home, the first person I call is always Bruno.

UNIT 2 Recording 2

M=Man W=Woman

M: These days many companies motivate their staff in new and different ways. Internet companies are a good example. At Yahoo there's a free bus ride to work for the employees. There's also a dentist and a hairdresser at the office. And one day a month the staff watch films together. These are all great ideas for motivating your workers.
W: Well, Google also has some interesting ways to motivate staff. Lunch is free. And after sitting at your desk for hours, you can have a cheap massage in the office.
M: Wow.
W: Another nice little bonus – you can take your dog to work.
M: Yahoo and Google are quite famous for this type of thing. But what benefits do other companies give their employees? Well, we found one company that takes its employees on a surprise holiday every year. The staff go to the airport but they don't know where they are flying to. In the past these trips included Amsterdam, Iceland and even the Caribbean.
W: At Starbucks employees get free coffee, of course, but they can also bring their children to work.
M: And there's a phone company that has a party for the staff on the last Friday of every month – with free drinks.
W: Finally, a very interesting idea: an insurance company keeps fish in a little river next to the office. The employees go fishing after work and they take home all the fish that they catch.
M: Fantastic.
W: Isn't that a great idea?

UNIT 2 Recording 3

Conversation 1

I=Interviewer M=Man

M: Hi. I work at Kinko's coffee shop across the street. But, er, at the moment I'm having a break here in the music shop.
I: And what are you doing on your break?
M: I'm choosing my free CD for the week.
I: Free CD? Can you tell us a bit more? Why are you doing this?
M: Sure. Kinko's, the coffee shop, has an agreement with the music shop. The employees at the music shop get free coffee at Kinko's. They all come in during their break. And we get one free CD a week from the music shop.
I: Great!
M: We all know each other and it works really well.

Conversation 2

I=Interviewer W=Woman

W: So, this is the clothes shop. And this is the study area.
I: Right. So you have a study area?
W: Yeah. As you can see, David over there is studying. And these two are doing an online course.
I: And this is during company hours? Does the boss know about this?!
W: It's the boss' idea. The company pays for employees to do courses. So during our breaks or after seven when the shop closes, we can stay on and study.
I: That's excellent. And are you studying at the moment?
W: Yeah, but I'm not studying anything connected with fashion.
I: What are you studying?
W: I'm studying history.
I: And the company pays?
W: The company pays. It pays for about six of us. I think six of us are doing online courses.
I: Brilliant.

Conversation 3

I=Interviewer E=Employee

E: Hi there. I work for a software company.
I: And what are you doing now?
E: Well, I'm checking my emails at the moment because I need to see what work I have to do today.
I: At one o'clock?!
E: Well, the company has flexible hours. You can arrive when you want and go home at any time.
I: That sounds good.
E: It's great. We get a salary for good work, not for the time we spend in the office. So, really, the important thing is to do your job well. That's what the boss says, anyway!

UNIT 2 Recording 5

I'm a marine biologist. I work mainly in the sea and also in the lab. The good things about my job are … um … I like working outside. In fact, I can't stand sitting at a desk all day, so this job is perfect for me.

What else? I absolutely love travelling and I travel a lot, particularly in South America and Australia. Also I don't like working in a team – I prefer working alone – and most of my time is spent alone or just me and nature. Um, what else? One thing that's very important: I don't mind getting my hands dirty. That's important in my work because it's a very practical job. You're working with animals and plant life the whole time. Also I'm keen on learning new things – and you do learn all the time in this job. So overall, it's the perfect job for me. I couldn't do an office job because I hate working under pressure. And I'm not very keen on working for a company. I want to be my own boss.

UNIT 2 Recording 6

A: The company is called VocationVacations.
B: VocationVacations?
A: Yeah, and the idea is that you go on holiday with the company …
B: Right.
A: But during the holiday you try out a different job – your dream job.
B: Oh, I see. That sounds interesting.
A: So if you can't stand your job any more, you can try something new!
B: Great. So how does it work?
A: The holiday is usually just one weekend. You work one to one with an expert who shows you how to do the job …
B: Right.
A: Say, for example, you want to be a cheese maker. You spend the weekend with a real cheese maker who teaches you all about cheese.
B: That's great. So how many jobs can you try?
A: I looked on their website. There's a lot, actually. You can try over seventy-five jobs.
B: Wow! Really? And what type of jobs?
A: You can learn how to make wine. You can learn to be a TV producer, a fisherman.
B: A fisherman?!
A: Yep. A magazine publisher, um … a marine biologist … and lots of other jobs.
B: Well, I absolutely love the idea. Actually, I'm really keen on working as a chocolate taster.
A: What?
B: Do you think VocationVacations has a holiday for chocolate tasters? I don't mind getting up early …

UNIT 2 Recording 10

A=Alistair Z=Zeinab

A: Zeinab, can I ask you a few questions about your work/life balance?
Z: Of course.
A: OK. First question: how much time do you spend sleeping?
Z: Lots! Probably about eight or nine hours a night!
A: Really?!
Z: Yep.
A: OK. And what about studying?

Z: Well, I suppose usually about five or six hours a day, although it depends. I mean if I have an exam coming up or something, it's probably more.

A: And do you ever have a holiday?

Z: Oh yeah. Probably twice a year I try and go abroad and just completely relax.

A: OK. What about your weekends? Do you ever study at the weekend?

Z: Not usually, but once in a while I open a book!

A: Right. And do you think you have a good work/life balance?

Z: I think so, yeah. I'm not too stressed or anything.

A: Easy life being a student.

Z: Oh yeah!

UNIT 3 Recording 1

P=Presenter K=Ken

P: Hi – this is George Thomas on *The London Show*. Now, London is one of the world's top five expensive cities to live in. But did you know that there are lots of things you can do in London for free? That's right. This morning we're talking to Ken Smith, a tourist guide from Going Out in London. So, Ken, what can we do in London for free?

K: Hi, George. Well, many people come to London to visit its famous museums and art galleries. But did you know that many of London's museums and art galleries are free? You can go to the British Museum or see paintings by Raphael and Picasso in the National Gallery. And you don't need lots of money in your pocket.

P: Free museums – that's good, because they can be very expensive.

K: That's right. And another thing. If you go sightseeing, some of London's most famous sights: Big Ben, Tower Bridge, Piccadilly Circus and Trafalgar Square are all free. And the parks, too. If you want a really good view of London, you can walk through one of London's many parks.

P: That's a good tip. Now what about shopping? People love to shop in London, but you can't do that for free?

K: No, you're right. But go to one of London's famous markets to experience the atmosphere of the city. Try the busy markets in Camden, or Covent Garden. Or for something different, go to the flower market in Columbia Road. It's beautiful.

P: OK. I love markets. They're a great place to meet people. You meet all kinds of people in a market, don't you?

K: Yes, you do.

P: Right. So, we've got culture, museums, sightseeing, parks, markets. Is there anything else? What about entertainment? Going out?

K: Well, yes. Lots of comedy shows are free in the city, and many theatres offer free (or very cheap) seats too. You can find free concerts with all kinds of music, from classical to jazz. In Hyde Park in the summer, you can go to the 'Proms', a free classical music concert. And you find lots of free music in pubs, too.

P: Thanks Ken. That sounds brilliant. I had no idea you could do so much for free in London. Now, you know what we're going to do next. We've got this week's £15 challenge. Here's the challenge.

UNIT 3 Recording 2

P=Presenter D=Dominique R=Rob

P: … on this week's £15 challenge. We're going to send two people out for a night in London, and their challenge is to have a good night out, but not spend more than £15. So, is it possible? Well, we're going to find out. We've asked Dominique and Rob to spend an evening in London, and not spend more than £15. So, let's speak to Dominique first. Hi Dominique.

D: Hi, George.

P: Tell us, Dominique, what are your plans?

D: Well, first of all I'm going to see a free art exhibition at the Tate Modern. I don't normally like modern art, so I hope it's OK. Then I'm meeting some friends and we're going to a concert at a pub called The King's Head. There's a free band playing and so I only need to pay for my drinks. Afterwards we're having dinner in Brick Lane where there are lots of Indian restaurants. They've told me that if you go to one of the restaurants there at 10p.m., you can get a free meal. I don't know if that's true, but I'm going to try anyway. Then I'm getting the bus home. A taxi is too expensive.

P: That sounds great. Have a good evening, and you can tell us all about it tomorrow.

D: I will.

P: Our second volunteer is Rob. Rob, can you tell us about your evening?

R: Yes. I'm starting the evening with a visit to a museum, too. I'm going to the National Gallery to see the paintings there. They stay open one night a week, and it's free. Then I'm going to Covent Garden to watch the street entertainers. Um … that's free, too. And after that, I'm going to watch some comedy. There's a really good comedy club just near Covent Garden. It's £8 to get in. I'm not having dinner. There isn't enough time.

P: Thanks, Rob. Enjoy your evening, and don't forget …

UNIT 3 Recording 4

W=Woman M1=1st man M2=2nd man

W: Who's got the answers then?

M1: I have.

W: What did you put for the first one?

M2: That one's easy. It's Michelangelo, isn't it?

M1: It's Michelangelo. He painted the Sistine Chapel.

W: What about the second one?

M2: Michael Jackson?

M1: Yep. It's Michael Jackson.

W: And number three?

M2: I don't know very much about art, but I'm guessing it's Pollock.

M1: It is Jackson Pollock.

M2: Thought so.

W: Is number four *Candle in the Wind*?

M1: 'A' is correct. *Candle in the Wind*.

W: What about number five?

M2: Well, it has to be 'C', doesn't it? If no one noticed for two months that it was upside down …

M1: Correct. Though I didn't know this story.

W: That's quite funny. Where was it, The Museum of Modern Art?

M1: Unbelievable, isn't it?

M2: What about the next one, number six?

W: Live 8.

M2: Live 8.

M1: Yep. It was Live 8.

W: Number seven, I have no idea. I guessed 'B', *Heavenly*.

M1: Nope.

M2: So is it *Scrambled Eggs*?

M1: The answer is 'C', *Scrambled Eggs*.

W: No way!

M1: Yep.

M2: So how about the last one? It isn't Shakespeare, I know that.

W: It's not Shaw either, is it? I guessed Samuel Beckett.

M2: Me too. What's the answer?

M1: Correct. The answer is C, Samuel Beckett.

M2: I got them all right.

W: Aren't you cultured?

M2: Not really.

UNIT 3 Recording 5

Conversation 1

A: King's Restaurant.

B: Hello, I'd like to book a table for four on Friday night. Around eight thirty, if possible.

A: Let me just have a look. Sorry, we're completely full on Friday. There's nothing at all.

B: Ah, what about Saturday?

A: Saturday, Saturday. Um … the best I can do is a table at ten o'clock.

B: Ten o'clock? You haven't got anything earlier?

A: Nothing at all, I'm afraid.

B: OK, let's go ahead. Ten o'clock.

A: Can I take your name, please?

B: The table is for Rodney Collins.

A: Rodney … Oh! Can you repeat that, please? Did you say Rodney Collins?

B: Yes.

A: OK, that's all booked. Table for four, ten o'clock, Saturday.

B: Great. Thank you.

A: Thank you.

Conversation 2

C: High Tower Productions. Paul speaking. How can I help you?

D: Hello, I was wondering if you could help me. I've booked a ticket for the show on the fifth of June, but I'd like to change the date.

C: OK, one moment. Can I just check? What's the name please?

D: The tickets are booked in the name of Judy Starr.

AUDIOSCRIPT

C: Sorry, I didn't catch that. Did you say Starr?

D: Judy Starr. S-t-a-double r.

C: OK, yes. Two tickets for June the fifth. What date would you like to change to?

D: What dates do you still have seats for?

C: There's nothing on the sixth or seventh. There are two seats for the eighth but they're separate. We have …

D: Sorry, can you slow down, please? Two seats for?

C: Sorry, two seats for the eighth but they aren't together. We can do you two seats together on the ninth of June.

D: Ninth of June. That's fine.

C: OK. I'll just go ahead and book that.

Conversation 3

E: Hello?

F: Hello, it's Wendy here.

E: Oh hi, Wendy. How are you?

F: Very well, thanks. And you?

E: Yeah, fine.

F: Are you doing anything on Saturday? Because a few of us are going out for dinner.

E: Sorry, Wendy, can you speak up, please? I'm on Oxford Street and I can't hear a thing.

F: D'you want to go for dinner on Saturday?

E: Oh, that sounds nice.

F: There's going to be a few of us, Tom and Zoe, and Steve.

E: That sounds like fun.

F: Are you free?

E: I think so.

F: Alright. Eight-thirty, Saturday. Zanzibar's.

E: OK. Zanzibar's on Saturday at eight-thirty.

F: That's right. Brilliant. See you soon.

E: OK. Thanks for calling.

Conversation 4

G Thomson and Co. Who's calling?

H: Hello, this is Andy. Andy Jones. Can I speak to Sarah Hobbs, please?

G: I'm afraid she's not here at the moment.

H: Ah, do you know when she'll be back? I've tried her mobile three or four times and left messages, but she hasn't called back.

G: She's visiting a customer. She should be back this evening. Can I take a message?

H: It's about dinner tonight. I've had to cancel because of work.

G: OK. I'll ask her to call you back.

H: Thanks.

G: Does she have your number?

H: It's 0988 45673.

G: Can you repeat that, please?

H: 0988 45673.

UNIT 3 Recording 9

I'm going to tell you about my perfect day in Prague. First of all, we're starting the day in the main square. It's a beautiful place to have breakfast in one of the cafés. It's a little bit expensive, but we're going to sit outside so we can watch the clock tower. After breakfast, we're going to walk through the old city, and go to Charles Bridge. There are some interesting statues on the bridge, and there's a market where you can buy some souvenirs. From the bridge, we're walking up to the Castle. And we're going to have lunch in a restaurant near there. In the afternoon, we're taking a tram around the city. It's a good way to see the sights because it's cheap and easy. Afterwards, we're going to relax in the park at Petrin Hill. There is a tall tower here, where you can see wonderful views of the city, too. We're going to a coffee shop in the afternoon, in the Municipal House, where they do wonderful coffees. And then, in the evening, we're planning to go to a classical music concert in St Nicholas church. You can come here to listen to Bach, Mozart or Vivaldi, and the atmosphere is very special. When it's finished, we're having dinner at Kolkovna, in the old town, which serves traditional Czech food, and then we're going to spend the rest of the evening trying different bars in the old town, which serve very cheap, local beers. It's going to be fantastic!

UNIT 4 Recording 3

Conversation 1

I=Interviewer R=Ralph

I: So Ralph, can you tell us a bit about your secret talent?

R: Um, well, I started drawing people when I was very young.

I: OK. What sorts of drawings do you do? Mostly cartoons?

R: What I do is I draw cartoons of people when I'm sitting in cafés or when I'm on the train. And I can do a face in about fifteen seconds.

I: So they're like caricatures?

R: Exactly. They are caricatures.

I: Has anyone ever asked what you were doing or caught you drawing them?

R: It's happened a few times …

I: But usually you do them in secret?

R: Usually. And occasionally I tell the person that I've drawn them.

I: Oh really?

R: Yeah. Actually, while sitting here I've drawn you!

I: No way!

R: Yep. It's right here.

I: That's brilliant! Definitely a secret talent. So tell me, how do you do it? Is there a special way to do it?

R: No, I just love drawing and I practise.

Conversation 2

I=Interviewer C=Carly

I: What's your secret talent?

C: I can say sentences backwards.

I: Backwards? That's amazing. How fast can you say them?

C: Well. I can say them at normal speed but backwards.

I: Can you give me an example?

C: What, my last sentence?

I: Yes.

C: Backwards but speed normal at them say can I.

I: Wow! Can you give me another example?

C: Yes, I'll say your sentence. Example another me give you can.

I: Can you do it again?

C: Sure. Example another me give you can.

I: How do you do it?

C: I don't know. I think I visualise the sentence, I see the words in my head, and it just appears to me.

I: Amazing. Have you ever done it in public?

C: Yeah, I've done it at parties and with friends. They all think I'm very strange.

UNIT 4 Recording 5

P=Presenter S=Sally

P: Hi. You're listening to *Ask the expert* and in today's programme we're talking about languages and how to learn a language. Our expert today is Sally Parker, who is a teacher. Hi Sally.

S: Hello.

P: Sally, our first question today is from Andy. He says, 'I've just started learning English. My problem is that I am too frightened to speak. My grammar is not very good so I'm worried about saying the wrong thing.' Have you got any advice for Andy?

S: OK. Well, the first thing is I think Andy should practise speaking to himself.

P: Speaking to himself? I'm not sure that's a good idea.

S: I know it sounds silly, but talking to yourself in a foreign language is a really good way to practise. You don't have to feel embarrassed, because nobody can hear you. You can talk to yourself about anything you like – what you had for breakfast, where you're going for the weekend – anything. And the more you do it, the more you will get used to hearing your own voice and your pronunciation, so you won't feel so frightened in the classroom. Andy should try it.

P: I suppose so. Anything else? What about his grammar?

S: He has only just started learning English, so he is going to make lots of mistakes, but that's not a problem. That's how he'll learn. Andy shouldn't worry about making mistakes.

P: You're right. So Andy, try talking to yourself, and don't worry about making mistakes. Our next problem comes from Olivia in Brazil. She is worried about pronunciation. She says, 'The problem is I can't understand native speakers. They speak so fast and I can't understand their pronunciation.' So Sally, any ideas for Olivia?

S: Well, first of all it's a good idea for her to practise her listening skills. She should listen to English as much as possible to get used to how it sounds. Listen to the news, listen to podcasts, watch English television.

P: OK – that's a good idea.

S: And another thing she should do is to focus on listening and reading at the same time. If you listen to something on the internet, you can often read the transcript. If you listen and read at the same time, it will help you see what the words sound like and how the words sound when a native speaker is talking.

P: Great. Thank you, Sally. I'm afraid that's all we have time for today, but …

UNIT 4 Recording 6

A: OK, so we need to think of the best ideas for taking tests.

B: Yep.

A: Well, how about this one? It's a good idea to study with friends at the same time each day.

B: In my opinion, this is a really good idea. You can make it a regular part of your daily life.

A: You mean like having breakfast at the same time, lunch at the same time, studying at the same time.

B: Yes. And also I think it helps when you study with friends.

A: Yeah, I think it's more motivating.

B: And you can actually talk to someone, not just look at books. I find that if I'm only reading my notes it's easy to lose concentration. I start thinking about other things. But when you are talking to someone, it really helps you concentrate. So, yes, I agree with this one.

A: OK. Another idea is not to eat too much before the exam.

B: Oh really?

A: When I eat a lot, I get sleepy.

D: Oh I see. I think it depends. Because if you don't eat enough, you start to feel hungry in the middle of the exam.

A: That's true.

B: And then you can't concentrate.

A: Yeah, that's true.

B: So, I'm not sure about this advice, for me. As I said, I think it depends. I always try to eat a good meal before an exam. I'm so nervous that I never get sleepy.

A: OK. What other ideas do you have?

B: Well, there's one thing I always do before an exam.

A: What's that?

B: I go to bed early the night before.

A: Right.

B: I always try to sleep for eight hours the night before the exam.

UNIT 5 Recording 3

1 These days we always expect to hear English in tourist areas. Most people working in tourism speak it, but I always want to talk to local people and many of them don't speak English. So I try to learn a few words of the language, especially 'please' and 'thank you', and I always take a small dictionary.

2 I love walking when I go on holiday … 'cause I think … I think you see more, so I always take a really good pair of walking boots.

3 I think a good digital camera is important when you travel. I always seem to take hundreds and hundreds of photos. And I also take binoculars.

4 When I'm not travelling for work, I usually choose to go to a warm place for my holidays, so I always take a sunhat. But when I go somewhere during the winter or rainy season, I always take waterproof clothes.

5 I think it's a good idea to buy a really good suitcase. And when you pack, leave enough space for souvenirs. On the other hand, I enjoy travelling in wild places, so quite often I take a rucksack not a suitcase. If you decide to go walking, a rucksack is much easier to carry.

6 It's best to avoid carrying too much money because you don't want to look like a rich tourist! 'Cause of this, I always take a money belt on holiday.

7 I need to write things down to remember them so I take a notebook and pen.

UNIT 5 Recording 4

There's one point in the centre of Foz do Iguaçu city where you can get to Paraguay and Argentina easily. From this point, it only takes half an hour to get to both countries. It's great because you can visit three countries in one hour. And of course you can see the falls!

UNIT 5 Recording 5

1 To get to Paraguay, you have to go left. You go along the main road, past the turning for the international hospital. Then you turn right and you're on the main street called Avenue Kubitschek. This goes through the centre of the town. From there you just keep going until you reach the highway, Highway 277. Go left and the bridge is at the end of the highway. You cross the bridge and you are in Paraguay.

2 To get to Argentina, you wait at the corner for the bus. It takes you down Avenue das Cataratas and right into Avenida Mercosul. The bus goes straight on for about 25 minutes. Cross the bridge and you're in Argentina.

3 To see the Iguaçu Falls on the Brazilian side, you turn right and just go straight on down Highway 469 and the falls are in front of you. You can't miss them – they're the biggest in the world!

UNIT 5 Recording 6

Conversation 1

A: Excuse me. We're trying to get to the carnival. Is this the right bus stop?

B: Yes, but you don't need the bus. It's very close.

A: Oh! Can we walk?

B: Yes, it takes about ten minutes from here. Just go straight on. You'll hear the music!

A: OK. Thank you very much.

Conversation 2

C: Excuse me, can you help me? I'm looking for the Plaza Hotel. Is this the right way?

D: Um … Plaza Hotel, Plaza Hotel. Yes, keep going, past the cinema and take the first left.

C: OK.

D: Then keep going for about fifteen minutes until you reach the end of the road. And you'll see the sign for the hotel. You can't miss it.

C: OK. Can you show me on the map?

D: Sure.

Conversation 3

E: Excuse me, we want to get to The Grand Motel. Is it far?

F: Um … sorry, I've no idea. Jim, do you know?

G: What?

F: The Grand Motel?

G: The Grand Motel? Yeah, it's just over there. Just go to the end of this street. Go left and go past the … um … there's a restaurant. Go past the restaurant and it's on the left.

E: On the left. So I need to go to the end of the street, turn left, go past the restaurant and it's on the left.

G: Yeah, that's it.

E: Thanks a lot.

UNIT 5 Recording 9

OK, well, we would like to go to Easter Island. It is very isolated, very far from other places, and the nearest country is Chile, over two thousand miles away. We are going to travel there by plane and stay with different families and the trip is going to take three months. We want to experience the local culture, their music, food and way of life. So our plan is to speak to the local people about these things and to film them. We hope to find out about their traditions and to see what they think of their history. Well, finally, my husband and I always wanted to go to Easter Island. I read about it when I was a child and I saw pictures of these amazing stone heads on the island. So for us this is the journey of our dreams.

UNIT 6 Recording 1

1 Do you live in a town, or by the sea?
2 How long have you lived there?
3 How long have you lived in the house you live in now?
4 What is the name of your best friend?
5 How long have you known him/her?
6 Do you work or study?
7 How long have you worked or studied where you are now?
8 What hobby do you enjoy?
9 How long have you done it for?
10 Do you have a bicycle or a car?
11 How long have you had it?

UNIT 6 Recording 3

I= Interviewer W=Woman

I: Can you tell us a little about superfoods?

W: Well, superfoods include tomatoes, broccoli and spinach.

I: Mmm.

W: These have lots of vitamins, and they are really good for you.

I: Right.

W: Anyway, they may improve our health, but I don't think superfoods will be the answer to our eating problems in the future.

I: Can you tell us why not?

W: Well, the most important thing is to eat healthy food every day.

I: Right.

AUDIOSCRIPT

W: And this is more important than the idea of superfoods. Eating an apple a day is better for you than eating a kilo of spinach one day a week.

I: I see. So what you're saying is …

I: There's been a lot of talk about food pills.

W: Yes.

I: Are they healthier than other types of food? Could they be the food of the future?

W: Well, in the past astronauts ate a type of food pill when they were in space. It was dried food and they added water to it.

I: Right.

W: But I don't think food pills will replace normal food.

I: Right. Why's that? For health reasons or social reasons?

W: Well, cooking and eating together is an important part of family life and it always will be. You sit down together at a table and you eat and talk. It's a very old tradition, and eating pills isn't the same.

I: So we won't eat only food pills?

W: Food pills might become more popular, but no, we won't eat only food pills in the future.

I: Well, that's interesting because I was reading about …

W: In the future we may have special food that can change its flavour.

I: Can you give an example?

W: For example, imagine you like chocolate ice cream, but your friend likes strawberry. You eat the same ice cream but it will taste different for both of you.

I: The same food that tastes different for different people …

W: You'll think it's chocolate ice cream and your friend will say it's strawberry. It might happen with drinks, too. You take a bottle of liquid out of the fridge. You press the button which says 'coffee' or 'lemonade' or 'hot chocolate'. You put the bottle in the microwave and the liquid becomes the drink that you choose.

I: So it starts off as the same food or drink, but then we change its flavour by pushing a button.

W: That's right. Just by pushing a button.

I: So how does it work?

W: Well, this is possible because of nanotechnology. The technology might not replace normal drinks and food but it may become common in the future.

I: And nanotechnology is something that's used in different …

UNIT 6 Recording 4

Conversation 1

D=Doctor W=Woman

D: Hello. I'm Dr Andrews. Now, what's the matter?

W: Well, doctor, I feel terrible. I get these headaches and I feel sick.

D: Oh. How long have you had this problem?

W: A few weeks now. And I can't sleep at night because my head hurts.

D: You can't sleep?

W: That's right.

D: And are you very worried or under pressure at the moment?

W: No, I don't think so.

D: Do you have a healthy diet?

W: Hmm. Quite healthy.

D: Do you drink tea or coffee?

W: Yes, I do.

D: How much?

W: Tea? Probably about eight cups, or ten.

D: A day?

W: Yes.

D: I see. And has that changed in the last few weeks?

W: Not really.

D: OK. Well the first thing is I think you should stop drinking so much tea and coffee. Try to drink just one small cup a day. I'll give you some painkillers for the headaches. Take two of these three times a day. I don't think it's anything to worry about, but if …

Conversation 2

D=Doctor M=Man

D: Good morning. How can I help?

M: Well, I'm worried about my foot.

D: Your foot?

M: Yes. It hurts when I walk.

D: I see. Did you do anything to it? Did you have an accident?

M: Um. Well, sort of.

D: What happened?

M: I kicked a wall.

D: I see. When did you do that?

M: About a week ago.

D: OK. Did you go to hospital?

M: No.

D: Can I have a look?

M: Yes, of course.

D: Where does it hurt? Here?

M: Argh. Yes, there.

D: Can you move it?

M: Yes, a little, but it's very painful.

D: Hmm. I think it might be broken. It's nothing to worry about, but I think you should go to the hospital for an X-ray. I'll write you a note and if …

UNIT 6 Recording 7

A: Does exercise make you feel relaxed?

B: Yes, I think it really does. Sometimes it's difficult to find time to exercise, but I play football after work on a Monday, and I play tennis at the weekend, and I feel so much better. If I don't play one week, I feel terrible. So, yes, doing sport makes you feel really good. You feel much better, and more relaxed.

A: How much exercise do you do in a week?

C: In a week, well I probably do about two or three hours of exercise, maybe more. I go to the gym once or twice, if I have time, and I sometimes go swimming. Oh, and I ride my bike at the weekend, so actually, probably three or four hours a week. More than I thought. Yeah, four hours, that's OK.

A: Do you have a sporting hero?

D: Oh yes, Pelé. He's a hero, not just for me, but probably for all Brazilians. I think he is one of the greatest football players ever. He was such a good athlete, and he had so much talent. He was 'King of Football', and scored more goals for Brazil than anyone else. And he was born very poor. You know he didn't have money for a football so he used to practise kicking a grapefruit, or a sock stuffed with paper.

A: How much do you walk a day?

E: Oh my goodness. Well, I suppose. I don't walk very much actually. I … um … I drive, the car everywhere. That's terrible, isn't it? Umm. Yes, I probably only walk about, about maybe five minutes every day.

UNIT 7 Recording 1

P=Presenter A=Anita J=Jasmin

P: Have you ever felt stuck in a rut? Well, this morning we talk to two women who have made big life changes and they are here to tell us about it. Jasmin Wells used to work as a doctor in York. In her thirties she gave up her job and became a professional musician. Anita Jacobs used to work in advertising. But she sold her house, gave up her job, and decided to travel around the world. Anita first, what made you decide to change?

A: Well, I was nearly forty. I was in a job that I wasn't really interested in. I used to work long hours and I didn't enjoy the job much any more. So I decided to follow an ambition I've had for a long time. I always wanted to travel, but I never had the chance.

P: Your ambition was to travel around the world?

A: That's right. The idea was to take a year off. I started work when I was eighteen and I never had a break in all that time. I never had time to travel or see the world. So I decided to take a year off and go travelling. The time was right, so I left my job and went.

P: And you earned some money while you were travelling, didn't you?

A: Well, a little. I worked on a farm for a while in Australia. They didn't pay me very much, but I stayed on the farm and ate for free, so I was happy.

P: I see. Now, Jasmin, doctor to musician is quite a big change. What happened?

J: Well, it is a big change. And it happened quite suddenly. I was working in a hospital doing more than a hundred hours a week, looking after elderly patients. I didn't use to have time for anything else. It was just work, work, work. And one morning when I left the hospital, I saw a piano in the corner of the room. I sat down and started to play. I remembered that I really enjoyed making music.

P: So, did you use to play the piano before, as a child?

J: Yes, I used to play, but I wasn't very good! Luckily, I'm a bit better now. Anyway, I decided I wanted to learn the piano, so I started piano lessons, and learnt about writing songs. It became a passion for me, and I realised that it was something I really wanted to do. So, I decided to make more time for it, and eventually I gave up medicine altogether, and started playing my own music.

P: Fascinating, now tell me …

UNIT 7 Recording 3

Conversation 1

A: Excuse me, where do I register for my course?

B: Do you know where the main reception is?

A: Sorry?

B: The main reception.

A: Oh, yes.

B: The registration desk is there.

A: Thank you so much.

Conversation 2

A: Excuse me, where's the study centre?

C: It's next to the cafeteria.

A: The cafeteria? Where's that?

C: Follow me. I'll take you there.

A: Thank you. That's very kind.

Conversation 3

A: Where can I use the internet?

D: You can use the computers in the library or in the study centre.

A: Do I have to pay?

D: No.

A: So it's free for students.

D: Yes, that's right.

Conversation 4

A: Excuse me, what time is the library open?

E: It's open every day, from 9a.m. until 6p.m.

A: Did you say 'every day'?

E: Yes, that's right. Every day, from nine in the morning until six in the evening.

A: Thank you.

Conversation 5

A: Could you help me? Where can I get a new student card? I've lost mine.

F: OK. If you go to the main reception, you can get a new one.

A: Thank you.

Conversation 6

A: Excuse me, can you help me find my classroom?

G: Sure. What number is it?

A: 301.

G: OK. You need to go up to the third floor. And it's on the right.

Conversation 7

A: Where can I buy a notebook?

H: There's a stationery shop downstairs.

A: Sorry?

H: There's a stationery shop downstairs.

A: Thank you so much.

Conversation 8

A: Can you help me?

I: Yes, maybe.

A: I need to find out about my accommodation. Can you tell me where to go?

I: Accommodation? I think you have to go to the welfare office, over there, next to the book shop.

A: Thank you.

UNIT 7 Recording 6

Well, when I first arrived in the USA, it was a very interesting time for me. The biggest problem was that I couldn't really speak the language very well. I learnt English at school and at university in Poland, but it's very different when you are living in the country and you need to speak it all the time. I felt very nervous when I had to speak to American people, like in the shops or when you meet friends, and I couldn't understand what people were saying to me. It was terrible. I used to stay at home, and watch loads of television to try and understand what people were saying. Luckily, I made friends very quickly with some American girls, so we used to go out together, and that really helped me. After a few months my English was much better. I felt more confident. And now I talk to people all the time, but it was hard at the beginning.

UNIT 8 Recording 1

Welcome to *Money Matters*, presented by Jimmy Stevens. Today we're going to talk about four of the best money-making ideas in history.

What do you think this is? It's a food which you don't eat. It's a sweet which is made of rubber. It's chewing gum! Chewing gum was originally made from chicle, a plant from Central and South America, but now many gum companies use rubber. No one knows who first used chewing gum, but it was in 1891 that Wrigley Company started making and selling it. Many people say it helps them to concentrate, and the US army gives gum to its soldiers for this reason. Today the industry is worth nearly twenty billion dollars a year.

On to our next big money maker. The first telephone that could be carried around was invented in 1908. In the 1954 film, *Sabrina*, a character played by actor Humphrey Bogart made a call from the back of his car! But it was in 1973 that the modern mobile phone was invented by an American, Martin Cooper, and in the 1980s 'mobiles' started to become popular. Many countries, including the UK, now have more mobile phones than people.

Next is the iPod. It's small and light. It plays and stores music. A company called Apple invented it, but Vinnie Chieco was the man that gave the iPod its name. He saw the machine and thought of a line from the film *2001: A Space Odyssey*, 'Open the pod bay door, Hal!' The iPod arrived on the market in 2001. In 2007, from January to March, Apple earned 1.8 billion pounds from iPod sales.

Our final big money maker is all about making money. In 1934 Charles Darrow showed a game to a company called Parker Brothers. Did they want to invest in it? No, they didn't. So, with a friend who worked in a printing company, Mr Darrow made 500 copies of the game and started selling them under the name 'Monopoly'. The idea of the game is to buy streets where you can build houses and hotels. It soon became popular and Parker Brothers agreed to produce it. Today the owners say they've sold over 200 million Monopoly sets and 750 million people have played it. The game is truly international. it's sold in 103 countries and in thirty-seven languages.

UNIT 8 Recording 3

A: Personally, I think these footballers earn too much money. They're twenty years old and they're already millionaires. I think it's crazy.

B: I agree. They earn enough money in one week to buy a house, a car – anything. Now if you look at, say, fire fighters, who risk their lives …

A: Fire fighters don't earn enough.

B: They don't earn enough.

A: Or what about doctors? Certainly in Britain they work very hard.

B: They work too hard. One of my friends is a doctor and he sometimes does eighteen-hour shifts.

A: That's crazy.

B: Eighteen hours without a break. Again, they're saving people's lives.

A: Teachers, too. I think they should get much bigger salaries. They also work really long hours.

B: Yeah, although they do get good holidays.

A: Yeah. That's true.

B: Actually, I think they get too many holidays. There's Christmas and half-term and Easter and the summer. What is it in the summer – about six weeks?

A: Yeah, but I think teachers need it 'cause of all the stress.

UNIT 8 Recording 4

Conversation 1

W=Woman S=Shop assistant

S: Can I help you?

W: No, thanks. I'm just looking.

S: OK, just let me know if you need anything.

W: Thanks.

Conversation 2

M=Man S=Shop assistant

S: Hi there. Are you looking for anything in particular?

M: Yeah, do you sell those things that soldiers wear? Er … it's like a jacket.

S: Um, a type of jacket?

M: Yeah, a light green jacket with lots of pockets.

S: Ah, you mean a flak jacket?

M: Yes.

S: They're just on your left.

M: Ah, yes. Thank you. Can I try this on?

S: Of course.

M: Where's the fitting room?

S: Just over there.

M: Thanks.

Conversation 3

M=Man S=Shop assistant

M: Excuse me. Do you have one of these in a larger size? It doesn't fit.

S: Is that the Large? I'll just go and check for you. I'm sorry. This is all we've got in stock at the moment. There are some other T-shirts over there on the other side. There might be some Extra Large sizes there.

AUDIOSCRIPT

Conversation 4
W=Woman S=Shop assistant

W: Hello. I was wondering if you've got any of that stuff you use for cleaning swimming pools.

S: Um … yeah, we usually sell a liquid cleaner. You pour it into the pool. There's one here.

W: Can I have a look?

S: Yep.

W: How much is it?

S: This one's twenty-eight pounds ninety-nine for a litre bottle.

Conversation 5
M=Man S=Shop assistant W=Woman

S: Hi. Are you paying by cash or credit card?

M: Credit card.

S: Can you enter your PIN, please? Thanks. Here's your card.

M: Thanks.

S: Thank you. Who's next, please?

W: Do you take Mastercard?

S: Yes, that's fine. Can you just sign here, please?

UNIT 8 Recording 6

Our business is called 'The Very Special Cake Company'. Our idea is to make delicious birthday cakes for children. We want to make interesting cakes shaped like animals or trains or faces. In fact, you can choose any shape you want and we'll make it for you. We'll also make the cake personal, by writing your name or a special message on it. We hope to make money by selling the cakes at local markets, in shops and on the internet. We don't need very much to start our business, because we can make the cakes at home. To be successful, we need to advertise in schools and have a beautiful website with lots of colourful photos. And we plan to go to markets and give people a free taste of the cakes, so they can try them, and then they'll definitely want to buy them!

UNIT 9 Recording 1

Welcome to *Save the Planet* where we talk about the world's environmental problems. Now, did you know there are more than six billion people on the planet, and by 2050 there might be more than nine billion? People are living longer and healthier lives than ever before, but a big population means big problems for the planet. Let's look at three of the most important problems.

The first problem is water. Many people in the world can't get enough water. But in some countries we use too much. A person in Gambia, Africa, for example, uses much less water than someone in the United States. In Gambia, one person uses four and a half litres of water a day. But in the US it's 600 litres. And to make the problem worse, the deserts are getting bigger. The Sahara desert is one of the hottest places in the world, and is already the largest desert. But each year it gets bigger than before, so it gets more difficult to find clean water.

Our second problem is the animals. There are more people on the earth than ever before. This means we use more space. And for the animals this means that there is less space than before. One example is the Amazon rain forest. It has the highest number of plant and animal species in the world, but it's getting smaller every year. People are destroying the rain forest to make more space for houses, roads and farms. In the last ten years we have destroyed more than 150,000 square kilometres of forest – that's an area larger than Greece! So in the future, many plants and animal species will become extinct.

And the last problem on our list, but not the least important, is the weather. The world is getting warmer. The ice in Greenland is melting faster than ever before and on Mount Everest there is less snow every year. Also sea levels are rising. This means that soon some of the world's most important cities, like New York, London, Bangkok, Sydney and Rio de Janeiro might all be under water.

UNIT 9 Recording 5
Question 1

A: The best sense of direction? Perhaps it's the butterfly.

B: Er, I'm not sure.

A: It's hard to say. Well, it could be sea turtles.

B: Maybe.

A: They swim everywhere, don't they?

B: Um, it might be, but I think it's the butterfly. It can't be the taxi driver, can it?

A: It's definitely not the taxi driver.

C: OK, here are the answers. Sea turtles travel 3,000 miles a year. And when they lay eggs, they go back to the place where they were born. So they have a great sense of direction. New York taxi drivers drive 37,500 miles a year. They know the fastest way to any address in New York. But sea turtles and taxi drivers do not have the best sense of direction!

B: So it must be the butterfly.

C: The winner is the monarch butterfly. At the end of every summer, they fly from Canada to Mexico. And no one knows how they do it.

Question 2

A: Er, so who's the best athlete? That's a good question.

B: I'm not sure.

A: It could be triathletes.

B: Or rats.

C: Rats are the winners. A rat is the superman of animals. Rats can kill animals that are much bigger than they are, and they can eat electric wires. They can swim a mile and survive in water for three days. They can also jump three feet and fall forty-five feet and survive.

A: That's amazing.

Question 3

B: Who sleeps the most? Let me think. Erm, it can't be the human baby, can it? And it's not the black bear.

A: It must be the sloth. They spend most of their lives asleep.

B: So what's the answer?

C: Well, the black bear sleeps for about seven months a year. The females are even half-asleep when they have their babies.

B: Wow.

C: Human babies usually sleep about eighteen hours a day, but only in their first few months. So sloths are the winner. They sleep fifteen to eighteen hours a day for their whole life.

Question 4

A: Who has the best memory? That's a good question. It's hard to say.

B: It must be humans. We remember things for years.

A: Or elephants?

C: Here's the answer: female elephants remember friendly elephant faces and this helps protect the group. Jays store their food in secret places and always remember where they put it. But humans are the winners. We have the best memory because we are able to organise time. We have concepts like 'yesterday', 'last week', and 'tomorrow' and these help us to remember things better. We also have ways to record information like writing and photos.

B: I thought so.

UNIT 9 Recording 8

A: OK, the most beautiful place I've been to. Well, a few years ago I went to Fish River Canyon.

B: Where?

A: Fish River Canyon. It's the second biggest canyon in the world.

B: After the Grand Canyon?

A: After the Grand Canyon.

B: Where is it?

A: It's in Namibia, in Africa.

B: Wow. And what did you think of it?

A: It was amazing. The first thing you notice is how big it is, of course.

B: Of course.

A: It just goes on and on as far as your eye can see. But the best thing about it was the silence.

B: Right.

A: It was so amazingly quiet. We went there in August and there weren't many tourists and it was just so quiet.

B: Would you like to go back?

A: I would love to go back. One day!

B: One day.

UNIT 10 Recording 1
Conversation 1
I=Interviewer R=Rick

I: Rick, you've lived in Dubai for … what, four years, right?

R: Yeah, four years.

I: So what's it like, living in Dubai?

R: Well, I read that Dubai is one of the world's fastest growing cities, so there are a lot of people, and it's very crowded. It's a great city for shopping, and going out. And it has really good nightlife, with lots of bars and clubs.

I: Is it a safe city?

R: Yes, there isn't a lot of crime. The streets are very safe. But one of the biggest problems is the traffic. Everyone drives a car here – petrol is still cheap, so the traffic's terrible.

One good thing is the taxis though. There are lots of them, and they're cheap, so you don't have to drive.

Conversation 2
I=Interviewer S=Sasha

I: Sasha, you live in Tokyo, don't you?

S: That's right.

I: And, do you … do you like it? Do you like living in Tokyo?

S: Yes, Tokyo is a great city to live in. People think it's very expensive, but actually you can buy Japanese food in the supermarkets quite cheaply, and eating out in Japanese restaurants isn't expensive either.

I: How about getting around? What's the public transport like?

S: There's a really good public transport system here. The metro system is fantastic. It's very fast, and it's cheap, so lots of people use it. That's the only problem. It gets very crowded.

I: And what do you like best about living in Tokyo?

S: The food, definitely. I love Japanese food! And the green spaces. There are lots of parks and green spaces, so it's less polluted than you think.

Conversation 3
I=Interviewer C=Charlie

I: What about Sydney? What's Sydney like, Charlie?

C: Sydney is one of the best cities in the world. There are lots of young, friendly people living here, so there's a really good atmosphere. The streets are clean and safe and there are lots of things to see and do. There are beautiful buildings, like the Opera House. You can sit and watch the boats on the harbour. And it has one of the most beautiful coastlines in the world.

I: What's the weather like? Is it really hot?

C: The weather is perfect. It's never too hot and never too cold. You can eat outside all year round, so there's a great café culture with lots of places on the streets selling really good coffee.

I: So, are there any problems?

C: Problems? Not really. Traffic, I suppose. Too much traffic and a terrible public transport system.

UNIT 10 Recording 3

Conversation 1
G=Guest R=Receptionist

G: Oh hello. Could you help me? There's a problem with the air conditioning.

R: Oh yes?

G: I've just tried to switch it on, but it doesn't work.

R: Is it completely dead?

G: Completely. Absolutely nothing.

R: OK, we'll look into it right away. I'll send someone up. It'll be about five minutes, OK?

G: Thanks.

R: You're welcome. And sorry about that.

Conversation 2
W=Waitress D=Diner M=Manager

D: I'm afraid I have a complaint. Could I speak to the manager, please?

W: Yes, of course.

M: Good evening, sir. I understand there's a problem.

D: Yes. I'm afraid I have a complaint.

M: Oh?

D: Well, we got here at eight. And then we waited about twenty minutes for a table.

M: Right.

D: This is for a table we'd booked for eight, OK? Then we waited another hour for our meal.

M: Right.

D: One hour. Then when the bill arrived they put this extra charge on it.

M: An extra charge? That's probably the service charge.

D: Well, could you check this for me, please?

M: Yes, that's service.

D: Well, to be honest, I don't want to pay this.

M: Of course not. Well, sir, I am really sorry about that. It's a very busy time of year.

Conversation 3
W=Woman M=Man

W: Excuse me. Do you work here?

M: Yes.

W: Do you know when the next train will be arriving? I mean, I've been here for over an hour.

M: I'm sorry but there's nothing we can do at the moment. Everything is delayed.

W: And you don't know when the next train is coming?

M: No.

W: Or why there's a delay?

M: Snow.

W: What?

M: Snow on the track. It was the wrong type of snow.

W: What do you mean 'the wrong type of snow'? You're kidding, right?

UNIT 10 Recording 5

A: One of the things that really annoys me is when I buy food in the supermarket, and I see that, for example, I buy apples, yeah, and here in the UK we grow a lot of apples. And I go to the supermarket to buy some apples, and they come from New Zealand, or South Africa, or something. And, I just think it's crazy. I mean, I don't understand why we pay for apples to come millions of kilometres, from the other side of the world, when we grow them right here in this country. It really makes me angry.

B: I get very fed up with public transport, you know, buses and trains, and that kind of thing. I mean the government says that we shouldn't use our cars, and we should travel by public transport. But it's horrible. It's crowded and there are delays. I use the train to get to work, and so many times I arrive late because the train gets cancelled, or delayed, and you know I'm paying a lot of money for my ticket, so I just think it should be better. I think the service should be better.

UNIT 11 Recording 1

1 I use my phone for everything. I text most of the time because it's quick and cheap, so I text my friends and my boyfriend. We send each other texts during the day. It's a nice way to keep in touch. I like texts because they are quiet – nobody knows what you are saying. My mum used to call me all the time to check that I'm OK, but now she can text me, which is much better. I get really annoyed when you're talking to someone though, and they are texting someone else. I think that's really rude.

2 I use the internet a lot now. I use it for phone calls – you know – what's it called … Skype. I use Skype to keep in touch with my family because my daughter lives in France you see, so I don't see her very often and the phone is expensive. With the internet I can see my grandchildren – it's wonderful. My son sets up the computer for me. I haven't learnt how to do that yet. And sometimes it crashes during the phone call, which is annoying, or I can't see the picture properly. But usually it's fine. Generally, I think the technology is wonderful. When I was younger we only dreamed of having video phone calls, but now it's possible and it's free.

3 We use a blog. We've never done it before, but it's a great way to tell people about your travel experiences. We've been to so many places already and it's nice to be able to tell people about them. And you can put photos there of the people you meet and the places you visit. It's better than writing postcards because you don't have to wait for them to arrive. As soon as you write the blog, people all over the world can read it. And you only have to write it once! The only problem we have is when we can't find an internet café.

4 I've just started to use networking sites, like Facebook and MySpace. They're a great way to keep in touch with people you don't see very often. You can post photos or send jokes and funny videos. I found some friends I haven't seen for years and it was great to see their pages. The only problem is that I keep looking at the website when I should be working.

UNIT 11 Recording 3

A: I use the internet all day at work. I 'wilf' and I get my work done.

B: Yeah, me too.

A: I'm sorry, but I really don't see what the problem is.

C: I think the problem is that lots of workers spend all day on the internet instead of doing their work.

A: Hmm.

C: And students at university are failing their degrees because they spend all their time checking Facebook and watching the videos that friends send them.

B: Yes, that's true, but … um … I don't think, you know, I don't think that the problem is the internet. You know, I think the problem is with the websites like Facebook.

A: Yeah, MySpace …

B: Some companies stop you from using certain websites. And I think that's OK.

C: But it's such a waste of time. I don't think people should use the internet at work, unless you need it for your work.

A: I'm not sure about that. Using the internet helps to give you a break. It's like having a cup of coffee or talking to someone in the office. People should use the internet as much as they like.

B: Yes, that's right. I think it's good to use the internet. I run a small business and all my staff use the internet as much as they want to. I don't check what they are doing. They do all their work and they are happy. I don't think it's a waste of time at all. It's the same as going to a bookshop …

C: No, but …

B: or looking through a pile of magazines.

C: I'm afraid I totally disagree. The problem is that people are addicts. People aren't addicted to reading books, but the internet is different. People spend too much time in front of the computer. They choose the internet over sports and going out. They forget how to live in the real world, and 'wilfing' is a part of that.

UNIT 11 Recording 6

1 OK – mobile phone? That's essential. I love it. I use it all the time. I love talking to people, and texting. I couldn't live without my mobile. MP3 player? I suppose it's not essential, although I do like listening to music. Television? Not essential. I don't watch much television. Digital camera? Not essential. I'm terrible at taking photos anyway. So, what's left? Er … laptop? That's essential really. I use my laptop for work, so yes, I need that.

2 Which are essential? All of them! Goodness. Right. Mobile phone? Essential. I don't go anywhere without my phone. I need it in case there's an emergency and I have to call someone. Or if there's a problem with one of the children. Yes, I definitely need my phone. TV? That's essential really. I couldn't live without my television and DVD player. Umm. Laptop? Well, I need a computer to go on the internet and keep in touch with people. So, that's essential. Digital camera? I suppose I don't need that. Someone else can take the photos! What else? MP3 player. No. I can live without that.

UNIT 12 Recording 2

1 If I could be famous for anything, it would be art. I love painting and if I had more time, I would love to paint seriously. If I could have a painting in a museum, I'd be really happy.

2 I'd be a famous politician. If I was a politician, I would try to change the world. To stop all these wars and do something to help poor countries. You know, I think it's terrible how most politicians don't seem to worry about things like that.

3 If I could do anything, um … I think I'd be a famous footballer or something like that. Imagine if you scored a goal for your country in the World Cup, that would be such a good feeling. You would remember something like that forever.

4 I'd love to sing. If I could be famous for anything, I think I'd be a singer. Or a dancer. I'd love to be a famous dancer. I'm terrible at both of those things – I can't sing or dance! I guess that's why we have dreams, isn't it?

5 I would love to be a famous writer, or poet, like Shakespeare. I think it's a wonderful thing to be able to write a book that people all around the world want to read. To be able to speak to people in that way. Yes, I'd like to be remembered as a great writer. But I don't think that'll happen.

6 If I could be famous for anything, well, let me see … for being beautiful! That would be good. One of those beautiful actresses who wins at the Oscars. If I was famous, I would be rich, live in a big house, and have all those clothes. Oh yes, that would be nice.

7 If I could be famous for anything, it would be for inventing something, like a medicine or a cure for cancer. Not for being an actor, or a musician. If I invented something that made people's lives better, that would be good.

8 What would I want to be famous for? Hmm. I wouldn't like to be famous. If I was famous I wouldn't be happy. No, I prefer just being me, thank you.

UNIT 12 Recording 3

Conversation 1

A: Hello Mr Pietersen. What can I do for you?

B: Hello, Tom. Um, I'd like to go on a private tour of the White House.

A: The White House? In Washington?

B: Yes.

A: OK.

B: And I'd like to go maybe tomorrow afternoon.

A: Tomorrow afternoon in the White House. OK.

B: Yes. If it's OK with the President.

A: Right, let me see if I have a number … hang on … ah, here it is. OK, I'll call the President's office and I'll get back to you later.

B: OK.

Conversation 2

A: Hello, Clara. What can I do for you today?

C: Hello, Tom. Would it be possible to book a ticket for that space flight?

A: What space flight is that?

C: I just saw it on TV. They're sending a flight into space next week and I would really like to go.

A: OK. I know the one you're talking about. Would you like me to get a ticket for your husband, too?

C: Yes, please.

A: OK. Just a moment. I'll call Mr Branson.

Conversation 3

A: [...] 7 DAY [...]OOK

D: Hi, [...] like to rent a boat and take it [...] the River Thames for about three or four days. And it needs to be a big boat for about eighty people.

A: Eighty?

D: Yes, we're inviting a few friends along.

A: And when would you like it?

D: We told our friends this weekend. Would you be able to organise it for us?

A: Yes, of course. Can you give me a moment? I'll make a few calls. Do you want me to get a boat with a cook and restaurant service?

D: That would be wonderful.

Conversation 4

A: Hi, Maggie. How can I help?

E: Hi, Tom. We're in London and we're going out for lunch and we were wondering … well, could you recommend somewhere in Paris?

A: In Paris?

E: Yes, we're going to take the helicopter.

A: What type of food?

E: Any type really. Well, French.

A: French. OK. Um, there's a very good restaurant near the Eiffel Tower.

E: Oh good. That's perfect.

A: Shall I book it?

E: Yes, please. And can you give us directions?

A: Have you got your laptop with you?

E: Yes.

A: Hold on. I'll email you a map.

UNIT 12 Recording 5

I'm 28 and I live in South Wales. I've grown up here. My dream began from an early age. As a child I always used to listen to my Dad's records on a Sunday afternoon. And the music really excited me. I knew I wanted to be a rock star. As a teenager, I had music idols; Jimi Hendrix, Keith Moon, Jim Morrison, Nick Drake. Many of them died before they were 27. It made me think that I had to do something about my dream, before it was too late. When I was 15 I bought myself a second-hand drum kit. I joined bands, and we played concerts. And then I started to write songs. I played all the time. I played for pleasure, I played for money, I played when I was angry. It was like everything I ever wanted. But although we had songs on the radio, we never got famous. I don't know when my dream started to change. But at 28 it was like I woke up and I realised there was something else. I was watching my son grow up, to have his own dreams and ambitions. I woke up to my family, and my friends. I still play, but it's just for fun because I'm 28 now and it's time to live.